To Bonnie Bressette, Marcia Simon,
Carolyn (Cully) George-Mandoka, and
Kevin Simon, my Nishnaabe teachers
on this transformational journey

"Healing happens if you want it bad enough, and that's the trick of it."

– *Richard Wagamese*

"Relationships don't just shape Indigenous reality, they are our reality."

– *Shawn Wilson*

"Kinship, like empathy, is as much an act of imagination as it is lived experience."

– *Daniel Heath Justice*

Meeting My Treaty Kin

Meeting My Treaty Kin

A Journey toward Reconciliation

Heather Menzies

on point PRESS | a UBC Press imprint
Vancouver . Toronto

32 31 30 29 28 27 26 25 24 23   5 4 3 2 1

Printed in Canada on FSC-certified ancient-forest-free paper (100% post-consumer recycled) that is processed chlorine- and acid-free, with vegetable-based inks.

Library and Archives Canada Cataloguing in Publication

Title: Meeting my treaty kin : a journey toward reconciliation / Heather Menzies.
Names: Menzies, Heather, author.
Description: Includes bibliographical references.
Identifiers: Canadiana (print) 20230486061 | Canadiana (ebook) 20230486711 | ISBN 9780774890663 (softcover) | ISBN 9780774890670 (PDF) | ISBN 9780774890687 (EPUB)
Subjects: LCSH: Reconciliation. | LCSH: Canada – Ethnic relations. | LCSH: Indigenous peoples – Canada. | LCSH: Menzies, Heather
Classification: LCC E78.C2 M46 2023 | DDC 971.004/97—dc23

Canada Council   Conseil des arts
for the Arts   du Canada

Canadä

BRITISH COLUMBIA ARTS COUNCIL

BRITISH COLUMBIA

UBC Press gratefully acknowledges the financial support for our publishing program of the Government of Canada, the Canada Council for the Arts, and the British Columbia Arts Council.

On Point Press, an imprint of UBC Press
The University of British Columbia | Musqueam Traditional Territory
2029 West Mall
Vancouver, BC V6T 1Z2
www.ubcpress.ca

Contents

Prologue

November 2018

On a cool, grey day in late autumn, I stood outside the former Ipperwash army barracks where Cully (Carolyn) George-Mandoka has lived since 1995, the year her brother Dudley was shot by the Ontario Provincial Police. I knew this was where she lived because a former band council chief had brought me here, to what – beneath the army camp structures – was still the Stoney Point Reserve, to meet her. I'd stood at the bottom of the stairs leading to the small stoop outside the door as the former chief knocked on the door. I thought I'd seen the curtain over the door's window move, then nothing. The door never opened, and we left.

A week later, I now stood on the stoop by myself, with no one to introduce me and legitimize my presence. There were two hundred years of social, cultural, and political alienation between the woman on the other side of the door and me. Yet somehow, according to Indigenous ways of thinking about which I was starting to learn, this woman and I were related, as was Dudley, through a treaty. We were even treaty kin. I knocked on the door, my mouth dry, my heart thumping in my chest. I waited, my eyes on the small square window set in the faded wooden door. The curtain moved. I stood there waiting, feeling conspicuous as a pickup truck drove by on the road just beyond where I stood, slowing down as it passed. Someone had noticed me. I felt self-conscious, clearly a white person (zhaganash) on this remnant of ancient Nishnaabe territory. I continued to stand there, not wanting to knock again, but not wanting to give up either.

The door opened a few inches. In the darkness of the opening, I saw a short woman, brown skin, dark brown eyes, chin-length grey hair.

"Yes?" she said, her voice hard.

I told her my name. I knew it was pretty late, I said. But I'd come to offer her my condolences at the death of her brother.

She looked at me hard. I held her gaze: brown eyes on blue, blue eyes on brown.

She stepped back, pulled open the door.

"Come in," she said.

I entered the space: a big open room that had once been separate bedrooms for army cadets before the walls were taken out. The pale linoleum flooring was scuffed and worn through in spots. In the centre of the room stood a big Arborite and chrome table and, hanging above it, a Tiffany-style lamp with a Coca-Cola motif, bingo cards stuck along the edge.

"Have a seat," Cully said. She went around to the other side of the table, sat down, and pulled a pile of fabric toward herself. It was a quilt. A bear-paw design, she said, opening it out so I could see the pattern.

Meeting My Treaty Kin

Introduction

I still can't identify everything that drew me to Cully's army-barracks home that day, or what prompted me to accept an invitation to help her and three others pull their collective stories into a book about the Ipperwash crisis and the broken treaty behind it. I can only say that, nearly five years into the journey, I'm glad I took up the challenge that accompanied their invitation: the challenge to learn to listen, and to change at a level deep enough to be called transformation. This memoir is the story of my journey, a very personal account of how I came to implicate myself in Canada's colonial history. Finally! I'd spent most of my life conveniently ignoring it.

I was probably fairly typical of my generation, growing up with a short, early history of Canada's Indigenous Peoples at school. The Indians, as they were referred to at the time, featured in the fur trade – the European fur trade. After that, they disappeared. Even when Section 35 of the 1982 Canadian Constitution came into effect, recognizing and affirming the treaty rights of Canada's Aboriginal peoples, these realities were just abstractions. Add-ons. Peripheral to what really mattered. I didn't consider the early treaties as founding constitutional documents of this country, which is how the Anishnaabe legal scholar John Borrows describes them. I didn't even know about them. I didn't know there was a treaty part of my heritage; I only knew about the colonial part – and not much even of that.

I grew up in a tightly knit nuclear family in a post-war suburb of Montreal, with streets named after the species of trees that had been removed, their roots bulldozed away, to make way for the perfect pavement of Maple Avenue, Elm Street, and so on. There was no sense of history, and at the time I didn't miss it. The past was past, end of story. I didn't even think of myself as a "settler" at the time, just a Canadian pure and simple. And my sense of that – what it meant to be Canadian – was grounded in the time when European people like me came here, and the values and institutions they brought with them.

I knew that my father's people, the Menzies and the Crerars, originated in the Scottish Highlands and had settled in southwestern Ontario in the early 1830s and 1840s. I understood that they'd bought their original hundred-acre lots from the Canada Land Company in North Easthope Township, Perth County. I didn't question how the Canada Land Company had acquired all this land in order to sell it. I assumed it had just been lying there vacant. Empty. There for the taking.

I wasn't aware of anything missing from the story I'd been told, and it never occurred to me that there might be some avoidance going on – some dissociation and unconscious denial. The contradictions remained buried, blithely ignored and unexamined, even after I began to show up for social justice causes involving Indigenous people, and even when these involved land claims. Yes, I support you, I thought as I joined the Idle No More march to Parliament Hill in Ottawa on a snowy day in December 2012. Yes again, as I brought food and firewood to support Chief Theresa Spence during her hunger strike in a teepee on Victoria Island in the Ottawa River, just behind Parliament Hill. Three years later, having moved to British Columbia, I travelled north to join a Paddle for the Peace protest against the provincial government's plans to flood the traditional territory of the West Moberly and Prophet River (Treaty 8) First Nations as it constructed the mammoth Site C dam on the Peace River. I spent some days at the Unist'ot'en Action Camp, also in northern BC, supporting the Wet'suwet'en hereditary chiefs in their struggle to assert their sovereignty and, with it, their collective right – and responsibility – to protect their vibrantly alive territory against an invading pipeline project.

But even as I leaned in, wanting to be part of all this, I somehow remained on the outside. Each time, it was like jumping over a fence and landing in a different country. I couldn't map my being there against, or into, my map of Canada. There was no connective link to my narrative as a Canadian in this same space. But then I wasn't adding that other descriptor: settler Canadian. In other words, someone descended from people who had settled here. Here not being there, where my people's original home was; here being the place of origin of other people, then and now. Here being *their* place.

There was something unresolved here, two unreconciled realities latent with contradiction and unacknowledged truth.

I didn't confront this contradiction as much as sidle up to it. Around the time the Ipperwash Inquiry into Dudley George's death was winding down and the Truth and Reconciliation Commission was being launched, a vague sense of being at a loss in my life had sent me to Scotland seeking my ancestral roots. I was flying home after yet another trip to the Highlands, this time exploring the glen where the Crerars – my father's mother's people, part of the MacIntosh clan – had lived out their lives, seemingly since before recorded time. I'd tracked the faint remaining evidence, dating from around 1000 BCE, of their ancestors having built stone-circle huts on one slope of the glen, and knew these signified their transition from hunter-gatherers to hunter-gatherers plus farmer-herders. On the other side of the valley, I had wandered among the more recent (1830s) ruins of a *clachan* village where the people had lived as more settled farmers, especially as the surrounding common land began to be enclosed as private property; hunting and gathering then became "poaching," a punishable offence.

As I drifted in and out of sleep, flying high above the vast Atlantic, I found myself wondering what had been going on in North America in 1832, when Peter Crerar and his family, and in 1842, when James Menzies and his family, had crossed the Atlantic by sailing ship. Had there been any people around when they landed and settled here? If so, how had those people lived out their lives on the land? It wasn't much of a thought – just a small crack in the head space I had grown up in. But the questions lingered.

I started reading anything I could get my hands on, catching up on all the Indigenous history I'd missed without realizing it or paying attention. And as I read, I began to understand that North America wasn't just First Nations *territory*, not just "native" space. It was native *mind space*, too, as Abenaki scholar Lisa Brooks puts it. A different way of thinking and being in the world prevailed at the time. A different world. It probably still did when my forebears arrived, I thought; it possibly still prevails in the here and now. Could my forebears have related to this then? Could I now? This fascinated me. It also kept me safely in the past, and conveniently in my own little world inside my head; it was all about me.

In *The Common Pot*, Brooks recovers the story of how the Indigenous peoples of the Atlantic seaboard negotiated their first relations with European newcomers, first through peace and friendship treaties, and then gradually through the sharing of land. She also reveals some of the thinking they brought to these treaty-making or "treating" sessions, referencing what Indigenous leaders, including Joseph Brant, recorded at the time on birchbark scrolls, as well as the memory embedded in wampum belts, one of the earliest being the Two Row Wampum. The land itself is also a memory device, I learned; walking one's ancestral land was, for Indigenous people, a way to connect with memories of that inhabited space.

I read that, to the Abenaki and the Haudenosaunee at least, these lands, often bounded by the slopes of a river valley, were understood as a "common pot." It was a pot that all the inhabitants of the valley were part of, contributed to, and were fed from. Yes, I thought, sensing similarities to what I'd learned about how my ancestors had lived on commonly shared lands in their Highland glens.

I also learned that the treaties weren't so much contracts as vows and covenants, even sacred ones. They were a way to formalize relationships that were both political and personal, understood as between kin. The relationships connected the people who shared a habitat over time. Moreover, the responsibility to maintain and regularly renew that relationship was ongoing, from generation to generation. Renewal began with gestures and rituals of condolence and reparation, both acknowledging harms done and restoring balance to the relationship.

I kept nodding as I read, identifying with this way of connecting with the land, with the idea of these intergenerational relationships, and the responsibilities too.

As my reading transported me across space and time, I found the Royal Proclamation of 1763 and its follow-up in the Treaty of Niagara, 1764, in which Indigenous leaders promised to live in peace with their British allies in return for the promise King George III had made in his proclamation: to respect the sovereignty and self-determination of the Nishnaabeg and other Indigenous nations in their territory, with any ceding or sharing of that land subject to treaty making with the crown. Symbols stitched into the shell beadwork encoded these understandings in wampum belts made for the occasion. One of these was the Covenant Chain Belt depicted on the cover of this book. When its ends are brought together, they complete the second of two diamonds, symbolizing the council fires of two sovereign nations.[1] In the middle, two stick figures holding hands and with beaded hearts visible in their chests signified the closeness of the treaty relationship.

Next, I found and read what was recorded by colonial authorities about the 1827 Huron Tract treaty. Under its terms, somewhere between two and three million acres of fertile land in what became southwestern Ontario, mostly west of present-day London, were "ceded" and "surrendered" by the resident Ojibwe-speaking Nishnaabeg[2] to the Crown. One million of those acres were given to the Canada Land Company to sell to prospective settlers like my forebears.

Aha, I thought: the missing piece of the story! I took that in. But there was more involved in the treaty negotiations. Four large tracts of land, thousands of acres each and often on spots considered sacred – though representing less than 1 percent of the Nishnaabeg's territory dealt with in the treaty – were set aside for their exclusive use, in perpetuity. One of these was at Sarnia, another at Walpole Island on the shores of Lake St. Clair, close to Windsor and Detroit. Two were bordered by an extensive stretch of fine-sand beach on the shores of Lake Huron, northeast of Sarnia. One was called Kettle Point; the other became the Stoney Point Reserve.

I felt a prickling in my eyes and a tightening in my throat as a memory surfaced. Stoney Point had been in the news in the 1990s, something about an army camp called Ipperwash being reclaimed as this reserve. Now it occurred to me: this might be part of my settler heritage, a heritage reaching closer to the here and now. It was a treaty side to my heritage about which I'd known nothing.

I found myself wanting to know and even claim this heritage, wanting to take on what it had to teach me about myself as a Canadian, including my responsibilities toward that treaty. I bought a copy of the 2007 report of the Ipperwash Inquiry into the 1995 shooting death of Dudley George during that land-reclamation action. I worked my way through its four volumes of comprehensive history and detailed account of what happened in the early 1990s.

In 1942, the federal government invoked the War Measures Act to legitimize its appropriating the entire Stoney Point Reserve to create an army training camp. It was understood that at the end of the war the land would be returned, and the people who had been displaced, including Cully and Dudley George's father, could get their homes back. But the land was not returned. Year after year, for decades, repeated letter writing, petitions, demonstrations, lobbying by regional and national Indigenous organizations, and even a report by a parliamentary committee urging the land's return changed nothing. Canada's Department of National Defence maintained it still needed the land.

In 1993, six elders, all of whom had been born and at least partly raised on the reserve and were by then getting old, decided they'd had enough. They simply moved back home, many of their children and children's children coming with them. At first, they lived in tents and trailers along the edge of the bush, some distance from the barracks, offices, mess hall, and parade ground where the army still ran its training programs, now for young army cadets. Someone's old hunting tarp sheltered a shared eating area.

Gradually they built more substantial accommodations, including small cabins and a council meeting hall. They revived their language and customs, such as the sweat lodge and peacekeepers, and they restored their self-governance traditions. They drew widespread support from non-native groups as well as from other reserves, in Canada as well as the United

States, support with which they tried to advance the return of their land. To no avail. In July 1995, they took over the by-then largely unoccupied barracks,[3] which, amazingly, prompted the remaining army personnel to leave. A few weeks after that, at the end of the Labour Day weekend, they went one step further. They extended their reclamation efforts into Ipperwash Provincial Park, a beautiful stretch of the lakeshore adjacent to the army camp, which had originally been part of the reserve. After Labour Day, the park was closed for the season.

The newly elected Ontario premier, Mike Harris, decided to treat this action as a law-and-order issue: these people were illegally trespassing in the park. The fact that they were Indigenous and reclaiming their homeland guaranteed to them in a treaty didn't matter. Two days later, on September 6, 1995, there was a police boat in the waters offshore, a surveillance helicopter hovering overhead, and a massive police presence throughout the area, with roadblocks on all the access roads. In the moonlit darkness of that night, a contingent of thirty-five body armour–clad provincial police – some with semi-automatic weapons on their shoulders and guns in their holsters, and all with special-issue steel batons swinging from their belts – marched down the road to the park. In the melee that ensued, the police opened fire. Dudley George, a short, slightly stocky, and unarmed man dressed in sneakers, jeans, and a T-shirt, was fatally shot.

I don't remember those details having been on the news at the time, or that Dudley George, like the others, was unarmed. I only remember that a native man called Dudley George had been shot. I remember thinking, that's too bad and, if I'm remembering right, making a donation to a peace group that was trying to help. But otherwise I carried on with my life. Now I didn't know what to do. But something had changed, something had gotten through to me. I'd found a way through the fence; the Huron Tract Treaty was the gate. It was the connection between Indigenous people like Dudley and Cully George, and me – or at least a way of connecting.

This was my treaty heritage as a settler. I focused on that, not the fact that it was buried under a colonial heritage, an ongoing colonial heritage I was still shying away from. What had happened at Stoney Point was my way in; all I had to do was get there.

I'd been an activist all my life, part of the post-war generation of idealists who believed that direct action could change the world. At university in Montreal in the late 1960s, I'd joined anti–Vietnam war marches and Quebec sovereignty rallies. At the university itself, I'd been part of a sit-in at the sociology department to demand more critical (Marxist) perspectives in what we were being taught. In 1970, the year I graduated, I participated in a teach-in on the North American Indian, with Harold Cardinal as keynote speaker denouncing the 1969 White Paper proposal to abolish the Indian Act and, with it, the things that formally recognized Indigenous peoples as nations, including treaties.

The impulse, and with it the confidence, to just show up had served me well both in my career as a journalist and writer, and in my continued involvement in issues of the day as a peace and social-justice activist and a feminist. So why not implicate myself in what happened at Ipperwash? I was retired now and had more time.

Dudley George had been shot not so much because people like me had chosen to deny his treaty rights and heritage, though some in decision-making authority certainly had, but because, at least in part, people like me had remained indifferent: ignorant of this heritage and the responsibilities flowing from it. And at some level, I was now willing to admit (at least privately, and only to myself) that remaining ignorant had been a choice. I was determined to repudiate that choice.

This book tells the story of what happened next, starting in the moment of my first contact with the Nishnaabeg, with whom I hoped to establish some sort of relationship and learn what my treaty responsibilities toward them might be. Starting with that glorious hour when I arrived, unaware of how I might be intruding, unaware that there might be protocols of approach when entering their territory – or that small remnant of it that was the Stoney Point Reserve. Unaware of my white settler privilege in presuming that my turning up would matter to anyone beyond my own smug and righteous self.

Page by page, chapter by chapter, I chart my often-painful experience as I entered Nishnaabe space and mind space, a space of unknowns and unknowing; my initial procrastination, being locked in self-consciousness and the need to prove myself; the anxiety of stumbling around in the darkness resulting from all I hadn't learned or had wrongly learned; the struggle to break out of my own apartheid; the compulsive need to make the unfamiliar into something familiar and comfortably under my control. I wrestle with that need to control and my colonial heritage operating through it. I share moments of embarrassment and shame when I responded defensively to being challenged, with excuses or obfuscating bullshit under the cover of which, and unbeknownst even to my conscious self, I was asserting my "professional" authority – even my white, privileged superiority – in controlling the conversational agenda. I relive the panic of being lost in not knowing; the confusion I felt as I let what surfaced in conversations with the Nishnaabe I was getting to know unsettle me, rattling the cage of my unconscious assumptions. I relive my discomfort and self-doubt, revisit moments when I wrestled with guilt and self-recrimination to the point that, to end the pain, I nearly left. The desire to do this was strangely seductive.

Over the course of many visits in the next four years, each lasting between one and two weeks, I began to face up to what I had denied: that colonialism was alive and well and at work inside me, replicating the larger harms of colonialism in the minutia of how I related to the Nishnaabe I was encountering. I challenged myself to confront this, to take responsibility for changing. As I did, I began to learn to listen to my Nishnaabe hosts on their terms. I learned to listen deeply enough that I could take in the cadence of their voices and the rhythms of their lives. And I began to change. In what I can only describe as a raising, expanding, or transformation of my consciousness, I began to sense the Nishnaabe way of life that has persisted through all the annihilating actions of the Indian Act, the Indian agent, and the local residential school. I began to learn how to tune in to it, this way of being in the world. I did this by becoming the minority person in the room, the non-native, the zhaganashi-kwe, the white woman. I left the comfort zone of my familiar.

This book is a memoir in the personal-is-political sense, building on all I've learned in the women's movement, which started with some often awkward "consciousness raising" circles in my early twenties. After a lifetime of reading, thinking, and engaging, I've come to understand the power dynamics of gender and how these operate, not just through institutional power structures but through the stories we're told about ourselves versus those we tell ourselves, and in the narratives of daily-life relationships as we conform to what's expected or dare to break free and speak a truth that has been suppressed or sugar coated. Not only does the personal reveal the flexing of sometimes lethally powerful forces like patriarchy built into the structures, systems, and narrative lines of lived life, but it's in the realm of the personal that the contradictions are experienced and felt, and can therefore be named and challenged. And it's in the realm of the personal, particularly personal relationships, where change often begins. Relationships can be healed and repaired here; counternarratives can be explored and brought to life as words and institutional action.

I'd carried that personal-is-political credo into my work as a journalist and author, always seeking out direct experience, always looking for the people whose voices had been silenced, trying to surface if not a counter-narrative then at least ways to show that the mainstream storylines weren't the whole story: family farmers being squeezed in the rise of agribusiness, small-town telephone operators losing not just their jobs but their place in the community to automation.

I'd always identified myself as something of an outsider to the status quo, without really considering how affiliated I was with it because of the circumstances of my life and upbringing. I felt comfortable (and safe) seeing myself on the side of the oppressed rather than the oppressor. Being a woman also seemed like a carte-blanche membership card. In the back of my mind at least, I allowed it to excuse me from how as a settler I was in fact on the side of the oppressor, inside the systems that adjudicated these roles.

I'd learned enough to take my settler hat off, ready to smudge, to acknowledge being on unceded territory, and to condemn racist stereotypes and slurs. I wasn't yet aware of how settler colonialism was stitched into the patterns of my thinking, even into my posture and how I walked into a room. I didn't realize how much this blocked my ability to see and to hear, let alone to move beyond mere words and symbolic gestures of so-called reconciliation with Canada's Indigenous Peoples. When I began the journey that is the subject of this book, I hadn't a clue about how daunting it was going to be to take up the challenge to really change, and how much inner resistance I was going to put up – my colonial capacity for control unwittingly at work in the subtlety of my self-deception. I only knew that mere words and gestures had grown hollow with repetition, and this was a chance to get real, to grapple with the hard realities.

And so while I begin by concentrating on the Nishnaabeg and the treaty relationship I assumed I could walk into simply by turning up at Cully's door offering condolences, the focus of my journey, and this account of it, gradually shifts to myself in my own journey as I came understand how my colonial heritage as a settler – in other words, the power dynamics of colonialism – stood in the way of any authentic relationship building. That was the real work to be done here and is the heart of the story I'm sharing. The real work I had to do was on myself, not the book I was helping Cully and others write. And work it was. It was a struggle, a shame-laced, sometimes excruciating, and long, drawn-out struggle to recognize the colonizer in myself, to acknowledge it at play in the relationships I was starting to form, and to take responsibility for dismantling its scaffolding in my mind. It was a struggle to endure the anxiety of letting go of the old and familiar, and of letting the new in.

Decolonization as personal experience is not easy. What kept me going, though, was the relationship building, my determined desire to nurture real and lasting relationships with the Nishnaabe I was encountering, who might one day regard me as treaty kin. It was their hesitation or silence, always polite but signalling that I'd said something inappropriate, that knocked me off my pedestal, that challenged me to change. These budding relationships were the context in which I came to see and to struggle to dismantle colonization in myself, and also the incentive to keep at it. All that bumbling-into-being of relationships became the crucible of decolonization, or my experience of it.

Becoming involved with the Stoney Point Nishnaabeg as a writer, helping them weave their stories into an oral-history account of the Ipperwash tragedy, complicated things enormously. On one hand, it gave me an excuse to keep visiting, to come back to see them again and again, and that was good. It was a means to the end of forming relationships. But it also insulated me from the work I had to do on myself, forestalled it, and made it more complex. Because being the writer (even as I scrupulously defined myself as their "writing assistant") was loaded with colonialism disguised as professionalism and expertise. As a successful writer, I knew how to express things, how to organize thoughts into coherent order. I knew what publishers would want, and what might best guarantee that the book would be reviewed. Or did I? And, if so, on whose terms?

I knew I wasn't appropriating their stories, trying to steal them or take them over. But still, I wasn't the appropriate person to be there helping, because of all my professional assumptions – the arrogance of them, the inherent sense of superiority that I carried with them into the project – and because I was white. The Canadian cultural space I was familiar with had largely been filled by people like me for most of my adult life. Its ways of telling stories and conveying what matters were second nature to me, and the almost total absence of Indigenous voices telling Indigenous stories was just the way it was. It wasn't easy considering – let alone acknowledging – that colonialism was part of this; this might diminish the legitimacy of my own status as an "award-winning author" in that space. So I resisted, a lot, hiding behind this supporting role I'd welcomed their invitation to play. It was a convenient mask, behind which I hid even from myself.

It was only as I began writing the book and encountered resistance from some of the Nishnaabe co-authors – not so much as I recorded their stories as when I showed them the first drafts of the book – that I began to really question my role. It didn't matter if my intentions were honourable. Good intentions weren't good enough; not if my mind was still steeped in colonial thinking.

It wasn't appropriation of story that was at issue, but appropriation of voice. Can a non-Indigenous person serve a supporting role in situations like this? I am still struggling with the question. Meanwhile, in the messy particulars of lived reality, I struggled to get out of the way of their telling their story, struggled to listen with integrity, because as two years of visits became three and four, I had come to deeply care for Cully and the others. I'd come to respect them and to feel fully accountable to them. And so I stayed the course I had embarked on, stayed even while remaining uncertain, full of self-doubts that kept me awake at night. I wrote draft after draft after draft, sending each by mail and then flying back to Ontario to review them. Slowly the co-authors took charge, and I truly became their assistant, not just in self-designation. It felt as if I were graduating from a school I hadn't even been aware I was enrolled in.

Being a writer became an additional lens through which I learned to look at myself, to question myself, and to change. Writing has been my life's work. It's been how I have engaged with the world: as someone who names things, as an author with published authority. In my journey of unlearning and opening myself to the new, I've changed as a writer, becoming more responsive to, accountable to, those whose stories I'm helping to tell. (I also look back at my career and regret how much I presumed to speak for others, to think that I knew how their stories should be told.)

Working for the Nishnaabe co-authors also helped me move from the personal to the political, and realize how important it is for the momentum of change to move this way for it to be lasting: from the private realm of relationships to the more public realm of institutions. As I changed, I brought my committed sense of accountability in the relationships I had with the Nishnaabeg to the editors I was working with at UBC Press. From past experience, I knew that publishers, as the authority figure behind the author, reserve final say over a book's title, its cover design and art. They will consult with the author, but that's all. Over the course of my writing career, I'd sometimes chafed against this, but had never seriously challenged it. Now, though, having been deputized by the Nishnaabe co-authors as their go-between with the publisher, I found myself doing so; being shown options was not enough. The Nishnaabe co-authors felt strongly about what the title should be, what image and feel the cover should convey. They rejected the choices the publisher came up with. On yet another visit to their territory, I sat with the co-authors as they came up with the options they preferred. Then I championed these to the publisher. And the editors listened. They put the respect for Indigenous voices to which they'd committed in principle into practice. They changed their practice.

And so this book is about my transformation not just as a settler but as a writer engaged in the institutions of culture in this country. Toward the end of the book, I explore the implications of what I learned: for the changes needed at this level, and for people like me to feel implicated in those changes, even at the cost of privileged status.

I don't know if my experience of decolonization has anything to teach others. If it does, perhaps it will be by modelling the journey of decolonization, or part of it.

I began to change and to take on the implications of being part of a larger change, not because I'd decided this was the right thing to do, although it certainly was, but because justice demanded it and genuine reconciliation requires it. I found myself being changed because I wanted to be worthy of a treaty relationship with the Nishnaabe women and men I'd set out to meet. To get to even the possibility of this, I had to acknowledge their colonial heritage – everything from colonial authorities' lip-service commitment to treaty promises to the genocidal agenda at work behind the Indian Act and its ongoing amendments, the residential schools, and child-welfare agencies still scooping children. I had to acknowledge it as ongoing lived reality not just for them, but for me too. As I helped them write one part of that heritage into a book, the relationships I was forming around this work also forced me to acknowledge colonialism as an ongoing dynamic, including in myself and, through me, in institutions of power that shape reality. And as tentative early and ongoing working relationships deepened into friendships and I began to really change, I also became more motivated to advocate for larger change.

So much hinged on the dynamics of relationship and communication. I wanted to fully take in all that these would-be treaty kin were saying as a way of respecting them for who they are. And this meant letting myself be touched, affected, and then motivated to change.

It was a case of I see you, I hear you. I–thou. In the messy particulars of the relationships that were developing, in which I allowed myself to be moved by what they were sharing with me about the traumatic past through to the troubled present, they challenged me to change my thinking – about practically everything. And so even though I began by seeking a treaty relationship for some very suspect, self-deluding reasons, I'm glad I did. Because it brought me into the realm of encounter and of relationship building, where I could get on with the necessary work of decolonization and truly prepare myself for reconciliation and the new and renewed treaty relationships that will be part of this.

I end the book with a few thoughts on this longer journey of reconciliation. But first, how the journey began for one person: me.

1

At the Fence

It was a humid, hot day when I set out, and I was glad there was air conditioning in the car I'd rented. I hadn't bothered with GPS, an option for which you had to pay extra. I had my old paper road map on the seat beside me; that would do. I knew where I was going, sort of. I was heading for the Stoney Point Reserve, or the former Ipperwash army camp. Neither was marked on the map, though Kettle Point was, and I knew that the neighbouring reserve, Stoney Point, which had been turned into the Ipperwash army camp, was slightly north and west of there. Somewhere along Highway 21, on the shore of Lake Huron.

A family gathering in Dundas, outside Hamilton, had brought me to Ontario. I'd had to rent a car to get to the event, so it was easy to tack on some extra days, and I could visit my long-time friend Dona Harvey in Waterloo as well. She'd packed me some leftovers from last night's supper and wished me well as I'd set out after breakfast. She'd also Google-mapped Kettle Point, and how to find the band office there. But my instinct told me to go straight to the site of the 1990s action, to get my bearings from there.

I was going on little more than instinct, really, or rather acting on it before this impulse to just show up withered with too much rational thought. And here I was, passing Amulree, where both the Crerars and the Menzies had settled, named after the town at the end of Glen Quaig, in Scotland, from which they'd come in 1832. I drove down the road where they'd originally farmed. I'm in treaty territory, I thought. Huron Tract treaty territory.

The roads were a mishmash, with some running southwest and others running northwest. So I followed the zigzag pattern and finally emerged on what I guessed must be Highway 21. Good, I thought, getting close. But then, what to look for? The report of the Ipperwash Inquiry had recommended that the government "immediately return the former army camp to the peoples of the Kettle and Stony Point First Nation."[1] That was over ten years ago. Had this been done? If so, would any visible sign of the former army camp remain? Would there still be an official entrance gate where I should go to make inquiries? And even if there was, should I? Probably not.

As I drove, I noticed some dilapidated, look-alike buildings in a big open area. They were long and white, and low to the ground. Barracks? I'd never been close to an army base before, and of course this one dated back to the Second World War. I slowed down. Someone was driving what looked like a John Deere lawnmower across the grass on this side of them. I slowed down more, then pulled over and stopped the car. I should check this out; maybe this guy would talk to me.

I crossed the ditch and approached a rusted barbed-wire fence. A sign on one of the fence posts read "Danger: Unexploded Munitions. UXOs." I leaned across the sagging fence, felt the jab of one of the barbs pressing against the bare skin of my arm and pulled back. I placed my hands, carefully, between the barbs and leaned forward against the fence again. I kept my eyes on the man driving the big green lawnmower, willing him to notice me. He kept going back and forth, coming close, turning and going away, coming close again, but then turning and driving away. It was nearly noon by then, and the sun blazed down on me. I looked at my hands clutching the top strand of the old fence. Releasing my grip, I noticed rust on my sweaty palms. I wiped them on my jean capris and stepped back. I wanted to walk away but didn't. The guy was approaching another turn. He was closer now; each turn brought him closer. But then he completed the turn and moved away.

This was ridiculous! I should give up. Sweat was running into my eyes, stinging. What was I doing here, really? I watched the man on the mower move toward me down the line of grass, bumping up and down on the uneven terrain. Then, instead of turning, he drove up, turned off the machine, and walked toward me.

I watched him approach: not much taller than me, slight of build, black hair, a Blue Jays baseball cap pulled low over a lean, dark face. I didn't have a clue what I was going to say. I hadn't thought anything out, had laid no groundwork for this visit, going through my usual routine of getting someone to introduce me, to vouch for me being worth talking to. I'd just assumed I could drop in here, and whoever I encountered wouldn't mind.

He stopped a couple of feet from the fence. He looked me in the eye, gave a nod, said something like "Howdy," and I launched in. I didn't introduce myself at first. Plus, well, he was only the guy mowing the grass.

I tried to explain what had brought me to this fence: something vague about treaties and Ipperwash being a breach of one, and wanting to find out how things stood. I really can't remember what I said; I was nervous.

He told me that I wasn't the first one to stop by the fence. Once, he said, there was an old gent who had trained at the camp in 1942. The man said there was a house they'd started using for target practice back in the bush, and a woman had come out the door, a couple of children with her. "And he tells me he's been all over, Second World War, Korea, and this is what's stayed with him, haunts him" – that they were shooting at that house, thinking it was empty, when a Nishnaabe woman and her children were still inside.[2]

He knew the stories – the stories of what happened here! I'd arrived. I stuck out my hand and introduced myself.

"Kevin Simon," he said, shaking my hand briefly.

I'd heard of that name, just couldn't place it. I started to say something, to ask him a question. But he was already stepping away.

"Well, best be getting back," he said, half turning toward the lawnmower.

He took off his baseball cap and gestured down the road. There were a couple of campers permanently parked inside the fence but also along the highway here. I might find some people to talk to there, he said. Then he whacked his ball cap against his leg, pulled it back on, and gave it a good tug. He looked me in the eye again, quick nod, hint of a smile, and he walked away.

Back in the car, I found my list of names, people whom I hoped I might meet who'd been mentioned a lot in the Ipperwash Inquiry report. Kevin Simon's name was on the list. He was sixteen in 1993, when the elders led the way to reclaim their ancestral homeland at Aazhoodena/Stoney Point, and he followed, determined to support them. His grandfather Daniel and his grandmother Melva had been active in the efforts to regain the land after the war, organizing protests, writing letters, raising funds for lawyers. His mother, Marcia, had grown up surrounded by this, became part of it, and followed her aging mother back home in 1993 herself. Kevin was there that night in 1995 when his friend and cousin Dudley was shot. And he was still here?

I looked out the window and spotted him on his John Deere lawnmower. I started getting out of the car. But he must have just finished mowing the grass because he was driving off toward where the barracks and some other buildings were.

Ah well, I thought, closing the door again and starting the car. I'd get his number somehow, talk to him another time perhaps. I drove on and passed what looked like the official entrance to the camp. There was a barrier across the road and a gatehouse beside it. I carried on past the entrance, looking for the campers where Kevin had suggested I stop.

The first wasn't a camper; it was a container unit normally hauled behind a truck. It had a "Smokeshop" sign so big that it covered half the length of the unit. As I got closer, I noticed another sign, this one on the side door. It said Closed, so I carried on. Farther along, there was a sign for Medicines of the Earth, with a couple of marijuana flags fluttering beside a small camper, and a row of bright-red plastic cups along one side of it, the tips of marijuana seedlings visible above their rims. There was an Open sign in the window, and someone coming out the door. I waited till they'd driven away, and then I approached.

Inside, there was a set of deer antlers on a table, a Mohawk warrior flag covering the back window. Toward the front, there was a makeshift counter with jars of bud and leaf displayed under it, a tiny electronic scale on top, and a big man with scraggly long black hair standing behind it.

His name was Hubert George. In between customers, we talked. I told him that I'd been reading about his people's efforts to get their land and way of life here back.

"I'm assimilated," he told me. "We lost our heritage. We lost everything." Then he surprised me. He gestured toward the land behind the trailer, the terrain of the reserve where, he said, his grandfather and grandmother had grown up. "But the land's coming back," he said.

I asked if I could maybe drive around and take a look. "Sure, go ahead," he said. The events I'd read about had happened twenty-five years ago. It was ten years since Justice Sidney B. Linden, commissioner of the Ipperwash Inquiry, had submitted his report, recommending that the land be immediately cleaned up and returned. It was two years since the Final Settlement Agreement was signed. Had anything happened? Here was a chance for me to see for myself.

I simply drove through the back of the pot-shop's parking lot and there I was, facing the inside road. I was in the former army camp. It was as easy as pressing my foot on the accelerator of my shiny rental car.

I looked down the road to my left. There were remnants of what might have been a big sign for the camp on a spot set back from the road. Chunks of stone and cement littered what had been the base of it, looking jagged and sharp. Whatever had been on top had clearly been knocked off, violently. I could almost feel the force of the blows by the sledgehammer or whatever it was that had bludgeoned it to pieces. I didn't want to go any closer.

I turned right instead, and soon was driving past old barracks. The paint was chipped, and pieces of clouded old vapour barrier flapped from window frames, gray and opaque, like ghosts trying to get free. Kevin lived in one of the barracks, I learned later.

Meandering lines of grass and weeds filled cracks in the pavement, creeping in from the edges where the pavement had fallen apart. On either side of the road, mowed grass gave way to weed-filled – and even brush-filled – fields. In the middle of one, half hidden by weeds and bushes, there was a small, half-collapsed building standing by itself. I wondered if this might be the Nishnaabe council hall they'd built in 1993. It looked abandoned. The whole place looked abandoned, though I could see it wasn't. There was a children's play structure outside one of the barracks, the frame for a sweat lodge tucked beside a four-wheeler behind another. There was a vegetable garden nearby, with what I recognized as beans, squash, and corn growing together, the traditional Three Sisters. Clearly people lived here. This is their home, I thought. I was in their space.

I felt like an intruder. I was an intruder. I turned around and left.

I drove five kilometres down the road to Kettle Point, where the Kettle and Stony Point band office was located. After the shabbiness of Ipperwash, the smoothness of the stone and brick, the neat, clean lines of the building, struck me. Money had been spent here. I parked in the neatly marked parking lot and headed for the front door. Inside, there was a second, heavy door leading to the reception area. There was a counter with a plexiglass sheet running its length from countertop to ceiling, except at the centre, where a panel was slid back.

A woman came forward; how could she help me? I told her my name and explained that I was trying to locate some people. She asked if I had any names. I read from my list, mentioning Kevin Simon and also Bonnie Bressette, a former chief of the Kettle and Stony Point band council. Justice Linden had referred to her repeatedly in his report. He'd also singled her out as one of the "respected and trusted people" who might have helped resolve the Ipperwash crisis before it became a tragedy. The woman said she could give me one of the numbers, Bonnie Bressette's, because it was in the phone book. I didn't tell her that I wouldn't have known what phone book to look in – just took the number, thanked her, and left.

2

Showing Up

I'd only given myself a day for my little trip to Ipperwash. Still, I could have tried Bonnie's number when I was back at my friend's place that evening. But I didn't. I'd call as soon as I got back to BC, I'd told myself, and yet I kept putting it off. Maybe I shouldn't bother, I thought; it had been so long. What was the point of showing up now?

The fall rains arrived and I still hadn't made the call. Rivulets of water zigzagged down my office window, warping the trees beyond. Once again, I had the phone in my hand. I'd created an entry in my contact list: Bonnie Bressette. I scrolled down to her name, and lethargy swamped me again.

"What took you so long?" I imagined her saying. Not "so long" since July, because she wouldn't know about that, but since the 1990s. Why had I remained ignorant for so long? Not just unaware but indifferent too? It was embarrassing.

But I recalled what I'd read in Paulette Regan's *Unsettling the Settler Within*, how emotions like fear, shame, guilt – what she called "coping mechanisms" – keep us "mired in a colonial relationship."[1] I got the book off my shelf and leafed through it to find the phrases I'd marked: the importance of "encounter," of entering an "uneasy, unsettled relationship, based on learning (about difference) from the Other, rather than learning about the Other."² This was my chance.

I kept looking at the screen of my iPhone. Whoever was behind that name and number was an opportunity for encounter, like that moment by the fence with Kevin Simon. I wanted to continue what I'd started there that day. A sense of beginning had stirred alive in me. I wanted to keep showing up.

I kept remembering what I'd seen that day in July: the tattered vapour barrier flapping from the frames of cracked and broken barrack windows, the shattered stones and mortar where the base of some big and official sign had once stood. My mind kept going back to that, the violence of it. Colonial history as the Nishnaabeg must have experienced it, repeated here in a second round of colonial authorities taking Nishnaabe land – though they were called Canadian authorities by the 1940s, not colonial ones. The sign that was there would have renamed this place as the Department of National Defence's domain, one of its army training camps; I was sure of that. The evidence I'd seen, of it having been violently removed, even its base broken, shattered into bits, told me something of whatever that sign had meant to certain people, their anger unleashed in the act of its removal.

I had experienced personal violence in my life – an attempted rape, sexual harassment at work, sexual abuse when I was young. But I'd never experienced historical violence. Colonial violence. It was latent in the landscape.

I hadn't wanted to go any nearer at the time. Could I go back to that space now that I'd started to be aware? Whatever it had to teach me, it was part of my colonial heritage, from the Other side. This was my way into it. I just had to make the phone call, follow up on what I'd started already.

Finally, after months of intending and intending to call, I couldn't stand myself any longer. I pressed the Connect button and stood there at the window of my home in BC, watching the raindrops meander down the windowpane as I waited.

"Hallo?" A big female voice, sounding friendly. I asked if this was Bonnie Bressette.

"Yes?" Caution in her voice. My mouth went dry. I started to explain who I was. I wanted her to know that I was a writer, as if this lent me some legitimacy; people always seemed to give me the time of day when they knew that, if I called or showed up out of the blue. But I wasn't calling as a writer, I told her. I was calling as a descendant of the Huron Tract treaty of 1827. I didn't say *settler;* I still had trouble applying that word to myself.

"Oh yeah?" Her voice was neither encouraging nor discouraging, just, "I'm listening." I told her that I'd read the report of the Ipperwash Inquiry, that I'd read about her a lot there; her name kept coming up. Quick inhale, then: "I'd like to meet you."

"Sure," she said – essentially, come on over. She laughed: "I'm doing up beets. I'll give you a taste."

I asked her where she lived. She gave me her street address, Lake Road. I asked, uh, what town? Kettle Point, she said, with an "of course" edge to her voice. This was her territory. She'd lived here all her life, though she was born on the Stoney Point Reserve, down the road from Kettle Point, and had lived there till she was five, in 1942. I'd read about the family's forced eviction in the Ipperwash report: five-year-old Bonnie seeing her family's little bungalow hoisted onto the back of a flatbed truck. When the federal government turned her home into an army training camp, they'd relocated the family to Kettle Point, where there was family on Bonnie's mother's side to help them survive.

"See you soon," I said as I ended the call, as though this was as casual as seeing an old friend; trying to keep it light. Still, I had made a commitment.

Immediately, while I still had the momentum and the conviction that I could follow through, I booked a flight to Ontario. I rented a car – for ten days! Then I found and booked an Airbnb in the town of Forest, which seemed like the cheapest option close by, now that the small local motels were closed for the season. A week later, I flew first to Toronto and then to London. I picked up the car, drove to Forest, found the Airbnb, and moved my things in.

The drag of dread set in again, the excuse of food to buy, whatever. It had never occurred to me until then – the significance of it – that I'd never been on an Indian, or First Nations, reserve before. In all my life I'd only driven through two or three of them, on my way to somewhere else. They were my own terra nullius – "empty land, nobody's land," the land treated as if no one were there.

I forced myself to get in the car, to start the motor, to drive. This idea, that no one was there, was pure fiction, a false narrative of denial, known as the Doctrine of Discovery, dating from a 1943 papal bull, though subsequently revoked. But it was still alive in my head – at least its effects were there. It was a fiction denying the fact of other peoples being here, flourishing at the time when this edict – decreeing that any land without Christian people on it should rightfully be treated as empty, there for the taking – was issued. This fiction had then been acted upon as though it *were* fact, with these acts then becoming the facts of settler-colonial history. And this had entered my mind when I was growing up, as the landscape of my existence. Familiar, comfortable, and unchallenged. What other facts this fiction had covered up were still pretty sketchy in my mind.

I turned off the highway onto Lakeshore Road. Now I was entering Nishnaabe space. I was entering a reserve; this was the point, the destination, of my journey. And that's when it finally hit me: this was a terra nullius to me because nobody and nothing here related to me. It was a blank space in that sense, and almost in the original sense associated with the fifteenth-century Doctrine of Discovery, designating any land not yet Christianized as "terra nullius." Centuries of colonization in the name of Christianity had gone ahead, nullifying what had been here. And here I was in a spot where all this had gone on and all its effects had accumulated. I didn't know where to step. I didn't know what I might put my foot down on by mistake.

I passed the sign that welcomed me to the Kettle and Stony Point First Nation. This was it! I was entering the land of my treaty-settler heritage, the territory of the Nishnaabeg of southwestern Ontario, which had been reduced to this small scrap of land on the shore of Lake Huron. It occurred to me that a whole and wholly different way of life had been going on here since, and well before, 1827 when the Huron Tract treaty was negotiated, and I knew nothing about it. Instead, I had a head full of stereotypes and assumptions I didn't want to even admit were in there.

I nearly turned back. But I had made the call. I was expected. I'd paid to get here from my retirement savings. I passed a billboard advertising the Trading Post souvenir shop, the picture showing two figures in buckskin and head feathers waving from a canoe. Familiar kitsch put on for tourists, I thought, reassuring in their familiarity to people like me. I passed the brick band office where I'd gotten Bonnie Bressette's phone number three months earlier, and kept driving.

During the winter of 2012/13, when I'd brought food and firewood to Chief Theresa Spence's camp on the Ottawa River, I was invited to join the circle around the fire outside her tent. In the summer of 2017, I'd chopped firewood for Wet'suwet'en female chief Freda Huson as a way to give back during my time at the Unist'ot'en Action Camp. Maybe I'd cut up beets for canning with this woman, Bonnie; I could do that.

Finally I was on Lake Road, with vast stretches of an invasive water weed (Phragmites) blocking the view of Lake

Huron on one side, big old trees on the other. There were small houses, bungalows, among the trees, and bush stretching behind them. Bonnie's home was a bungalow, too, though looking like it had been added onto at both ends. There was a big walnut tree on one side and a big, drooping birch on the other. There was a gas barbecue on the patio in front of the door. I knocked.

"Come in," I heard. It sounded like Bonnie. So I pushed open the door and stepped inside. She was in a wheelchair, rolling it toward me with her feet in white, thick-soled running shoes.

"Take a chair," she said, indicating a wooden chair at a big wooden table by the front window. I took off my jacket, set down my bag, and pulled out the gift I'd brought: some vacuum-packed BC smoked salmon.

She thanked me and set it aside. She propelled her chair up to the table and looked at me. I looked at her, taking in the slightly red-blond hair, tightly curled as though in a perm, the small beaded earrings, and, behind her glasses, bright hazel eyes.

I asked about the beets. She laughed, told me that she and Fred had done up forty pounds of them. Any time there's a funeral, she said, "It's always, 'Bonnie, where's the beets?'"

Her daughter Shelly, she recounted, was down in the basement one day, and she came back up saying, "Mom, you've got enough to feed the whole reserve down there."

Bonnie offered me a coffee and we sat there for a bit in silence. The fingers of her hand were twisted sideways with arthritis; rheumatoid arthritis, I guessed. Yet she could hold a teaspoon and stir her coffee. She set down the spoon.

"So why are you here?" she asked, looking me in the eye.

I held her look but froze inwardly. All through my life, I've had a strong sense of social justice and the common good, and the confidence to act on it – like showing up to help organize a renegade version of the Women and the Constitution

Conference in 1981 when the official one was cancelled. I've always assumed that my stepping up, and whatever my contribution ended up being, would be appropriate. Now, as I tried to hold the gaze of this eighty-four-year-old Nishnaabe woman in a wheelchair, it struck me how presumptuous I was.

Yes, why was I here? What the hell was I thinking, rushing in here like this, using my wherewithal and self-assurance – I didn't think of it as my privileged white, colonial self-assurance at the time – to just invite myself here? As if my presence, showing up to acknowledge all the harm that was done all those years ago, was going to make a difference. I was probably just indulging myself in catch-up settler guilt. No, not even that: using my privilege to step around all that and script myself into a nice shiny new role as treaty kin. In fact, I was intruding on this woman and her family, in her home, on her territory, disrupting whatever fragile status quo she'd created over the years: making pickled beets, showing up at every funeral with a jar of them.

"I don't really know," I said, looking down. I was on the cusp of apologizing and clearing out. Instead, I looked up again. She was still watching me, not angry, not accusing. Her gaze was steady, quietly waiting for me to continue. I started telling her what had inspired me. I'd been learning about treaties from her side, from the Indigenous perspective, I said. I'd learned to think of them now as relationships, relationships that have to be renewed on a regular basis. I mentioned the Abenaki academic Lisa Brooks. I said that I'd been using what I'd learned in her book, *The Common Pot*, as a guide. In particular, I continued, what it said about treaty renewal: that it begins with condolences, expressions of remorse where wrongs have been done, taking responsibility for the treaty having been broken somehow. This is followed by reparations, the gestures and actions that are required to set things right and restore balance in the relationship.

I looked up from my coffee, met Bonnie's eye, and looked down again. "So I guess that's why I'm here," I said. "I feel like I'm in the condolences phase." I stopped, too choked up to continue.

Bonnie said she'd like to read that book and asked me to write down the title. She pushed back from the table and used her feet to manoeuvre herself up to the bookcase. Like every available surface in this big, open interior space with a TV in one corner, a wood stove in another, a counter and kitchen area opposite the dinner-kitchen table, the bookcase was cluttered. There were books, magazines, and flyers and, behind them, a crowd of photographs in wooden or plastic frames. Bonnie leaned forward, pushed aside some of the papers, and grabbed first one and then another and another of the framed photos. She pulled them all into her lap, backed up her wheelchair and returned to the table. She handed me a black-and-white photo of herself in a long white wedding dress, standing next to a man in a dark suit. "That's me and Fred," she said. They'd been married for sixty-four years.

She held up another old black-and-white photo: a man with a cigarette hanging from one side of his mouth.

"That's Uncle Bish," she said, looking at it herself. "He was just an ordinary old Nishnaabe man. He was six foot four. He was a fisherman. There's a company in Sarnia, called Purdy's Fisheries. They would never have been successful if they didn't have this man ... because he knew. There's thirty-three miles across this lake. He knew where the fish are. He knew where to set nets. And what kind of weather to get off that lake. And when the big ships started coming up the river, St. Clair, they got Uncle Bish; he was the one. He'd go, meet that ship, drive it up through the river." She handed me the photo.

"This man, he was the most generous man, the kindest man."

Bonnie looked at me, then took the photo back and put it in her lap. He and his sister Phyllis were allowed to stay home, she said, to help Grandma Flora on the farm. The Indian agent sent all the others, Bonnie's mother, Hilda, included, to the residential school at Muncey, nearly a hundred kilometres away.

Bonnie handed me another photo, this one more faded than the others: two little girls in smock dresses. "That's me and my little sister," Bonnie said. The picture was taken in May 1942, on the day the army came and took their house away on the back of a truck.

Bonnie shook her head. "I could never figure it out. Why did we have to get dressed up on such a hurtful day?"

I nearly said something, offered some soothing explanation about a mother's pride. I'd already blurted out some things I was kicking myself for: that I'd grown up with a wood stove in the kitchen, too; that I, too, had canned and frozen vegetables out of my garden. Drawing out the parallels, the similarities between us. Making a case for myself: sort of, sure, I was a "settler" but not with a capital S. I didn't tell her that my father had worked in management for the Canadian branch of a British multinational, and that his earnings had paid for me to go to university: McGill University, founded by James McGill, who had also founded the Bank of Montreal, in 1821, from the profits he'd made from the fur trade.

I was cutting and pasting a new c.v. for myself here, as qualified for the position of treaty kin, or treaty-kin apprentice ready to learn what my treaty responsibilities might be.

I was glad that Bonnie mostly ignored what I had to say, or glossed over it with a casual "Yeah?" Now I managed to keep my mouth shut, only shaking my head and saying something that simply commiserated.

Silence. Then, "You know, we don't even have a word in our language for surrender. We agreed to share the land, because to us, you don't have life if you don't have land."

I nodded. "Yes," I said.

"Land is life to us," she said.

"Yes," I said, my voice a little louder as I recognized the truth of what she'd said. I could never have stated it so simply, this knowledge coming through so clearly, foundational to her identity.

She piled the photos in her lap and started wheeling herself away from the table. I offered to put the photos back for her. "No, I'll do it," she said.

Over at the bookcase, she gestured up to the row of coloured photos: all her grandchildren graduating from high school, and this one, Summer, graduating from university.

She asked if I had any children. I told her one, plus two grandchildren. She told me that she was the first generation to be sent to the local public school, in Forest.

"I asked my dad, 'Are we dirty Indians?' Another time, 'Is it true, all the things they say in the history books about us?'"

She looked at me. Was she daring me to say something defensive? Was this a test?

I was past the awkward, knee-jerk defensiveness. Yet it was still there, only more inward: an instinctive avoidance, disassociation – out of fear. How to acknowledge the contradiction – the outright fraud and deceit – laid like thick cement into the foundation of this country? Land that had been considered a gift to be shared was instead considered as property to be surrendered for exclusive ownership by white people coming from Europe. And how to acknowledge its result? The cement wasn't just in the textbooks on which I was raised. It was inside me, in the foundations of how I saw myself in the world.

I grew up thinking it was normal for settlers to take up all the space, in every sense of the word. Now I wanted to repudiate this. And yet, I realized as I sat there, I perpetuate it, though at a level way below racist slurs and overt violence; it was much more subtle and between the lines. This unexamined sense of what was normal was the elephant in my head. And it made me the elephant in the room here; I couldn't even realize when I put my big foot down, squelching something before I could notice that there was something different from my normal to take in. It made me skittish, wanting to run away even as I was leaning in, trying to start a conversation with someone like Bonnie.

I stayed put. I returned her look, taking in what she was saying, letting myself fully acknowledge the pain and humiliation of it, day after day after day, even as I could feel a quiver running through me, the fear of taking on all that guilt-ridden truth.

There was movement to my left. A skinny guy with long grey hair roughly bound in a ponytail was moving slowly into the room, using a walker with rubber feet. One arm hung limp at his side and swayed slightly as he lurched his body forward, dragging one foot after him as he came.

Bonnie half turned in his direction, called out, "Eh, Buck. Gettin' some coffee?"

Some sound in reply as he moved to the counter, ignoring us. Bonnie made no move to introduce me.

I felt once again like an intruder. Whatever pain was going on here, it was none of my business. I felt out of place too. There was a birchbark log with ribbons tied around it propped up against the wall in the corner beside the front door. My eyes shied away from it. I was almost afraid of it even, because it signalled how much I didn't know, how much actually separated me from someone like Bonnie. I didn't know where to begin.

And yet I sat there, watching and not watching what was going on, my eye going back to the birchbark log, noticing too, something that looked like braided sweetgrass tucked away where a crossbeam met the front wall. Buck poured himself a coffee, added cream and sugar, then tucked his mug into a cupholder mounted on the walker. Without a word, he slowly made his way out of the room. Silence. Bonnie was looking out the window.

"My mom, this time of the year, she'd be getting antsy, wanting to get working on her wreaths," Bonnie continued after he left. Her father and his friend Sheldon Cloud would head into the bush at Stoney Point cutting Christmas trees and cedar boughs for wreath making. "And then we'd go into London, onto Richmond Street; that's where all the well-off people lived. Mom would have wreaths on this hand that were all decorated ready for the door. On this side was if you wanted to decorate them; they were a little cheaper. I'd have my arms full, and my mom's arms were full. And meantime, my dad was in what they call the market square in London now. My dad would go, him and Sheldon, they'd have a great big ol' forty-five-gallon drum with holes in it at the bottom, and they had three bricks. They would set that drum on the three bricks, and they had wood in the back of the truck with the trees. Make a great big fire. And Mom and I would go down the street, sell all our wreaths, turn around and get back there."

I loved the ingenuity, carrying on living off the land in a way. I smiled and nodded. "You carried on the old ways a lot, it seems." Bonnie snorted: "We never left them." She looked at me.

"You know, in all that time, Dad never had us on social assistance once. He always had a way to make money. And he taught us you have to share."

She was looking out the window again. Then, still looking out toward the lake, she said, "When my ancestors and yours made a treaty –" She stopped there. It seemed clear that she'd been thinking about this but didn't know where to take it. Or maybe she did, and it was my turn. She looked at me.

"Yes," I said, returning her look. "And it's broken."

She nodded. Then she called out, "Fred?" A faint answer from down the hall.

"Let's go for a drive." A slender older man dressed neatly in a flannel shirt and sweater walked into the room. "Where to?" he asked as he set his coffee mug down on the counter.

"Stoney," she said.

"Okay," he said. Not, "Why?" or "Why now?" He just picked up the car keys off the table, and we headed out.

I found myself in the back seat of a minivan big enough for Bonnie's walker, big enough to also sleep multiple grandchildren and, once, a very young great-grandchild determined to be allowed to go with them to Disney World in Florida because she'd met the bar, having learned to brush her teeth on her own. Bonnie and Fred took turns driving through the night, getting there the following afternoon.

Now we drove past the band office, the school and community centre, the daycare centre and mini-mall with its supermarket. Fred turned left and headed up the old wagon trail, now Highway 21. He turned left onto Army Camp Road, then right at the gates of the defunct army camp. A wave and a nod from someone inside the army gatehouse, and the barrier was raised.

We drove past a dilapidated trailer, part of its siding gone to reveal dirty yellow insulation. I learned later that it's the trailer where Dudley used to live. We passed a rusted little car with vapour-barrier in the passenger-side window, then a truck collapsed on one corner over a pancake-flat tire. Then we were on gravel, approaching the boundary of the former Ipperwash Provincial Park. But instead of going that way, Fred turned right and entered the bush. Tall trees on either side – chestnut, oak, maple – and it struck me: this land had been logged, but never clear-cut. We came to a fork in the road, one the main gravel one, the other not.

"No," Bonnie said, "don't go down that way." The fall rains had reduced these narrow back roads to mud. Fred carried on anyway, branches scraping against the side of the van. We came into a clearing, with pine trees on one side where the ground gave way to the sandy soil of sand dunes. Bonnie called a halt. She'd spotted a seedling she wanted to bring back for her front yard. I offered to help – sort of "treaty relation in training."

"No," Bonnie said. I sat in the back watching Fred, who'd already gotten out of the van. He used what looked like a tire iron to work the sandy soil around a small jack pine. I watched him tug it, work the ground some more and finally pull it clear, a lovely mass of root hanging like unbraided hair in his hand.

We drove on, and again Bonnie called out, "Stop." She'd spotted some lily of the valley; she wanted to transplant some of them. But they hadn't brought a shovel, and these plants were growing in solid earth. She looked around for something to mark the spot. There was a white plastic bag with Mr. Submarine written on it, lying on the floor at my feet. I held it up and offered to go tie it to a tree branch.

"Okay," Bonnie said. I jumped out, looked around. There was a bush close by. I went up to it, reached for a branch that I thought would do, and started to tie on the bag.

"No, put it higher," Bonnie called from the van. I undid the bag, quelling a flash of irritation, and reached for another branch.

"Yeah, that's good," Bonnie said. I finished tying it and got back into the van, and we drove away. As we bumped along on the muddy road, I turned around in my seat to see if I could see the bag, and there it was: a little flag of white plastic fluttering in the dark of the woods.

Back at their place, I offered to dig in the seedling. I've planted a lot of trees, I said, thousands, when I was a kid growing up on our farm.

"No," she said, but she was smiling, as though acknowledging my good intentions, accepting that much. "Buck'll do it later." Then she led the way inside. She was ready for another cup of coffee; I should have one too. She showed me her collection of ceramic and stuffed turtles, considered kin to the fish – sucker fish. That was her clan totem, she explained, leaving it for me to know what a clan totem was. She showed me more photographs, naming all the nieces and nephews, grandchildren's husbands or boyfriends, great-grandchildren, great-nieces and -nephews. Fred had disappeared into a back room. I was fading fast.

"Should I come back tomorrow?" I asked as I gathered up my stuff.

"Sure. Come back tomorrow. We'll talk some more," Bonnie said.

3

First Doubts

Back in my Airbnb, I kept remembering all the stupidities
I'd come out with – blurted out, really. Trying to prove myself, trying to bridge the gap between Bonnie as a Nishnaabe
woman living on a reserve and me, a white woman living
anywhere else. Trying to sweet-talk and pretend the gap away.
Going for the Get Out of Jail Free card. Meanwhile, the place
I'd rented was a dump. The ceiling was so low I could touch
it; they'd been smart to attach a wire cage around the light
bulb in the middle of the one big room it consisted of, or I'd
have bumped my head on it. There was no closet to hang
my clothes in, either, just three skinny hooks by the door
that I could tell wouldn't hold much. And the windows! They
were so small and high up that I had to stand to see out of
them. And even then, the view was of the back of the house
behind which this place squatted; maybe it was a made-over
garage. On the cheap, I thought as I tried to make myself at
home. I'd be here for over a week – if I could stand being here
that long.

At least the bed was firm. But I couldn't settle into sleep,
bits of what I'd heard and noticed at Bonnie's place tumbling

through my mind, the sound of Buck's walker scraping across the linoleum floor as he slowly pushed it toward the counter.

I'd gone online when I'd gotten back here, checking indicators of health among First Nations populations: the rates of stroke, of heart attack, of diabetes, kidney disease – all many times higher than the national average. I could have gone on, the stats on high school completion rates, university and college enrolment, incarceration rates, life expectancy. They piled up in my mind like roadblocks. Good sabotage, I thought as I turned over, trying desperately to get to sleep. But it was the little things that kept niggling me in the dark. When Bonnie had gone back to talking about the treaty, I'd jumped in to add the date of it, "1827." She'd looked across the table at me. Just looked at me.

I'd interrupted her. She was an elder. I was a guest in her house. This wasn't about getting the facts right, I realized. It was about getting to know people like Bonnie, getting the relationships right.

And then there was Buck, making his slow way first into and then out of the kitchen. Ignoring my existence. Carrying on as if I didn't exist. Concentrating on his own existence, I thought, finally; he wasn't necessarily judging me or especially ignoring my existence.

Buck was Bonnie's son, and he'd had a stroke. She had confided this to me after he'd left the big front room. But he couldn't have been more than fifty, I thought; too young to be having a stroke, surely! And what had happened when he had it? What failure in timely, appropriate intervention might have caused him to be left in such bad shape? I'd heard so many stories.

Eventually, grey light was coming in through the window. I slept some more and then got up. I took a shower and washed my hair, took my time drying it. I made myself some breakfast, then took my tea to stand by the little window looking out.

I had no mission here, no defined purpose that would justify leaving my usual space and entering this other space, clearly marked as Nishnaabe space. If I went back, it was to step into complete not knowing, with no map and no sense of direction. It was a blank slate of possibility – not entirely a figment of my imagination, either, I thought. From what Bonnie had said about when her ancestors and mine had made a treaty, there was a similar sense of possibility at work in her imagination too. A dialogue had begun. Something had begun, however tentatively. And so I went back. After all, she'd invited me to come back, said we'd talk some more.

I'd left her place through the back door the previous evening. So I headed that way as I returned. Coming round the corner of the fence, I saw Fred and then Buck. Fred was half perched on the old grey picnic table near the back door; Buck was sitting on the padded seat of his walker. The seedling we'd brought back from Stoney Point was flopped sideways in a plastic bucket between them. They both looked up as I approached.

"Good morning, Fred," I said. "Good morning, Buck."

No response from Buck. A nod from Fred, and a small sideways motion of his head.

"Go on in. She's there."

I passed through the closed-in porch, a large freezer on one side, a washer and dryer on the other. I knocked on the inner door and, at what sounded like a shouted "Come in," I stepped inside.

Bonnie was leaning forward toward a round mirror on a metal frame she had set up on the table, applying lipstick. Then she dabbed a bit on her cheeks and rubbed it in. Satisfied, she leaned back.

"I didn't sleep so good," she said. "Charley horse, I get it so bad."

She pushed all her stuff into her makeup bag, rolled it up and pushed it to the back of the table.

"Get yourself a coffee," she said. "Cream's there on the counter."

I put the box of chocolate-covered cookies I'd brought on the table and settled myself in the chair I'd sat in yesterday.

I told her about passing Fred and Buck outside, as if naming them helped establish my claim to know them.

"Oh yeah," she said. "They're gonna plant that tree for me."

The back door opened and an older woman came in: Janice, one of Bonnie's younger sisters. She had sunglasses on, and kept them on even as she took a seat at the far end of the table, plunking her big purse down and zipping open her jacket.

Coffee? Bonnie asked. She said no, she wasn't staying; she wanted to get home and clear out her garage. She nodded hello to me when Bonnie introduced us, and then started talking about the trouble she was having with the ophthalmologist. She'd finally gotten an appointment because she was seeing almost double and it was hard to drive, and the doctor had given her these drops to take, she said. I nearly asked if that was why she was wearing sunglasses, just to get myself into the conversation. Instead, I just nodded and smiled as she kept talking.

I asked Bonnie if I should open the cookies I'd brought.

Sure, she said. "I'll have one of those; they look good." Janice took one too and started talking about the funeral feast she'd gone to the other day; so many desserts. She laughed, patting her middle. Bonnie said something about it becoming a competition, people putting out more and more food for these things.

"It's getting too expensive to die around here." She laughed, then asked Janice if she remembered McCracken and the food vouchers he'd had.

"Those Indian agents, they were so crooked," she said. "This one, McCracken, his sister was married to the man who ran a local food store, so he made out food vouchers for it, so you had to buy there."

I listened, rapt; Indian agents, this was important. Heritage stuff.

"Oh yeah," Bonnie continued, putting down her coffee mug. "You couldn't do anything without the Indian agent. He used to come down here, and if he didn't like what someone was saying, he'd close the books and close the meeting."

"Or he'd write it down the way he wanted it," Janice added.

I had my pen and notebook out, ready to jot all this down if I could. A history lesson from their side.

Fred and Buck came back inside. Bonnie called out, "Coffee's on." But Fred turned and went away, Buck following behind him. I could hear the rattle as he manoeuvred his walker up the short flight of stairs leading to the back family room. Maybe this was their way of telling me to go away.

I sipped my coffee, looking around for something to latch on to. I asked Janice if she'd grown up in the bush. No, Janice said, but her Grandma Laura had. "I remember her, 'I'm goin' to the bush for my dyes.'"

Bonnie was in the kitchen area, making a racket. Something about looking for a pot or a pan; I hadn't quite caught what she'd said. A woman came into the room, with a mop in a bucket on little wheels.

Bonnie called out, "That's Colleen. The band office pays her to come here and give me a hand."

I said hello and told her my name. Bonnie added, "That's the writer I was telling you about."

Colleen went around to where Bonnie was making a noise with the pots and pans. Bonnie shooed her away. "I know what I'm looking for," she said.

Colleen wheeled her bucket into the entranceway.

"You looked at them windows yet?" Bonnie asked when she returned. She handed Colleen a dented tin pan. "Put that over there, will ya?" she said, indicating the chair near the back entranceway. Then she wheeled herself over to the table. They'd had pipes freeze out there last winter, she said, nodding her head toward the back door. No water out there for months. What a mess! So they were putting plastic over the windows this year.

I offered to help. I was used to putting my time to some purpose, and there didn't seem to be any purpose to my just sitting here watching everything going on around me.

"No," Bonnie said. Then she smiled. "Have another coffee."

The back door opened and a young woman strode into the room. Worn, ripped jeans, her black hair short and spiky around her face. "Hi, Nana," she said, leaning down to hug Bonnie around the shoulders. She walked around, checking out what was on the counter, the table. She seemed to be at home here; she was one of Bonnie's granddaughters.

"Did you get a hold of those people I told you about?" Bonnie asked. When the young woman disappeared in the direction of the bathroom, Bonnie explained that she'd been stiffed on the money she was owed. Some casual work she'd picked up helping clean up and prepare a growing bed for the winter at one of the local market gardens. And they'd short-changed her. Bonnie had warned her, told her to keep careful track of her hours. Now she had to file a complaint with the Ministry of Labour.

The young woman came back, stooped down next to her grandmother.

"Okay, see those baskets out there," Bonnie said, pointing out the big front window. There were numerous hanging plants, plus fallen-over flower stalks in some window boxes lining the edge of the patio. Bonnie wanted her to clean all that up. Her hand came up, made contact with her grand-daughter's hand holding the arm of the wheelchair. Something passed between them, so fast and smooth I couldn't tell how much money Bonnie had slipped into her hand.

The young woman smiled, then stood up, slipped her hand into her pocket and headed for the door.

"And don't forget that pan," Bonnie called out.

"Chi-miigwech," she called back and went on her way. Janice got up and left too. Then Colleen grabbed her jacket and followed her out the door. Bonnie and I watched them standing by the mailbox at the end of the lane, talking. I asked Bonnie if she'd spent time in the bush back at Stoney Point when she was growing up.

She snorted, "Oh yeah. Dad would be sayin', 'Okay, we're goin' to the bush today.'" She gazed out the window, a smile lifting the lines on her face. "He had an old black-assed pot. He wouldn't go into the bush without that pot. Him and Sheldon, they were friends, almost like brothers."

"Was it an iron pot?" She looked at me, and I shrivelled inside; why had I asked that? To get her back on track of the story? But whose track? Whose story?

"It was just an ordinary old – just an old black-assed pot, and he always had tea and sugar, and they'd go back. And first thing, they'd go and get a few pieces of wood, like this." Bonnie put her hands together, teepee formation. "Make a tripod. Go and get fresh water out of the lake. Put it on, boil it. Put tea bags in there.

"And those guys would sit there. They had blocks of wood they used to sit on, and they'd sit on them, and maybe every five minutes saying something. Gawkin' away and then, 'Boy, I can hardly wait till we get back here.'"

Bonnie looked at me. "That was the issue with all these old people. They weren't asking for money. 'We just want our land back.'"

I nodded, said nothing.

"It's a feeling that don't come till you're older and you understand the meaning of the teachings about the land that were given to you. And it comes from the simple meaning of what the treaty meant, that this land down here at Stoney Point and Kettle Point was set aside for the use, enjoyment, and benefit of our people. And if anybody comes in here, we have the authority to tell you: this is where *we* are. We have laws, and eventually we will have our own judicial system down here."

She sat back. "That's my dream," she said.

Yes! I beamed at her. "I'd like to help make that happen," I said.

She ignored me. She picked up the dishtowel she carried on her lap and rubbed at a coffee ring left from where a mug had been, maybe mine.

Colleen brought in the mail, and Bonnie sorted through it, tossing aside flyers from the local grocery store in Forest. She gets Fred to drive her over to Port Huron in the United States. She'd already regaled me with the prices of things across the border. Eggs, milk – she buys them for others too. She used to go through fifteen dozen eggs a day sometimes when she and Fred ran their own little restaurant across the street.

I kept nodding and smiling, letting all this go in one ear and out the other. It was just background chatter to me, not quite noise but not adding up to anything important either.

"You going to bingo tonight?" she asked as Colleen took the flyers off the table and put them where Bonnie wanted them, over by the woodstove. Colleen said she might; there was a big jackpot. Then she poured herself a coffee and headed out the front door to the patio.

Bonnie leaned toward me, lowered her voice. "She smokes," she said. And sure enough, through the window I could see Colleen lighting up a cigarette.

We both gazed out the window without speaking. Bonnie took the dishtowel from her lap again and wiped the tabletop in front of her. "I'd like to see something done, to be a bridge between Kettle Point and Stoney Point." She looked up from her wiping. "The people here don't understand what went on back then."

I knew what she was getting at; it was clear in the Ipperwash report. The two reserves had been forced together as one band and then allocated only the one band council when the government assigned them a limited popular-vote form of local self-government under the Indian Act. Tensions from that forced union had deepened over the years, including as the band council and Kettle Point became more associated with modern commerce, while the small community at Stoney Point carried on more of the land-based ways. Not only had it left the people of Stoney Point, who'd struggled to reclaim their ancestral homeland in the 1990s, unsupported by the band council at Kettle Point, but they'd even been vilified by one councillor and called "thugs" in the local newspaper for giving Native people a bad name. Bonnie had sat on that council all through that time.

She pushed her dishtowel farther across the table. "We've never really thanked those people that went in there in 1995. Because I didn't."

She looked up at me; what was she getting at? It was as though she wanted to atone for something; but why was she telling me?

She looked out the window. "I was there with food or cigarettes or whatever. But those people have given up their lives since 1995 – no, 1993! – to do what we asked of them. And I'm a firm believer that we wouldn't be at the level we're at today if they weren't still occupying the land, and the government realizing we're not going away." She wiped the table some more, then tucked the dishtowel back into her lap. I said nothing but hoped she'd continue. This was something I could relate to because it was about treaty land, treaty rights and responsibilities. If there was an outstanding issue, maybe

I could help get it resolved. I'd read the Ipperwash report, so at least I knew what Bonnie was talking about.

Bonnie was gazing out the window again. "Right now it bothers me – how many of us are left?" She shook her head and started listing the elders who'd led the way home to Stoney Point that sunny day in May 1993, despite the fact that Canada's Department of National Defence was still actively using it as a cadet training camp. All of those elders have since passed on. Plus, many of their children have moved away or are sick or have also died. Only a handful, like Cully George and Kevin Simon, are still left living in the barracks – buildings so dilapidated that many of the roofs leak and the faucets in the bathrooms no longer work. Some are so full of toxins – asbestos, lead, and mould – that when they are finally ready to be replaced by Nishnaabe housing, the people who do the demolition will have to wear hazmat suits and respirators. How much longer could the few there now carry on?

Colleen came back inside. Was I finished my coffee? she asked. She took my mug to the sink. Then she rolled the wash bucket into the kitchen area and started washing the floor.

The back door opened, and a young man poked his head in. He was looking for Fred; something about his car having a flat and he needed some card. Bonnie sent him off into the back room but told him to come back when they were done. "I have something for your mother," she said.

Colleen wheeled her bucket into the middle of the floor and started mopping the space around us. I shifted my chair away from the table so she could reach under it, then lifted my feet as the mop sluiced closer to where I was sitting. Should I leave now? I wondered. I was bloated with coffee and cookies. I was only getting in the way.

I lifted my bag off the floor, put my notebook and pen away, thinking I'd use the excuse of Colleen to get myself out of here. But no. Bonnie told me to stay. She wheeled herself out of the room toward the bathroom, leaving me to watch

Colleen wash the floor, feeling useless, awkward, and out of place.

Bonnie wheeled herself back, and then Colleen was done for the day. She put on her jacket and came over to where Bonnie and I were sitting. They talked about putting up the plastic. Colleen had some box cutters; she'd bring them in the morning. No, no, we have some, Bonnie insisted. They're in the basement somewhere. Colleen shrugged, shot me a look and a little smile that made me bet that she'd be bringing her own tomorrow anyway. Then she was gone.

Fred came back into the room, set down his coffee mug, and headed out to the front porch for something. When he came back –

"We're goin' to Stoney," Bonnie announced.

4

A Chance to Really Engage

Once again, I was heading to Stoney Point, the place where the treaty that had brought me here had been so utterly broken, the place that called to me the most. Fred was at the wheel of the big family van, and Bonnie's walker was in the back. We were going to see Barb and Worm. Bonnie was saying that she'd been talking to them about me. "I told them, 'I think we can trust this person.'" Had she been checking me out somehow during my visit yesterday? But why? Maybe they were going to ask me to do something for them, sort of reparation for the broken treaty. I tried to keep the smile off my face.

Then, half turning in her seat, she said that their people had been misrepresented before. She mentioned a book that was written shortly after Dudley died: *One Dead Indian*. I recognized the title. It was written by a Toronto journalist who'd been covering the story of the Nishnaabeg struggle to reclaim their land, the occupation of the Ipperwash Provincial Park after the Labour Day long weekend in 1995, the increasingly tense standoff with the police, and finally the shooting death of Dudley George.

Bonnie twisted around more toward me and quoted something from the book, referring to one of the elders, Clifford George, who'd led the return to Stoney Point in 1993. She snorted in disgust. "Clifford would never have said that," she said. I stared at the grey upholstery of the seatback in front of me. What was she getting at? I felt excited.

Fred slowed and began to make the turn into the former army camp. As he did, the barrier at the gatehouse began to rise, and Fred kept going. Once again, Fred waved and received an answering wave from the gatehouse; one insider to another, I thought as he drove on. It was easy getting in through the main gate after all.

Then I thought, hardly! It had been easy for Fred because he'd followed the rules, rules set by the federal government to police access for people like Bonnie – onto her ancestral homeland, the land where she was born! Rules that other local Nishnaabe were paid to enforce. Whereas I had flaunted the rules. Actually, I'd done more than that: I'd basically made up my own as I sought my own private, privileged permission to drive in from the back of the pot shop. Who was the insider here?

Fred was pulling off the road into a large open space, broken pavement all around. He parked beside an old red truck; like others around here, it had no licence plate on the back. There were oil stains everywhere, because this was where the maintenance garage of the army camp had once been. There was a big sprawling building on one side of it, where lawnmowers and other maintenance equipment were stored. On the side we were facing, the building had been used for maintenance supplies and an office. Abraham George's son, Stewart, known as "Worm," had adopted this building as his home in 1995, when the Nishnaabeg had expanded their land reclamation to include the barracks of the army camp itself. He was a mechanic.

We went inside, Bonnie bumping her walker over the doorsill and manoeuvring her way down an entranceway that had been framed in with drywall but never painted. We entered a large main room with no windows. A couple of table lamps and one standing lamp, its shade askew, illuminated at least the centre of the room. There was a large coffee table and, around it, some sofa chairs and a big sofa on the far side. People were sitting there, the light illuminating their laps and legs more than their faces.

Bonnie introduced me to her daughter Barb and then to Worm and, finally, to a man I recognized from my first encounter here, back in July: Kevin Simon. He ducked his head hello, a small smile acknowledging that we'd met before, but that was all. His grandfather Daniel George was one of Abe's brothers. Both men had been raised on the reserve, learning all the skills and ceremonies associated with the combination of hunting, gathering, and farming that had flourished there until 1942. Both had been dispossessed when the government took over the entire reserve that year and turned it into an army training camp. Both had been active in efforts to get Stoney Point back after the war, and had inspired their children, including Kevin's mother, Marcia, and his uncle Glenn to take the action they did of moving home, despite the army still running a training camp on their home reserve. Kevin had just finished high school at the time.

I felt conspicuous as the sole non-native in the room. But I was also keenly alert. Something was happening, and I was in the middle of it. I watched Worm get up from one of the sofa chairs, scoop a pack of cigarettes off the table, and settle himself at the far end of the sofa, almost in darkness. He was a tall man, broad-shouldered, grey hair pulled back in a ponytail. He said something briefly to Barb, then sat back smoking.

Silence. Bonnie broke it, talking about her wish to do something to heal the rift between the two communities. It would help, she said, if the people of Kettle Point could know the sacrifice people like Worm and Kevin and the others had

made to get their ancestral homeland back. She reminded
Worm of what he'd told her once: that no one has ever come
in here wanting to hear their story. She reminded Barb of
what she, Barb, had told her, about putting it in her prayers
that someone with journalistic skills might show up and help
collect their stories. Then she said something like, Heather
here is a writer, and stopped.

My turn. I looked around. The darkness beyond where we
were sitting pressed in on me. Not ominous or threatening in
an overt way; I wasn't afraid that I'd be attacked or anything.
Just inscrutable, unknown. I didn't know this terrain, this
lived-in, lived-through terrain that I'd walked into, so steeped
in pain and betrayal, trauma and distrust. I just knew that I
was sitting in the middle of it, right here in this decrepit,
windowless space. An abandoned maintenance storage building and office making do as Stewart and Barb's home, because
it had been almost twenty-five years since the government
had promised to return the land, and it was still in control,
its army barracks and buildings like this one still here. I
looked around at the people sitting silent and semi-obscured
in the dim lamplight. There was more than the brokenness
of the Huron Tract treaty going on here. It was as though I
was glimpsing terra nullius on the receiving end, the effect
of this thinking having shaped so much ongoing history.

I was the only one unscathed, untouched by this history.
I wanted to be scathed. I wanted to be touched, implicated. I
sat forward in the chair I'd taken, close to the standing lamp.
I took a breath, looked around. I felt like I'd been put on the
spot, as if the spotlight were on me, and something about
that didn't feel right. Some instinct said I should stay in the
shadows, let the darkness here get to me. I felt self-conscious,
unsure of myself. Yet if I could be useful as a writer ...

There was an eagerness in me I didn't trust. Because,
though I couldn't articulate it at the time, I'd be shining my
own light into this darkness, dispelling it by focusing on one

thing, by doing something. Some inner voice whispered that I'd be taking myself off the hook, the real hook in this real-life terrain I'd blundered my way into. The hook was here, in the darkness or semi-darkness. I was only beginning to be aware of it, pricking my skin, digging in, like the barb of rusted wire that had pricked the delicate inner skin of my forearm when I leaned against the fence that first day back in July. There was work to be done here; perhaps the real work I was meant to do, though I didn't know what that might be.

I fell back on the only thing I was sure of, even as I sensed that I was sidestepping. I told them that the Huron Tract treaty had legitimized my people settling not too far away from here in southwestern Ontario, because their land – Nishnaabe land – had been given to the Canada Land Company, which surveyed it and turned it into private lots that settlers could buy. I recapped what I'd been learning about treaty making from the Indigenous side of the negotiations, repeating what I'd told Bonnie about the rituals of condolence, admitting the wrongs that have been done, and taking responsibility for a broken treaty and treaty relationship. I ended where I'd ended with Bonnie the day before, saying that I was trying to learn how to act on this responsibility. Again, my voice quavered and broke. This was all becoming very real to me, whatever it was that I'd entered into. I was sitting in a room surrounded by Nishnaabe descendants of the Huron Tract treaty, individuals who are living its brokenness every day. Of course, there was more involved than one broken treaty. But this was my point of connection.

Barb sat forward in her chair, dark eyes shining, possibly with tears. "Treaties," she said, "they're spirit paper. Spirit energy moves in them."

I looked across the coffee table at her, the standing lamp with its crooked shade shedding just enough light that I could see her in the gloom. I nodded and smiled, trying to communicate that, yes, I heard her. I didn't understand what she meant, but here she was, sitting forward, reaching out – to me! Offering to at least give me the benefit of the doubt by responding, with this notion of treaties as sort of spirit bonds. I wanted so much to identify with this, to take it on, whatever it meant. Here was an opening for me. Might helping out here be a gesture of condolence and reparation, and at the same time a chance to learn?

There were tears in my eyes. I was afraid to say anything to break this delicate thread – this lovely energy of pure possibility and connection – hovering in the air between us.

I took a breath, ready to say something, anything, and was aware that Kevin was speaking – to me. He was asking if I wrote books. I told him, yes, I'd written ten. Worm looked like he was going to say something, too, but instead reached for the ashtray and stubbed out his cigarette.

Silence. Then Barb got up, grabbing her jacket off the chair arm.

"Come on," she said, gesturing for me to follow.

We got in her truck. She drove down the gravel road that flanks the paved Army Camp Road outside the camp, the road that connected the barracks area to the former Ipperwash Provincial Park. She drove past the remnants of a ribbon-decked frame of lashed-together poles. It was left over from when a powwow had been held here, Barb said. She bumped the truck off the gravel and along a rutted path that led to the lake, then revved the motor to pull up onto a grass-covered sand dune facing the water. She turned off the motor. She reached for her pack of cigarettes, took one out, then offered me one.

"I don't smoke," I said.

She smiled. "To put your tobacco down."

Oh. Right. I smiled at my stupidity and followed her.

She led the way down the sandy slope and over the low embankment onto the stones of the beach. She'd brought us to a point of land that juts out into Lake Huron and marks one end of the long crescent moon–shaped beach that stretches from Stoney Point to the Kettle Point Reserve, seven kilometres to the south. The entire stretch of beach was once reserve land and considered sacred.

Barb stood right on the edge of the water, waves splashing over the stones at her feet, an empty plastic water bottle caught among the stones beside her. She'd already broken open the cigarette and held the spilled tobacco loosely in her hand. I watched her as she closed her eyes and started speaking. She was speaking in Nishnaabemowin. I recognized "miigwech" repeated several times, and "Manitou" as well. Then she leaned forward and released her tobacco onto the water-washed rocks.

She turned to me and said that she'd been praying to the spirits of her ancestors, especially the grandmothers. She'd asked them to guide her in how she should relate to me, what she should tell me, share with me.

Something like an electric shock went through me, a sense of awe and wonder, that I could be on the threshold of something this big. A sense of dread, too; I didn't know what I was getting into. What ancestral spirits could I count on to guide me?

I steadied my feet on the rocks, broke open my cigarette and, holding the tobacco in my closed fist over my heart as Barb had done, I too offered up a prayer. I didn't speak it out loud; I was feeling far too shy and self-conscious for that. Yet I knew with a quiet certainty, which had come to me while listening to Barb speak her prayer, what I wanted to say. I called on the spirits of my ancestors, the ones who I sometimes felt had followed me back across the Atlantic once I'd visited my ancestral homeland in the Scottish Highlands a few years back. I also called on the spirits of those who had crossed the Atlantic by sailing ship in 1832, determined to create a new life for themselves here in this strange and unknown land; I felt that what I was doing I was doing for them too. If treaties are relationships, and my forebears were part of breaking this one, they might want to help me repair that relationship now.

Standing on the rocky shore, the waters of Barb's ancestral water territory glimmering through my half-closed eyes, I asked these spirits to be with me, to guide me on the journey I had begun. To hold me as I journeyed into my own new world here; to discover, or rediscover, this land on the terms that prevailed here, not on the terms provided by the colonial powers that were intent on pre-empting them and obliterating all traces of their distinctive presence.

When I finished, I copied what Barb had done. I bent over the water and scattered my tobacco. The two of us stood there watching the water take the tobacco, toss it back onto the stones, draw it outward into the lake, then push it back as it scattered and disappeared.

Back in the truck, Barb was full of energy. She talked about getting a decent car. She told me about her children and asked if I had any. She put the truck into reverse, bumping us back onto the gravel road. As she drove back to the barracks area, she talked about how much this place meant to her.

"I was physically raised in Kettle Point," she said. "But I was spiritually raised here."

I asked if she was a language speaker like her dad. She said no. A flash of anger.

"It was all disrupted," she said. "I'm still like a child compared to what I could be if my mom and dad had been allowed to stay here ... if I'd been born and raised in a traditional community."

I felt her bitterness move through me. This is why I'm here too, I thought: to take this in, and let it teach me about my accountability here.

Barb manoeuvred the truck around a big pothole. She's been trying to get her language back, she said, more than just the clusters of phrases and words she's learned from different ceremonies. She gestured down a gravel side road as we passed. It led through the bush to the chain of inland lakes. Sometimes when she's walking back there alone, she said, "the words seem to come to me."

I looked around, again marvelling at the rich diversity of trees standing tall and beautiful behind the line of bush and brambles that lined the road. They'd been growing like this, or rather a seamless continuity of them had been growing here, probably since before recorded time. These old trees and their forebears had been helping to sustain life for Barb's people for centuries. The Nishnaabe had cut trees as they'd needed them. But they'd never clear-cut this land. It had remained unchanged, their ancestral hunting and gathering grounds for generation after generation, even as the acreage involved was steadily diminished, first to put through a highway and then as a result of at least two shady land deals – until 1942, when it was taken away from them completely.

We re-emerged at what had been the main operations centre of the army camp, the parade ground on one side and various outbuildings on the other. Most dated back to the 1940s, except for some trailer units sitting by the fence. This was headquarters for Department of National Defence personnel in charge of the cleanup here. All the unexploded mortar shells, grenades, and other munitions that had been fired by soldiers and cadets in training over all the years since 1942 had to be located, dismantled, and removed. Apparently, the preliminary work had barely begun.

Barb pulled the truck into the space beside her parents' van. She turned off the engine and sat there looking through the windshield. She said something about setting up a time to sit down with Worm and others who might want to tell their story. I knew that Barb was a photographer as well as a journalist in her own right; she'd helped to found a Nishnaabe newspaper. I mentioned the cameras I had. Maybe she could use some of these while I operated the audio recorder. She could be my assistant. No, I could be *her* assistant.

She looked across at me and smiled. I smiled back. And it was that simple, or so it seemed.

I was in! If I could be of service here – wow! It would be a means to an end, too – of building a treaty relationship, of learning what my treaty responsibilities might be. I hadn't yet clued in to how much work I'd have to do before I could be worthy of such a relationship, let alone prepared for its responsibilities. I was focused on reconciliation. How had Paulette Regan put it? "Reconciliation as encounter."[1]

If we were pulling everyone's stories together, this would give me an excuse to be here, to keep coming back, to get to know people like Barb, Bonnie, Kevin, and Worm, to form relationships with them. Working relationships, at least; maybe friendships eventually.

And then the phone rang.

When we got out of the truck and went back inside, Worm was putting on his jacket and preparing to leave. He'd just gotten a call that his sister who was in hospital had died. He had to go. I fished in my bag for my business cards and gave one to Barb. Kevin came forward, took a card, and left before I could seize the moment to get some contact information for him. Still, it wasn't the right time, not now. It was time for Bonnie, Fred, and me to leave too. Fred had already brought Bonnie's walker over, and she was pulling on her windbreaker.

I stood there in the midst of all this swirling, disappearing activity, feeling the darkness around me once again, once again unsure of myself. Then Barb walked over and put her arms around me and called me her treaty partner.

"I look forward to working with you," she said.

"Miigwech," I said, hugging her back.

5

Who Do You Think You Are?

I woke up the next morning full of confidence and a sense of purpose. I had something to focus on; my path was clear. I was going to help Bonnie, Barb, Worm, and the others pull their stories together into a book. It felt like I'd skipped a couple of grades – maybe for good behaviour. No matter. I'd passed some kind of test and I was in. I was on track to serve and support, to help heal a broken treaty relationship by taking on this project of reparation. I thought that was all it would take, that was all that would be required of me. I'd complete this task and I'd have arrived: clearly decolonized and qualified to call myself a responsible treaty person. Barb would be in touch.

I made myself a nice breakfast, then a second cup of tea, and sat on the rickety rocker that, along with a small, vinyl-covered sofa, marked the sitting room of this Airbnb, facing the wall with its high-up window.

I got up to turn the heater fan off again; the noise was grating on my nerves. Of course I'd be cold again soon, so I grabbed my jacket off the hook by the door and put it on. By now my tea had gone cold. I got up again and stuck it in the microwave. It was a big, noisy old thing and was perched on a ledge along the wall that doubled as a dining table, with a bar stool tucked underneath. I had my laptop on the ledge, too, and now I checked it. Still nothing from Barb. No text or phone call either. I should have asked for her number before I left yesterday.

I sat back down on the sofa facing the window, only with the window so small and high up, I was staring at the wall. Should I go over on my own? Go back to Bonnie's place? Was I sort of working for her here? That didn't feel right somehow. As a writer, you're supposed to be independent, accountable only to yourself. Still, Bonnie was an elder, a Nishnaabe elder. This would be different, too, with me working as a writing assistant to Barb, Bonnie, and the others. I'd be accountable to Barb, to Bonnie – to all of them, really. I'd never done this sort of thing before, scribed for somebody else. I'd just have to get myself out of the way.

I went for a walk, following the town road my little rental unit was on till it emerged in the countryside. Clouds lay low on the horizon, heavy with unshed rain. A damp wind blew in my face and up the sleeves of my jacket. I turned around and headed back. I'd make myself some lunch. Maybe by then Barb would be in touch.

Still nothing. I got in the car and drove. I ended up turning in at the Kettle Point reserve, going back to Bonnie's place to get my bearings. Maybe I could get Barb's number from her, find out for sure whether she lived with Worm or somewhere else.

There was no one out back when I got there; only the big old family dog who I knew enough to call Beau.

Hello, Beau, I said as I approached. He was lying at the base of the back stairs. He didn't move. Didn't wag his tail either, and a flash of memory went through me. Decades back, when I'd been a farm reporter with the *Edmonton Journal,* I was doing what I normally did: jumping in my car to go out and talk directly to farmers affected by whatever was going on, wanting to let them tell their own story, or their side of it. As I typically did, I'd pulled in at this farm at random, unannounced and unexpected, confident of a welcome once I explained that I was from the Journal.

Only there'd been no one at home. Then, when I got no answer at my knock and turned away, the dogs that had followed me to the door with tails wagging suddenly turned. Their hackles went up and they started to growl. One, a German Shepherd cross of some kind, lowered its shoulders in what some instinct in me recognized as a pending attack. I used all the authority I could muster to my voice and ordered the dog to go lie down. It broke the spell enough that the dog turned away, and I got back to my car. Totally rattled but okay.

Now I gingerly stepped around the old dog and went inside.

I knocked on the inside door, then opened it, calling out, "Hello, hello."

"Oh, it's you," Bonnie said, her wheelchair half turned from the table. She was wearing a peach-coloured blouse in some lovely silky material; nice pants too.

"Shelly's coming to pick me up," she said, turning back to the table. Shelly was one of Bonnie's daughters. She gestured to the chair at the end. "Sit down," she said, "I'm just putting on my eyebrows." She'd lost her eyebrows during her cancer treatments years ago, and for some reason they'd never grown back. Now she leaned toward the round mirror in its collapsible metal stand sitting on the dinner table, a stick of eyebrow pencil clamped in her hand.

She looked sideways at me. "Maybe you don't know it, but Indian children are big business out there. People are making a fortune out of them kids."

"You mean, foster care?" I asked.

"Yeah, foster care," she said. I knew that Children's Aid or its equivalent routinely sent social workers to the hospital when an Indigenous woman was giving birth, basically assuming that this would be an "at-risk" baby they might have to apprehend.[1]

I took a breath, ready to tell Bonnie that I knew about this as well, to show off how much I knew, to show her that I was on her side. I was feeling unsure of myself, and my habit of covering it up ran long and deep. I watched as she furiously bundled up her makeup bag in her awkward but efficient hands.

"And you end up with a Nishnaabe kid comin' back to the reserve, don't know who the hell they are. They're ashamed of being Indian." She looked at me hard. I nodded: I hear you.

"Ninety percent of the kids that are in care are Nishnaabe. So we said, enough of this." She paused, her hands on the makeup kit. She looked up at me.

"We decided, we're gonna take over not just prevention; we're gonna take over protection too."

She collapsed the mirror and pushed that to the back of the table, plunked the makeup bag on top.

She pushed herself back from the table. "What did we call it? Customary care." She looked at me, smiled.

"It's the way we've always done it. So we called it customary care." She laughed, letting me in on how they'd learned to play the bureaucrat's game.

Bonnie, I learned later, had helped create a Nishnaabe alternative to the Children's Aid Society in Ontario, called Mnaasged Child and Family Services. That was in 2006 and, well over a decade later, the provincial government still hadn't recognized its authority.

Now I listened as Bonnie let me in on what was going on. There were a lot of drugs around the reserve, including these new ones, fentanyl and OxyContin, she told me. There was this one young mother; she was into something, and Children's Aid were going to take away her children. Instead, the plan was to foster them in the community. Bonnie was involved, and there was a meeting planned. Shelly was taking her; Barb was going too.

I should leave; maybe for good.

"Come back later," Bonnie said as Shelly came into the room.

"Or maybe tomorrow?" I asked.

"Yeah," she said. "Give me a call."

In other words, don't just come barging in here, I thought as I got back into my car.

It was starting to rain, and the wind was up. It blew straight in off the lake; I could feel it buffeting the car. I glanced at the dashboard; it was a new and fancy enough car that it had a gauge showing the temperature outside and I was glad of that. The last thing I wanted was freezing rain, the roads treacherous with ice.

I drove slowly, carefully, watching for potholes and the slick possibility of black ice. I might not have much money, but it was privilege that had brought me here. Not just materially, but psychologically. Plus, I'd taken it for granted that I could barge in on these people's lives. In other words, whatever was going on here didn't matter all that much.

This is Indian Country, I thought. It's guaranteed as essentially Nishnaabe sovereign territory by treaty, at least, and I was on record, from things I'd said to Bonnie and others, as wanting to learn how to live under their jurisdiction, their priorities, and their realities. Yet here I was, presuming to show up unannounced at Bonnie's family home, without having asked permission of the band council chief to enter this reserve in the first place. All along, too, I'd been assuming that my intentions in coming here were honourable. And I'd assumed that I could be the judge of this. Ha!

I couldn't be trusted, and this was why. I was so unaware! Of myself!

It wasn't that I needed to take charge or even to seize the initiative. It was just so normal for me to do so that I wasn't even conscious when I did it. I had the power and the self-assurance to go with it – and always had. It was the water I swam in.

I looked down at the steering wheel, all the gadgets built into it. Here it is, I thought, hidden in plain sight. It's embedded right here in the steering wheel of this shiny rental car. Embedded, too, in my ability to turn that wheel toward wherever I felt like going. It's not just personal power; it's colonial privilege – at least in this context, and the history behind it.

I continued driving, the windshield wipers flicking back and forth, the wind still bumping up against the car in gusts. This isn't just privilege driving either, I thought. It's superiority, maybe even "supremacy": colonial power and white supremacy, one reinforcing the other.

And it's not just in the car, I thought as I turned onto the paved highway. It's in the landscape I'm driving in. It's like there's a gravitational force field at work, in which I implicitly assume a position of authority: knowing what needs to be done and getting on with it. I automatically become the one taking the initiative, colonizing the space all over again.

What's the difference between me stepping past the dog to walk into Bonnie's house unannounced and the Indian agent or Children's Aid coming through the door to take away the children?

6

Showing Up Again

The next morning, I went back and forth, back and forth: to the table by the wall to check my laptop, then to the window with its pitiful view. The tacky polyester curtains in some homesteading settler motif would *not* stay back, no matter how hard I pushed them to the side. I went back to the vinyl-covered sofa, which by then was cold against my bum. I picked up the phone, put it down again. The dread I'd felt back in the beginning was back: Bonnie wouldn't want to talk to me. I shouldn't bother calling.

I stared at my phone. I was afraid. Afraid of their anger, blame for all the injustice that had gone on and was still going on. But now I was also afraid of myself. Afraid of outing myself. I was afraid of the fact that I was less decolonized than I'd thought. I didn't really know what decolonized meant, but clearly I hadn't gotten there yet. So I shouldn't be here, contaminating things with my presence.

Just make the call, I told myself. Take your cues from Bonnie. She was giving me the benefit of the doubt as someone trying to honour a treaty, trying to learn what honouring a treaty relationship and its obligations might mean. So you haven't got it all figured out yet? So what? Do you have to in order to visit this woman who is anxious and upset about some children in the community at risk of being taken away, about some young mother struggling with addiction? You're a mother and a grandmother too, I told myself, with an adult child who struggled with addiction too.

I called. "Come on over," she said.

There were two cars by the fence in the laneway when I pulled up. One I recognized as Colleen's. The other I thought might belong to Bonnie's sister Janice. Should I go in the front door? I started heading that way, noticed that things looked nicely cleaned up around the patio, and remembered the granddaughter who'd needed a bit of money.

No, I thought. I can go in the back way.

Beau came waddling toward me as I approached, wagging his tail in slow motion.

Hello, Beau, I said, reaching down to rub behind an ear.

I knocked on the inner door, heard a shout, and came on in.

Bonnie wheeled herself over to the table. "You know Janice, eh?"

Yes, I said, nodding to Janice at the far end of the table, and feeling an inward sigh as I remembered how much she liked to talk.

"Colleen, get her a coffee, will ya?"

"It's okay," I said. "I can get it myself." I wasn't used to being waited on, and didn't want it here; especially here, and especially after what had happened yesterday. I didn't want to be treated like a visitor, like the outsider I was. But Colleen was already bringing me a mug, the carton of cream in her other hand. Plus a spoon.

I thanked her and helped myself to some cream, noting that the big carton was nearly empty. Next trip, I thought.

Janice was talking about the feast she wanted to put on for her granddaughter's graduation.

From college? I asked.

From high school, she said. Bonnie said she should make a jellied celery salad too. Janice wasn't so sure people wanted that sort of thing anymore. Sure they do, Bonnie said. It's good, and it's good for you.

She wheeled herself over to the sideboard, reached out and grabbed a couple of pictures.

Here, she said, showing me one, a man wearing a graduation gown and hat. "That's Marshall," she said. One of her brothers. "He was the first one in the family that wore that little flat black hat." She laughed. "Dad used to say, I want one of my kids to wear that little flat black hat." She laughed again, then told me about her brother's work as a counsellor with the local school board.

"Marshall made it his task to meet with the schools, see how they were doing. There were times when some of them kids were ready to give up, and he would show up. He did everything he could for them." She took the photo back into her lap, laughed again, then looked at Janice and said that it was because of her, Janice's big sister, that Janice had finished school after all. "Remember? It's because of a trick I played on you."

Janice laughed and admitted that she'd dropped out of high school, or wanted to.

"I just wanted money to buy cigarettes," she said. So she tried for a job at the Forest Basket Factory, where Bonnie worked, sometimes operating the big machines making wicker baskets for all the big canned-food factories in the area.

Bonnie turned to me, dropping her voice to sound conspiratorial: "I told the foreman, give her the dirtiest, most boring job!"

Janice laughed. "The worst was painting all those signs on the baskets; this one for del Monte, this one for Campbell's ..."

"How long did you last? A week?" Bonnie laughed.

The back door opened. A man came in, nodded and said something to Bonnie, went to the fridge and put something inside. Then he was gone.

Bonnie explained that her cousin down the road was a fisherman and would regularly send some fish over for her and Fred. I wondered where Fred was. Oh, Bonnie said, in the back room with the heater turned way up. He gets cold easily these days; his blood count's not so good.

She wheeled herself into the kitchen area, opened the fridge, then closed it.

Janice and I sat at the table listening as Bonnie rummaged around in one of the cupboards.

I asked her how her eyes were; any better? Janice said she was being referred to a new ophthalmologist, in London. "I still see double sometimes."

Bonnie came back to the table with a package of biscuits on her lap. She pushed it toward me and told me to open it. They're called Snowballs, she said. They have custard inside, chocolate icing, coconut flakes on top. She gets them when she goes shopping in Port Huron, across the US border.

Colleen came back into the kitchen, a box cutter in her hand, then disappeared into the hallway that led to the basement.

"She's gonna put up vapour barrier down there," Bonnie said.

I offered to help her. I'd done that a lot myself, I said, starting to get up.

No, sit down, she said. She laughed. "Have another coffee."

There was another carton of cream on the counter when I went over for a refill; so much for that idea.

Stop it, I told myself. Quit trying to contribute all the time, trying to be helpful, to prove yourself, on terms you know. And quit trying to redeem yourself by trying to find a role for yourself here, an active, speaking role. I was only getting myself in the way by thinking this way. So there might not be a role for me to play here? Okay. I didn't belong here. Or rather, this wasn't the space of my belonging – this piece of exclusively native, Nishnaabe space. That didn't mean I had to leave, just because I was feeling out of place. It meant maybe I should stay. If I had a role to play, a job to do, maybe it was this: to just let myself feel out of place and be open to what might follow.

In other words, I told myself, just shut up and drink your coffee. I added cream to my mug and headed back to the table. Just sit here taking everything in, I said inwardly. Listen and be grateful.

"Yeah, gimme that," Bonnie was saying; Janice was reaching for something in the pile of papers by the wall. She handed a booklet to Bonnie and then got up to leave. Bonnie handed the booklet to me. It's to go with some language nests[1] they're trying to get going, she told me. To get their language back. Because even when they had the Indian day school on the reserve, it was all in English. They'd gotten some government money to do up these booklets to help, she said. She and Shelly had done the stories. Gail had done the artwork.

Voices at the back door; more people coming in. It was Shelly and her sister Gail and Gail's daughter Summer. They settled onto chairs; Gail perched on a stool. I held up the booklet and said how beautiful it was. Bonnie said they'd all been sent to school in Forest; Summer was the third generation to go there.

"They started calling us the bus people," Summer said. "That was their step from calling us the Indian kids."

Remember "head-check" days?

"Some of the kids ran away from school on head-check days," Shelly said.

"It was the worst," Gail said, "braids out and they used these sticks, like chopsticks ... We tried to rebraid our hair before we got home so Mom wouldn't get upset ... The look on her face!" She put her hand to her heart. "That they would do that."

"And I made sure their hair was clean, put vinegar in the rinse," Bonnie told me, as if that needed saying. She was an education counsellor at the school at the time. So one day, she went to the school and took on the homeroom teachers in every class where her children were students. "I told them, you are the one responsible for my child when she's at this school. And I'm telling you as a parent, you are not to let them take my child for a head check! I told them, you're not going to look at my kids' heads, unless they do all the kids – white too!"

Gail sat on her stool beaming as she listened to her mother retell it: "And I'm sittin' there goin', *Yes!*, big grin on my face."

Summer worked on the school yearbook. And she made sure there were full portrait shots of Kettle and Stony Point students who graduated, she told me.

She laughed softly. "I heard complaints about 'over-representation of Indigenous people.'"

I sat there listening, eager to learn all this but also wondering if this was sidestepping whatever was going on with that young mother and her children. Still, why should they confide in me? And I was happy to listen and take it all in. Anywhere was a good start; everything was important.

Gail had been walking around, checking what was on the counter. She came back and sat down, laughing. She said that her grandson had come home from school one day saying that this old guy in a long black robe had come in, "and he marked the four directions in ashes on my forehead."

More laughter, then silence, but a comfortable silence. It felt comfortable to me, and I felt comfortable being a part of it.

Bonnie brought over some cheese and crackers, and more memories surfaced: After Dudley died, teaching culture was banned at the local school, they told me. No "Indian" dancing, one of them said, putting quote marks in the air. A kid got sent home for wearing moccasins to school. And someone was told she couldn't smudge there until they developed a smudging policy. There was a lot of anger, the people at Stoney Point feeling they weren't being adequately represented in negotiations with the federal government. They staged protests at the band council office, twice. One of those times, someone inside got everyone singing Christian hymns, to drown out the drumming and chanting going on outside. And someone scratched the luminescent paint off the sign for the Kettle and Stony Point First Nation, so at night the word *Stony* disappeared.

A shuffling sound, and Buck came into the room, heading for the kitchen counter. Buck and Dudley had been hockey buddies. Fred regularly drove the boys to out-of-town games.

Summer said hi. Buck looked up, smiled, and said something like hi back. Then he focused on dragging a slice of bread out of the plastic bag sitting on the lower counter with his left hand, bumping the bag back with his hip, then pushing his hand farther into the bag, his right arm hanging. Everyone left him to it and carried on talking.

A woman came in from the back entranceway, and this seemed to be a cue. Shelly, Gail, and Summer got up and headed for the door. Bonnie reached for what looked like a bottle of pills on the table. "Here, take this for Barb," she said. Then they were gone, and I sat there feeling like the water had all leaked out of the bathtub and I was still in it. I picked up my coffee mug and reached to take Bonnie's over to the sink too.

Then Colleen was back; she'd cut her hand.

"Here, let me look at that," Bonnie said, backing up her wheelchair and turning to inspect the damage. She sent Colleen off to the bathroom for Band-Aids and the hydrogen peroxide, then set to work cleaning up the wound.

I sat there marvelling at Bonnie's hands, her thumbs compensating for the fingers that were twisted sideways with arthritis, the joints like doorknobs, they were so swollen by the disease. She cleaned the wound. I opened two packages of Band-Aids, then got up to get Colleen a coffee and a cookie. She smiled as she took it, and made some joke about being pampered.

She went home, and eventually so did Janice. I wanted to ask about Barb; maybe Bonnie would give me her number. Or would that be asking too much?

I tried for something casual. "I haven't heard from Barb yet," I said, looking at the far wall.

"Oh yeah?" Bonnie said. She started gathering up the biscuit boxes, pulled them into her lap.

I pushed a little harder, saying something about our working together. Bonnie looked out the window.

"She's helping out with them kids," she said. She looked at me briefly, then pushed herself away from the table.

"She does too much; I worry about her." Then she trundled away across the kitchen floor.

I looked down at the little ring of coffee my mug had left on the table. How much damage was I doing by putting my foot down wrong, saying the wrong thing or speaking out of turn? I kept getting it wrong because I didn't really have a clue what was going on all around me here and the layers and layers of life experience behind it.

I watched Bonnie as she wheeled herself across the kitchen floor, her shoulders hunched, her head down. Silent.

So the project was off? Good! Some part of me was relieved. I could stop trying to pass as more progressive, more aware, than I actually was. I could stop pretending that I was fit to help these people write a book about their lives and their struggle to get back their homeland. I couldn't possibly get it right, because I wasn't one of them; I was an "other." A colonial "other."

I reached for one of the flimsy paper napkins, used it to sweep up the crumbs off the table. I'd get a rag from the sink and one of Bonnie's dishtowels too. Do a decent job of cleaning up after myself, at least.

7

Dwelling in Discomfort

There were still a few days left before I was scheduled to fly home. I texted Barb again, and eventually we got together for coffee and just talked. I kept going back to Bonnie's place too. One visit, she got Fred to drive us back to Stoney Point so she could introduce me to Dudley George's sister Cully. But Cully never answered the door, so we came away. By now I was starting to enjoy just listening to Bonnie's stories – including the local gossip. Ready, too, for whoever walked in the back door or into the big front room.

Fred came in, put his empty coffee mug on the counter, and headed for the bathroom.

"I'm hungry," Bonnie announced when he returned. She wanted to go to Forest for a submarine sandwich.

"You're coming with us," she said as I got up to leave.

The last thing I wanted was a submarine sandwich, but she insisted. So off we went.

"I'm paying," I said when we got there.

"No. Don't you go spending your money on us," she said. I insisted.

She laughed. "You're bone-headed, just like me. But I'm paying for the pop," she said.

We brought our sandwiches and drinks back to the van and ate in there. A car pulled up beside the van. Two older Nishnaabe women. Fred rolled down the window; Bonnie leaned across and they chatted. "You goin' to bingo tomorrow?" Bonnie asked.

Fred drove back to Kettle Point. But as he was about to turn left toward home, Bonnie told him to keep going straight. We'll go see Marcia, she said. Marcia Simon, Bonnie's cousin, had been part of the effort to get Stoney Point back almost from the beginning, along with her parents, Daniel and Melva George, and her then young sons, Marlin and Kevin. Marcia was there the night Dudley George was fatally shot. She'd driven to the nearest pay phone so she could call for an ambulance, and had been surrounded by cops, arrested, and held in a jail cell. She'd carried on living in the former army camp, in the army chapel, along with her mother, Bonnie's Aunt Melva, until shortly after Melva died, in 2000. Then she'd moved back here, to the old family home in Kettle Point.

Maybe she'd like to tell her story, Bonnie said as Fred drove down the road and turned in at her driveway.

There was a sandwich-board sign at the side of the road where we turned: Fish 4 Sale.

Fred swerved to avoid one large puddle, gently drove through another, then stopped where the mud gave way to a bit of grass. There was a weathered picnic table just to the left and, beyond it, a small bungalow, with two cinder blocks laid together, flat end up, serving as a step leading up to a small stoop and what looked like a side door. On the other side of the space there was an old camper and, in between, a patch of weeds, tall grass, and the drooping seedheads of some flowers I thought I recognized.

Bonnie wondered if there was a dog around. Fred sounded the horn, and a dog barked. It was a big, loud bark; clearly not a small dog, though nothing was visible at the moment. The door of the camper opened, and a tall man with long black hair emerged. He came over to the car on Bonnie's side and nodded hello.

"Is your mom around?"

"She's not been feeling too well," he said. "She's sleeping."

"Is she wake-able?"

Quick smile. "I think so," he said, and headed for the house. That's Marlin, her son, Bonnie said as we watched him disappear. A minute or so later, a woman with short grey hair peered out from the doorway. Bonnie started to get out. But Fred said, "Wait. Where's the dog?"

"I'll go check," I said, and slipped out before Bonnie could say anything.

Once I rounded the overgrown flower bed, I could see the dog: some kind of German Shepherd cross, and clearly chained up. I reported this as I came back to the van.

"Stay here," Bonnie told me as she got out herself.

The two women settled themselves on one side of the picnic table, its surface cluttered with garden tools, a hammer, and what looked like parts from inside a motor of some kind. I learned later that the table was Marlin's workbench.

After a while, Bonnie gestured for me to come and meet Marcia. Marcia offered her hand, stiff and formal, no smile on her face. I reached out, took her hand into mine, and shook it. But her hand stayed limp. I was shaking her hand; we weren't shaking hands. Still, she was saying yes. She gave a little nod, met my eyes briefly, and said she'd be willing to talk to me, to help with the project.

"Have you read the Ipperwash report?"

Yes, I said.

"What about the transcripts?" she asked. "Have you read all those too?"

No, I hadn't read those yet, I said. In fact, until that moment, I hadn't even known of their existence, or hadn't dug deep enough.

"Well, you should," she said emphatically. "They're all available online, you know." She shook her head and looked away.

I felt chastised, as I think I was meant to. It was as though this woman was putting me in my place. Irritation flared inside me. I was used to thinking I knew all that I needed to know; anything that I didn't know probably didn't matter. Then I remembered: I'm not the judge here. I'm here to learn how to be a treaty person, and I haven't even begun to learn. So begin, I thought; begin to learn.

I told her I'd look them up right away, or as soon as I got home. There were only two days left before I was scheduled to fly back to BC.

I gave her one of my cards. I asked if maybe we could meet for coffee. Or I could take her to Tim Horton's in Forest before I left. She made a motion with her head I couldn't read. Not necessarily no. Not necessarily encouraging either.

I asked if I could get a number for her. She hesitated, then dictated a number for me to write down. She told me to call her in the morning, not before ten. Then she got up from the picnic bench, turned her back, and went inside.

No answer when I called at ten the next morning. Just an answering service: a male phone-company voice telling me "We aren't home right now" and inviting me to leave a message. I did. I called half an hour later; still nothing.

I went for a walk. Got to the edge of town and kept going on the gravel shoulder, wanting to walk off this feeling of being off-balance, even being in the wrong. Just because Bonnie wanted me to do this didn't make it right. What about the others? Maybe I was reading too much into a few tentative gestures and ignoring the rest. Something wasn't right in what I was trying to do here: seizing this straw of an opportunity to help gather the stories of what these Nishnaabe women and men were trying to do back in 1993 to '95. Maybe it was too late. People had gotten on with their lives one way or another.

I remembered the handwritten Fish 4 Sale sign, and Marcia's son Marlin coming out of the small camper where maybe he lived now, though he had been one of the ones continuing to live in the deserted barracks, for a while at least. Like his mother, he'd given so much of his life to trying to get Stoney Point back as a functioning reserve.

Yet the story of what they'd been part of – and maybe still were, for all I knew – had never been told, not in their voices and from their point of view. The seasoned writer in me knew that this was an important story. Plus, the people who could tell it – clearly some more eager to than others – were growing old, ailing, and dying. Meanwhile, here I was. I could help by recording their voices, transcribing their individual stories, weaving them together. If they'd let me. If they could trust me.

Yeah, yeah, I told myself, feeling the grit in my face as a truck roared by. There was this desperate need to grab hold, to have something to focus on, something I could recognize as real. Anything to get over this recurring sense of being lost, being adrift in the minutia of life going on here. If I could be of service as a writer, a role with which I was familiar, I could regain my confidence, get my bearings, and prove that I could be trusted.

When I got back, I tried Marcia again. Maybe she'd be up by now. Nothing. Okay, eat!

I set to work making myself an omelette. I'd have to cook it on the pancake griddle since there was no stove, not even a hotplate. Just this large and awkward griddle. The paring knife wasn't very sharp, but I managed to cut up some green onions and mushrooms and slice the nice old cheddar cheese I'd bought.

As I worked, I kept coming back to it, this uncomfortable feeling I was stranded in. This sense of being totally in the dark, way out of my depth. That's the point of this, I thought as I hauled the griddle out of the bottom drawer of the counter by the sink.

So I was feeling uncomfortable? How inconvenient. How encouraging! This was a good sign. I was out of my comfort zone, where I knew what was what. You've chosen to enter this native space, I told myself. Chosen to become the sole white-skinned person in a place inhabited by brown-skinned people, these Nishnaabe women and men whose ancestry here predates yours by centuries – many centuries.

I got the butter out of the little bar fridge, turned on the griddle and waited for it to heat up. I'd chosen to inconvenience my settler-self this way – putting myself in a position where someone like Marcia could bump me up against some of the reasons I'd been such a convenient settler for so long: my know-it-all arrogance, which helped keep me ignorant of the history that people like her have lived and still live; an alienation and removal so complete that even when I set out to learn, I'd do it only superficially, according to what I judged was necessary to know.

I'd felt that bump in our encounter, in how Marcia responded to me when I admitted that I hadn't read the transcripts of witnesses like herself at the Ipperwash Inquiry. Don't sidestep this! Don't paper it over.

It was only a soft bump, really; a gentle rebuke, if that. So stay put, I told myself. Dwell in this discomfort. Be set straight by this Nishnaabe woman. Admit that not having done the work to find and read the witness transcripts was disrespectful of her reality, reality from her point of view. Be sorry; even tell Marcia that. Don't sabotage yourself by covering up, trying to pretend to know something you don't. You're not responsible for everything. Nor are you the judge of everything.

I scraped the cooked onions and mushrooms off the griddle, reached for the butter, and remembered what Marlin had said: She's not feeling so well. I remembered the weed-choked flower bed. I remembered that Bonnie and Marcia had not gone inside to talk but had sat outside in the chill of the late-fall day. What did that say? What was going on behind the scenes about which I knew nothing? Precisely!

I would respect this woman's priorities, and if there was no place for me in them, so be it. If she had no energy for remembering a painful, traumatizing time, accept this. Respect and honour it. Still, I'd welcome the chance to talk with her, maybe get to know her. Maybe I could weed her flower bed for her someday. And maybe not.

Marcia has told you what to do: read the transcripts, girl! And if you do, maybe then she'll be more ready and willing to talk to you. Maybe then you'll have earned a bit of her trust.

I poured the egg mixture onto the griddle and watched it spread across the heated surface.

Shit! There was a kind of gutter along the front of the pan, and a hole in the corner I hadn't noticed before. The egg mixture was running into the hole. I grabbed the griddle by the handle and tilted. Kept holding until the egg was cooked enough that it wouldn't run. I added the sautéed onions and mushrooms, the sliced cheese. There was a warped rubber spatula in the drawer. I used that to scrape the crisped bits in from the edge and folded everything together as best I could.

It was a mess, but edible at least.

8

Challenged

I didn't call again that day; if Marcia was home and didn't want to answer the phone, even the ringing would intrude. I waited until the next morning, and even then didn't call before ten.

She answered. That would be fine, she said when I invited her to come out for a coffee. She was ready when I arrived to pick her up, carrying a shopping bag made of thick plastic with faded and flaking decorations on both sides, plus a vinyl handbag with handles that stuck straight up. She kept both in her lap as I drove. We went to the Tim Horton's in Forest, and as we stood in line, I told her that the Airbnb where I was staying was just down the street.

Oh, she said, "I'd like to see that." So we took our coffee and muffins there. I fussed around trying to make her comfortable in the chilly room, turning up both knobs on the heater to the max, but leaving the noisy fan turned off.

She'd brought her own copy of the Ipperwash Inquiry report, she said, as she pulled it carefully out of the shopping bag. There was also something her brother Graham had put together as a submission. It was a history of Stoney Point, called Aazhoodena, she said. Did I know it was called that, she asked with a smile.

"No, I don't think so," I said, then corrected myself: "No, I didn't know." I'd seen the word on an old and faded billboard at the closed army camp and been mildly curious, but then let it go; some faded old sign, that's all.

Now I tried saying this Nishnaabemowin word out loud: Aazhoodena.

No, she said, and explained that in their language "e" is a long vowel. She repeated the word.

I tried again, and again I got it wrong.

She opened up the stapled-together document. It talks about our ancestors, the Potawatomi, she said, and the Three Fires Confederacy. She turned some pages, stopped at one with a hand-drawn map. Did I know about the "Trail of Death"[1] and the US Indian Removal Act of 1830? I'd heard of them, vaguely. I nodded so I wouldn't appear too ignorant. Her great-great-grandfather was one of the Potawatomis who escaped from the forced relocation imposed at the time. He fled with his family to Canada and settled in the Stoney Point Reserve at Aazhoodena. His name was Manidoka, she said. "It means a being with spiritual power."

She nodded as though to impress the importance of this name and its meaning, then pressed the paper napkin to her lips and folded it into the empty coffee cup.

She looked around. "It's cold in here. Can you turn the heat up?"

I explained about the noisy fan, then switched it on. She gave a little laugh when she heard it, but didn't seem to mind. I pulled the rickety rocking chair I was sitting on a little closer to her.

Did I know about the Three Fires Confederacy, Marcia asked. Again, I might have heard of it, but that was as far as it went. And what I knew was from way back, nothing to do with recent history. I needed to include this too, she said, nodding her head emphatically. I dropped my head. I made a note, but inwardly I was bristling. Just how far back did she want this story to go? I'd dealt with enough publishers over the years to know that they might not be interested.

I got up, went to the bar fridge and got out the cheese, then went to the counter to prepare a plate of cheese and crackers. Buying time, because I was being triggered by this woman. She was so insistent, so insistently the one in the know. Well, why not, I thought as I brought the plate over to where she sat. She was the one in the know and I was not. Simple as that. What was I thinking?

She'd done up the zipper of her jacket, I noticed, and pulled the sleeves down over her hands. She took a cracker and bit off a corner. "Hmm," she said, "this is nice." She smiled. "What kind of cracker is it?" I went and brought her the box. She nodded; she'd have to get some. She took another cracker and carried on talking about a leader, Tecumseh, who rallied the Three Fires Confederacy around the dream of securing a large Nishnaabe territory that would be recognized as entirely self-governing and sovereign, like one of the states in the United States.

That's why they fought alongside the British in 1812, she said – to secure that. But Tecumseh was killed, and the dream ... She sighed and pressed her lips together as though holding something back. Then she shrugged, shook her head, and gave a little laugh. Some of Tecumseh's descendants are still living in Kettle Point. Did I know that?

She looked up. No, I said, and made another note. She smiled. "And I'm distantly related – on my mother's side." Again an emphatic nod of the head and a self-satisfied smile.

Tecumsee? I asked. That's the name as I'd encountered it in all the history books I'd read.

"Yes, that's who I mean," she said. "But it's Tecumseh."

I tried pronouncing it. She corrected me. "No, not Tecumsee. Tecumseh."

I tried again. She nodded, smiling.

We didn't talk much more on that first visit. But I'd be back, I told her when I drove her home; I'd try to get back in a month.

BY THE TIME I got back to Kettle Point, six weeks later, I had done a lot more research, including working my way through some of the witness transcripts. But I couldn't find much on the Three Fires Confederacy beyond a brief mention in passing in various texts I consulted, and something on the Union of Ontario Indians website; the union traced its antecedents back to the confederacy. Its story of the three brothers who founded it and what each was responsible for differed from the account Marcia's brother had put together. I wondered which one to use. I found out only later that two people living in Kettle Point were considered the knowledge keepers for Tecumseh's story.[2] It's their responsibility to remember that Tecumseh had rallied the confederacy in a pan-Indigenous effort to secure an entirely sovereign Nishnaabe territory in what was still considered Indian Country under the 1763 Royal Proclamation. They'd fought on the side of the British in the War of 1812 with the idea that this would be the payoff for their support.

At the time, it hadn't occurred to me that all this knowledge might be available locally – an oral history faithfully preserved by Tecumseh's descendants. I hadn't thought to ask Marcia either, or to follow up on her reference to some of Tecumseh's descendants living in Kettle Point. I also thought that it was up to me, as the professional writer on the project, to do this research, using my usual academic sources. These were all written accounts that other authors, including academics, also considered reliable. And maybe, too, I wanted to bring myself up to speed quietly, so that no one, especially Marcia, a former teacher, even a native studies teacher and the co-ordinator of native studies with the local school board at one point, could discover just how out of touch with all this I really was. More covering up, of not just my ignorance but my anxiety around not being in the know. It didn't occur to me that this anxiety wasn't just personal insecurity; there might be some unexamined colonial and even white superiority in there too.

I hadn't yet read all the witness transcripts from the Ipperwash Inquiry, but at least I'd gotten through the testimony of the people I had begun to meet here. By the time Marcia and I got together again, too, I had taped a couple of conversations with Bonnie, had met Cully and recorded some of her stories, and had spoken briefly to her brother Pierre. Pierre had driven Dudley to the hospital on the night of September 6, 1995, in a futile attempt to save his life; Cully had been with him.

MARCIA WAS READY for me to start taping what she wanted to say for the book. She watched me set up the microphone on the coffee table, nodded that, yes, that was fine, then laughed.

"There was a Peace Tree; were you told about that?" She was referring to the burying-the-hatchet ceremony the Nishnaabe had held in 1993, shortly after moving onto the still-functioning army camp, a commitment that this would be a peaceful action, with no weapons.

No. I hadn't known about the Peace Tree. "Tell me," I said, and at her nod, turned on the recorder.

"Did you wonder where they buried the hatchet?" She laughed.

We talked for a couple of hours, and about many things, including our children and what they're doing with their lives. "I have pictures of Kevin and Marlin when they were just little wee toddlers out there," Marcia said when she was talking about the many protests she'd been part of outside the army camp, with many of these led by her parents, Daniel and

Melva. She talked about when she was young herself: her father would regularly take the children to Stoney Point, to skate on a pond that had once been a stone quarry the army dug for itself at one of the Nishnaabe family's homesteads. In other seasons, he took them to the dump near the back of the army camp to scavenge for bottles to sell and reusable nails.

"As part of his showing us, this is our homeland, he would take us there ..." and often to their own homestead which, like all the others, had been bulldozed to make way for the army camp during the war. "For years the well was still visible; the top of the well, the rocks and bricks – until they built another interior road in there. So we grew up knowing it was ours. And we were always told that they took it over, but their promise was that it would be returned at the end of the war. We had that ingrained in us! Too bad the politicians didn't."[3] She laughed, but there was bitterness in the sound and in the deep lines on her face.

I didn't want to push her or direct the conversation because, as I kept reminding myself, I wasn't the author. I wasn't the authority figure here. Marcia and the others were; this was their story to tell, however they needed and wanted to tell it. Still, I had such a confident sense of what good storytelling involved. Based on assumptions, really, but they were stitched tightly, if invisibly, into me, and part of what gave me self-confidence as a person was having this skill to offer as a writer.

I was hardly aware of myself steering her, respectfully, of course, and using words like "if you could ..." If there was going to be a book here, there needed to be more about what went on through that first summer, in 1993, when the Nishnaabe men and women simply went home, reclaiming their ancestral territory at Aazhoodena, the Stoney Point Reserve.

Marcia remembered: She used her lump-sum summer teachers' pay to buy a couple of trailers so that some of the young men who showed up, like her sons, didn't need to sleep on the ground. They all came together to build a council hall too, using wood donated by the United Auto Workers. They lit and tended a sacred fire, and Marcia's mother, Melva, who'd been forced to attend a residential school and give up her culture, taught some of the old songs and ceremonies, using a hand drum and the language she'd once been punished for speaking.

"Could you sense the old community coming back?" I couldn't resist asking, wanting to draw her out.

"We're not old," Marcia scoffed.

"Sorry. I meant the traditional ways of –" She cut me off.

"I hate that word, *traditional*. It's just being normal, being human," she said, looking at me hard.

How could I be so stupid? I wasn't being "traditional" in the way I lived, as though I was acting out a museum display. Nor were they. I sat there feeling small and ashamed. There's nothing blissful about ignorance once you're up against it, I thought, especially when faced with someone who's been paying the price of it. And still is. It becomes shameful, ugly even.

Marcia took the lid off her coffee, took another sip, put the lid back on.

"I'm sorry," I said. I opened the package of cookies I'd brought, offered her one, and put the package on the coffee table within easy reach beside my small recorder. I'd left it running, and now it recorded the sounds of us munching. I kept my mouth shut on all the explanations I wanted to offer. There were no excuses. I had a lot to learn, or unlearn, period.

She continued sharing her memories, how she'd carried on teaching school in London during the day and driving eighty kilometres back to the cadet training camp at night. She talked about the day in July 1995 when she and the others moved into the built-up area of the army camp, taking over the barracks that were by then largely empty because the cadet training program itself had been shut down, leaving only a few soldiers to keep the camp itself running.

Suddenly she was laughing. "I went in there and I told them, 'I want you boys out of here.' And to the female offi-cers I told them, 'I want you girls out of here as well. This is our territory.' Just said it calmly, told them what I wanted." She looked at me, nodding decisively and smiling, and I could see the teacher in her, as though she'd been talking to an unruly class.

"But some of them," she continued with a chuckle still rounding out her voice, "when they saw me coming, they would run and hide behind the trucks and things – and I was just an old woman going to town with my wish list!" She laughed again, helped herself to another cookie, and paused before eating it.

"If they only knew that we were a bunch of teenagers and old – they made us sound like were a bunch of real vicious warriors. Meanwhile, there was me and my mom, old grey-haired widows. Same as old Pearl." (Pearl George was one of the elders, along with Melva, who had led the way home in May 1993.) Marcia smiled, gave her head another nodding shake, and ate her cookie. Something in me began to unclench. Here we were, two grey-haired older women ourselves.

A few weeks later, she continued, the group decided to take over the provincial park as well. The park had originally been part of the Stoney Point Reserve, and contained burial sites – one of the things that bothered a lot of people, Dudley included. Because his grandfather was among those who had been buried there; he was called Albert George, but was also known as Kamaanii, Marcia said.

I said something like, "And then?" gently nudging Marcia to continue the story, because it was at the park after they'd taken it over that Dudley was shot.

Marcia didn't respond at first. Then: "When I heard that Dudley had been shot, I was just panicking and wanting to find my sons ... and there was a line of cars coming up from there, and one of the cars was Marlin, and his face was just ashen, and I said, 'What's going on down there?' and he said, 'Don't go down there. The cops have shot up everything.' So I reluctantly turned around – even though I still hadn't seen Kevin. But I had my mom with me. I forget when I did see him." She stopped and looked at me, the panic of that night plain to see.

"Yes," I said. "He was with Dudley when Dudley was shot, yes?"

"Yes." That single word repeated back, Marcia's voice like a ton of lead.

Silence. She looked up, locked her eyes onto mine.

"So," she said, "these guys have got some real heavy things on their psyche to tend with for the rest of their lives."

I nodded, still looking at her, and just sat there, letting the anguish on her face and what she'd said sink in. Her nephew Dudley had been fatally shot. Her sons had witnessed this.

Eventually she took a deep breath and carried on with what happened next: Dudley was bundled into Pierre's old car, she said, and they took off to the nearest hospital, fifty-five kilometres away, at Strathroy. Then she decided to take off, too, to find a pay phone to call for help, an ambulance for anyone else who might have been shot – her son, maybe. For all she knew, he was lying in a ditch somewhere. Then the police started chasing her, and when she got to the phone booth outside the McPherson Restaurant on Highway 21 some ten minutes later, they surrounded her and grabbed the phone out of her hand, twisting her hand behind her back.

"I'd had a shattered wrist and was undergoing physiotherapy at the time. I had to go every day," Marcia said. "You can see it here, the scar on my wrist."

I looked, saw the faint imprint of a scar, and nodded.

Marcia rubbed her wrist, then pulled her sweatshirt down over the scar.

Silence. "And then?" I gently prompted.

"I'm telling you. Just listen," she said.

"I remember hitting my head first on the hood of the car, and being knocked to the ground, and somebody was right on my back, and I remember my mom screaming at them, 'watch her hand!' So I was handcuffed."

She was taken to Forest and put in a jail cell.

"There was a mattress and an old grey wool blanket, and it just felt filthy. Just the idea that there were these criminals that had been in there before. It just felt ... These guys are nuts. They don't even know that I'm a respected schoolteacher. Same as my mom; she's a respected elder in the community. To be treated like that! People that knew me wouldn't expect me to be in jail!"

It was only when she was released into the custody of the Kettle Point Anishinabek police and when they, in turn, finally let her go that she found out that Dudley had died, she said. Her voice broke and she shook her head.

I reached for the recorder, to pause it. I didn't even have any Kleenex to offer her, hadn't thought of having some just in case.

"I'm so sorry," I said. She nodded. Silence. Then: "When I think of Dudley, it just makes me sob deep inside." Her voice broke again. More silence.

Dudley George's death, the reality of it – not just the historical fact of it – had entered this little room: the deep personal tragedy of it still living as a sob inside this woman who was Dudley's aunt. It moved down from my head and into my heart, lodging there. I'd never known anyone who'd died from gun violence, let alone at the hands of the police.

I reached out and touched her arm. "I'm so sorry," I said again.

She looked at me, looked away again, giving her head a shake.

"He was the heart of the community, that crazy old Dudley. He was almost like a clown. He would tell jokes that were old and stale. They weren't even funny, but he'd laugh the hardest himself." She carried on talking, about what happened next. So much time has elapsed, and so little has changed. But people like Kevin and Cully are still there, honouring what the elders had said back in 1993: that they needed to stay living on the land or the government would never give it back.

I wanted to say something affirming. "And they're honouring that," I said, "continuing the occupation."

Marcia snorted. "We don't think of it as an occupation. That's our home. We're living there in our homeland." She looked at me in my rickety rocking chair. "Have you heard any of us say: 'We're going to take part in the occupation today?'" She laughed, though gently, as if to soften her words.

"I'm sorry," I said, returning her look. "It's just that my mind has been schooled to think that way."

I wished later that I'd thought to thank her for setting me straight – not so much on the facts of the story but the point of view. Instead I told her that I was beginning to understand. I dared to go on, even though I didn't really understand, at least not yet. I just wanted Marcia to know that I was trying. "So carrying on hasn't been a choice," I said. "It's just carrying on until ..." I fell silent, leaving the blank in my mind blank.

"Yes," she said. "Until we get the government recognition that we need."

What will that mean? I asked, realizing that I had no idea what that might mean, though it was hidden in plain sight amidst the clutter and falling-down remains of the old army camp: people like Kevin, Cully, and the others were going about their lives, growing vegetables and sage, playing bingo. They were living the reality of a Nishnaabe community at

Aazhoodena/Stoney Point, whether it was officially recognized and supported or not.

Marcia told me about her vision that Aazhoodena would be restored as a fully functioning reserve in its own right, with its own jurisdiction and funding base, with the people free to choose their own leaders, to go their own way.

"And our little ones can grow up and have the right to live and learn and go after whatever they are created to be – and not to have to wage a war like this!"

She shook her head, looked at me. "You said you have children?"

Yes, I told her, a son called Donald. "And what does he do?" I told her about his work as a home renovator in Ottawa.

"Imagine if he wasn't able to do that, and had to contend with trying to get your land back that you used to live on."

I nodded, though I couldn't imagine it, really. My son's original plans for his life had been derailed by illness. But here the basis of a whole community living a shared life, with a distinct history and culture, had been derailed for all the kin-related people involved. People like Marcia's son Kevin were spending their whole life contending with this. I nodded again and looked at her.

"It's a real waste of our young people," she said. I nodded again. Kevin had been shot at, too, I knew, and still he carried on.

She looked away. "I remember when my boys were small. I had great hopes for them. I wasn't planning on them becoming – there's my Kevin cutting grass." Her voice broke and she fell silent. I reached out and touched her, remembering him on that John Deere lawnmower that day last summer.

Marcia heaved a sigh, glanced at me. "But I'm proud of them for what they're doing." She nodded emphatically.

I nodded, too, tears coming to my eyes. Time to turn off the recorder?

She nodded, yes. "Quite a bit for today," she said. Then her voice dropped to a whisper.

"Some things are difficult to talk about." She said it so softly that I didn't catch what she said.

"Pardon me?" I asked. She repeated what she'd said.

Yes, I said. "I'm sorry. I shouldn't have pushed you like that."

"But it's good that you come right out and ask me things."

She gathered up her purse, her hat and gloves, and I drove her home.

9

Challenging Myself

Time to download my audio files and give them at least a test listen. I cleared a workspace on the table ledge in the Airbnb I'd returned to, perched myself on the bar stool, and arranged my notebook beside me so I could jot down the odd phrase that stood out. By now I'd taped a session with Marcia's son Marlin too.

As I listened to what I'd recorded, I noticed my own voice when I spoke. It seemed to poke out at me, and I didn't like what I was hearing. I kept jumping into silences instead of just leaving them be. There were spots, too, where I blabbed away, telling a similar story, trying to draw parallels, still trying to close the distance between us, minimize our differences in a common, shared humanity, instead of recognizing and respecting them. And there were the spots where I put my foot right into it. Like when I started taping that first conversation with Cully.

While I'd been setting up, she'd gone off to collect some spools of thread from the stack of plexiglass drawers in her work area and plunked these on the table next to the quilt on which she was stitching the edge. Then she sat down and grabbed her baseball cap.

"I put on my hat when I get cold," she said.

She was nervous, I could tell. (And wasn't I, too?)

Ready? At her nod, I clicked on the machine: "If you could start," I said, "by telling me your name."

Listening now, I was so ashamed. I'd gone all formal on her, signalling my professionalism, setting the stage for a more official conversation, almost setting the rules of engagement. Taking charge!

Big sigh on the tape, then silence. Again, that was something I listened to again and again, taking in my impulse to control at work, and having its effect.

Finally she continued: "I do go by," pause, then "My name is Carolyn Joyce George dash Mandoka." She inhaled, continued. "I went back to my maiden name after I got divorced. And then I put my own name in there, my original name, Mandoka."

Another silence. I remember that she'd reached for a spool of thread at that point. She ran off a length, cut it, and started threading it through a needle; she had a bunch of these in a saucer beside her, straight pins in another saucer nearby. Then she continued.

"I asked my dad one time, how come we don't have an Indian name if we're supposed to be Indians? But we do!" The Mandoka name got taken away when this Potawatomi forefather had his family baptized in 1860. The missionaries baptized him as George and dropped his true name from the colonial records.

The power of naming, I thought now. There are so many ways it can be denied, and used against you too. I remembered my earlier conversation with Marcia: calling her and the others' action to reclaim their homes an occupation! No matter that the media had described it in those terms at the time, and that even her son Kevin had used it when he was on the witness stand at the Ipperwash Inquiry. But maybe he'd just been going along with using that word, so that he'd be heard in the hall of the inquiry, to be on the same page sort of thing. With Marcia, though, I had used that term in the space I had consciously tried to make into her talking space. I'd used it to her face – when it was the other way around: the Canadian army had been occupying *her* land! She and the others had been trying to repossess it, and still were!

I wasn't transcribing my interjections, I noticed. I wanted to erase them, like erasing incriminating evidence. Of what, though? Well, just being less than the perfect listener. Less than perfect!

No. There was more to it than just personal insecurity and the need to get everything right. I got up to warm up my tea in the microwave. Maybe it was impossible for me to get things right. Here I was, assuming that I could be of some use, but maybe I couldn't, or not this way, because I couldn't see my way clear of whatever in my mind had considered that word *occupation* so unproblematic. I couldn't assume that I was part of the solution. I couldn't even assume that I wasn't part of the problem.

I stopped myself. What was I saying, or admitting, here? That I might be part of the problem? Was this the evidence I wanted to avoid or erase? Yes. In fact, until I was willing to admit this possibility, or even to consider it, I very likely was perpetuating the problem – conveniently for the status quo to carry on. In fact, a symptom of my being the problem might be right here in my resistance to even considering this possibility. I shook my head. I was confusing myself; probably just more evasive thinking.

I took my tea over to the window, remembering how my mind had done a flip when I'd read Thomas King's *The Inconvenient Indian*. Indigenous people (like him) have been on this land all along, King writes. They still know it and claim it as the ground of their identity. They didn't die out. They might be "out of sight, out of mind, out of mind, out of sight," he writes.[1] But they have not disappeared. They're "still in the way. Still inconvenient."[2] On reading this, I realized that I was helping to perpetuate what left people like Thomas King inconveniently still in the way. I was the convenient settler helping to perpetuate the status quo and let it carry on unchallenged. So why not become an *inconvenient* settler by repudiating the status quo, and with it the idea that Canada was founded as a colony and grew to nationhood from that? Yes, I thought at the time, I could chart a more inconvenient course by embracing an older story: that Canada began with a relationship, a treaty relationship between European new-comers and the peoples who had long co-inhabited this land with multiple nations of animals and plants.

This new thinking had brought me here in the first place. But now I realized how facile, even arrogant, it had been to assume that I could undo all my old ways of thinking just with this flip of a phrase. I'd been pushing back against es-tablished ways of thinking all my life: as a student attending teach-ins, as a feminist embracing consciousness raising and, as a published author, joining other feminists in challenging men for presuming to tell our stories and speak our truth. Cultural appropriation. We'd debated what that was, fiercely, in the writing community, and I remember finding one of the earliest uses of the term, dating from 1635: "Christ cannot be so appropriated, or inclosed [sic]."[3]

I stared out the window. So much was in the enclosing: what was closed in and what was closed out of public per-ception, and the patterns of power behind this. I wasn't on the receiving end of the power here, however. I was on the other end, the enforcing end. And the evidence was in my continuing to think that I could ask the right questions. I could tell myself that I had been essentially invited to do so as an experienced journalist and writer. But who was I trying to kid? As if my merit as someone offering a professional service somehow cancelled out my biases as a colonized (and colonizing!) settler, however inconvenient a one I wanted to be! It just glossed them over, provided a convenient cover.

My tea was cold again, but I stayed where I was. My biases, however invisible to me, at least, were warping my perception. Maybe this wasn't just a symptom of the problem; maybe it was the problem itself or how I exemplified it. This stubborn assumption that I could ask appropriate questions, chart a reliable path to the truth. Gatekeeping on my own "professional" terms.

I went back to the table ledge I'd turned into my desk. I replayed the conversations I'd had with Marlin and Cully, noticing how often I intervened with a question, stopping the flow of the conversation and where they were going with it. Directing it here or there, along lines that made the story coherent – to me! Just the act of doing this was so normal for me, and I was so comfortable doing it, contributing from my self-assured professional know-how. I didn't recognize it as the exercise of power; the thought had never crossed my mind. It was that automatic.

"Can I bring you back to ..." I noticed how often I used that phrase, seemingly with such polite respect. Steering them back to what I wanted them to talk about, and away from where they were taking the conversation, off on what seemed, to me, to be a tangent. Deciding for us both! And worse, I thought: denying their sense of what was relevant.

I played back that little phrase over and over again, cringing at what I'd been doing, and how unconsciously too. It seemed so innocuous, yet I was denying their authorship! Their authority to speak as they saw fit. I was enclosing it!

Even as I considered this, though, I could feel myself resisting it. I wanted to stay snugly cocooned in my familiar, comfortable sense of things, in my own story, really, with me playing the treaty good guy, the role I'd scripted for myself to play here. I had to believe that I could play just a supporting role here. But supporting on their terms or mine? I hadn't considered how arrogant that was: assuming that I was playing merely a supporting role, not a leading one, by saying I was.

I recalled how readily, how eagerly, I'd seized this role, almost as an entitlement, simply because I was a writer. I'd embraced the invitation to help them write their story without pausing to wonder whether it was appropriate for me to play this role. Maybe it wasn't appropriate; maybe I should leave it to someone like Marcia if she could get her health back.

I preferred not to consider such questions, except maybe in passing. Meanwhile, I was leaving myself in the judgment seat, casually giving myself the benefit of the doubt. Not necessarily guilty of anything, but not innocent either.

I went back to the window, stared out at the blank wall of the house beyond. I was reproducing the same old colonial patterns, with me in charge, me adjudicating, me seeing and hearing through my eyes and ears, not theirs. It's been called ethnocentrism[4] or Eurocentrism. But knowing the terms didn't help me that much, because I was struggling to come to grips with this inside me, grasping for words that would pinpoint where and how I am the problem here so I could confront myself. It wasn't clearly labelled inside my brain; the power play at work was so subtle and elusive. It was in the dynamic of the relationships I was forming, in each moment of their unfolding.

Still, it was very real. And no matter how I disguised it – just doing my job, just bringing useful skills into play – this was the truth, or part of the truth, of what was going on. I could have kept getting away with it, too, because no one balked or challenged me. Maybe they were busy telling themselves to be grateful for getting their story recorded, even if it wasn't entirely on their terms. Meanwhile I was doing harm as I let myself play my professional role without challenging and questioning it. It was up to me, I thought now. It was up to me to recognize what I was doing and take responsibility for breaking the pattern. If I could.

I leaned against the window ledge. There was a squirrel running along the hydro line past the top of the house on the next lot. I watched it climb up onto the hydro pole, clamber around its fixtures, then run back along the line. Now what?

"Just listen." I could hear Marcia's impatient voice in my head. She'd said it more than once. I was warping the story they were trying to tell me with my preconceived ideas about it. I might be listening, all right. But I wasn't hearing right. I needed to listen inwardly, too, with my heart as well as with my head.

Yes, I thought as I turned from the window, because by now my heart really was engaged; I didn't want to hurt Marcia's feelings, didn't want to offend her. Same with Cully and Bonnie. If I could listen more with my heart, I could listen that much more deeply and stay with whatever people like Marcia were saying. Then maybe I could interrupt myself before I said something to steer and control the conversation. I needed to shut myself up. Or rather, shut up the "professional writer" and recolonizer in me, using my journalistic skills to distance myself from the realities they were speaking of, including from the pain.

I needed to show up just as me, or try to. Then maybe I could really start to hear them and what they had to say.

10

Conversations Deepen

I went over to Bonnie's, stopping for a carton of cream en route. This time I went to the grocery store on the reserve; I was getting this sort of thing right, at least. I noticed that the flags at the band office were at half-mast. Better check the news tonight, I thought; someone important has died.

Bonnie was in the kitchen area when I arrived. She'd hoisted herself out of her wheelchair and was leaning against the top of the counter, supervising Colleen as she poured what looked like macaroni into two large tinfoil pans. Next, Colleen started covering them up with cling wrap, saying something about taking them over herself.

"No, no," Bonnie said. Summer was coming over soon, Shelly too; they'd take them later.

She wheeled herself out from behind the counter, noticing the cream and another package of chocolate-covered biscuits in my hands.

"You shouldn't have," she said, but took the cream and told Colleen to put it in the fridge.

"Want a coffee?"

I said no, but Colleen was already bringing me one. There was an empty mug already in my spot – or the spot I'd kind of adopted as my own.

I asked Colleen how her hand was. She showed me where she'd cut it last month. All healed; not even a scar. Then she pulled a face, as though in pain.

"Maybe I need another cookie," she said. We both laughed, and I opened the new box.

Something was beginning to take root here.

When she went off to clean the bathroom, I fished out the language-nest booklets Bonnie had lent me, and put them on the table.

Fred came into the room and greeted me with a big smile. I smiled back.

"How are you?" I asked, getting up and guessing that this was his mug on the table. I knew he'd had some small procedure on his heart. Bonnie and I were friends on Facebook now, and she'd messaged me with the news.

"Oh, can't complain, can't complain," he said. He waved me back, went to the far end of the table, and sat down.

Bonnie told him that Shelly was coming over too. She looked at me, looked back at Fred, and nodded. "Fred here is a language speaker," she said. Fred looked up, smiled briefly, and nodded. Silence, then: "It was the worst thing that happened to me – going to school," he said. More silence.

"I grew up in the language. My mother was a Nishnaabe speaker. Up to six or seven years old, that's all I spoke. When I started school, I had to go in the English." He looked at me, then looked out the window. "I think even my mother, then, she kind of put the brakes on; she started speaking English too ... Put a real damper on."

He tightened his lips, something I'd noticed in him and others a lot. Then he nodded and leaned back in his chair. I hadn't thought twice about the fact that here we were, talking English as a matter of course, "the language" having been disappeared as the normal form of communication even here in Nishnaabe territory. At least that's how it seemed in my sense of things. There seemed to be no echo of the loss, nothing to make me notice the irony, nothing to make me feel.

Was this a residential school? I asked. No, Fred said. The local Indian day school, just elementary, he said. Here on the reserve.

Bonnie explained that when they started closing the residential schools, the teachers just moved over and got jobs in the Indian day schools on reserves like theirs. She laughed. "Remember Mrs. Orr? Oh, she was mean! You could tell she didn't like children. She didn't like Indians ... 'You lumps on a log,' that's what she used to call everyone ... There weren't enough pencils to go around, so she cut the pencils in half, and at lunch hour it was 'Get the tin, get the tin.' Someone was always stealing them."

The back door opened, and Summer came into the room. She smiled hello all around, then went over to Fred, her Poppa. She took his right hand into both of hers, and just quietly carried on standing there next to his chair, his hand pressed gently between hers. Bonnie told her what they'd been telling me, and carried on.

"They used to bring the Mounties into that school, line us all up, whoever was due for a strapping."

"No," she said when I couldn't stop myself from interrupting, "just to make sure we didn't bother the teacher. The teacher did the strapping ... I got it when they caught me washing my feet at the pump." She laughed at the memory. "But Fred was getting it on a regular basis." I looked at Fred. He chuckled. "Stealing sap from the sap bucket," he said. The man next door to the school tapped maple trees in the spring.

They told more stories, about having to do the schoolteacher's laundry, about the pranks the older boys pulled on Mrs. Orr. They explained, too, that the school only went up to Grade 8. Then Summer told a story of when her father's father was at school. He stole the math textbook one day. He and his friend were hiding with it under a table, teaching each other the math problems, and the teacher caught them. He ended up calling in a professor from the University of Western Ontario in London to demonstrate the boys' math skills in front of him. The professor was very impressed.

"But only Grade 8 for Indian kids," Summer said. She laughed gently. She looked at me, and went on to say that she'd heard this story again and again growing up. Her grandfather kept wanting to repeat it. "So I made a point of committing it to memory," she said.

Yes, I thought, not just remembering it, but committing it to memory. A commitment to honour that story and all the truth that it contained.

I remembered this kind of story coming up again and again in the report of the Truth and Reconciliation Commission, belying the notion that any of these had been genuine schools. The children spent at least half their school days working – in the fields, or the laundry or sewing room, or beyond, digging ditches. One school supervisor actually told a student that "your people are never going to get educated to be a professional worker." And at Mount Elgin, where local kids like Summer's grandfather were forcibly sent, the principal of the day actually wrote in a report that "classroom work is an important part of [the] training, but not by any means the most important," adding, "In the case of the Indian, 'a little learning is a dangerous thing.'"[1]

Summer touched my arm. She wanted to show me something, she said. She led the way into the back hall, off the entranceway, and pointed to a hat hanging from the wall above where the stairs led down to the basement. It was a round-rimmed sun hat. It had been made by Bonnie's grandmother Flora, out of wood. A log of black ash was pounded to loosen the fibres, then lengths of it were split thinner and thinner, to the point where the splints could be woven into baskets and, in this case, a beautifully brimmed hat. Bonnie had told me about this earlier. Flora sold these sunhats to local tourists and cottagers to help make ends meet. Bonnie had recognized this as one of her grandmother's when she spotted it hanging in one of the cottages she used to clean, and she arranged to get it back.

Summer had spent a lot of time here when she was growing up, and returned when she was working on her thesis – for a master's degree in Indigenous education policy leadership. One day, she told me now, she found herself looking at this hat, which had been hanging on the wall since she was a little girl, and something shifted. "A paradigm shift," she said with a mischievous smile at her use of this abstract, academic term. Instead of the usual academic texts, she decided to focus on her great-grandmother's hat as text, as primary source material for her thesis. She also vowed to keep doing this, paying attention to the stories told around kitchen tables like this one, the stories embedded in things like this hat, all the relations in its making remembered and treasured as knowledge.

She was doing that now, she told me as we walked back into the main room. She had a contract with a major archive to spend time with Indigenous elders in the area, recording some of their traditional knowledge and stories.

I wanted her to keep going, telling me more. I'd been reading about this sort of thing. In fact, I was sitting on the national steering committee for something called the National Heritage Digitization Strategy. The idea was to create a pan-Canadian portal of access to a digital version of anything that might be considered Canadian heritage, and to help digitize all that was still only in paper-based form. I'd been pushing for them to include an Indigenous person on the steering committee, especially for the working group I was on, developing policies on "access" to digitized material. All the others in the working group – archivists, museum managers, university and research agency librarians – wanted "free access" and "no barriers." But I knew enough to say there were certain protocols to follow around gaining access to traditional knowledge – including getting permission. Provision needed to be made to welcome doing things like this, I'd argued; the extra work involved shouldn't be treated negatively, as a barrier to access, or postponed so it would become an expensive add-on later. Nor should these stories be seen as merely more data to access, more product. I didn't know what was needed; that's why they needed Indigenous knowledge keepers involved, I told my colleagues on the committee. I only knew something was missing in the approach being taken.

But Shelly arrived at this point. She and Summer were taking the macaroni salads over for the funeral feast, Bonnie explained. She sent Colleen down to the basement for a jar of her pickled beets and sent them off with that too. Fred was also leaving, taking Buck to the doctor.

Bonnie wheeled her chair back over to the table, and we sat there in the quiet.

It was another OD death, Bonnie told me, shaking her head. A woman with kids still young enough to need a mother around. I mentioned seeing the flags at half-mast.

Yes, Bonnie said, that was why. And the wake was happening at the school there. The funeral would be later. She and Fred would go.

I took my napkin and wiped the spot where my mug had been. I asked Bonnie if it might be okay for me to drop in at the wake. It felt like the right thing to do: to bear witness. Not to just drive by on my way back to where I was staying.

Bonnie looked at me, nodded. "If you feel like you want to do that. Sure."

So I did. A throng of teenage guys stood by the doors to the school. They fell silent and stepped back, giving way as I, a white woman, approached. I walked inside, into a dark, gloomy foyer. Down a short hall to my right, I saw open doors. The gym, I guessed. I walked in and immediately saw a large white cross at the front of the room. It was the largest floral display there, and the only one entirely made from white flowers. There were rows and rows of metal chairs in the room, most of them empty. But there were small groups of mourners scattered here and there. I wondered if there were any people I might have met already, who might recognize me. I secretly hoped not, in case they thought my being here was wrong.

I took a chair near the back, and scanned the small folded program with a photo of the woman on the front. A slide show began. I watched the pulled-up white screen as it filled with baby picture after baby picture, followed by party pictures and family gatherings. I watched it through twice, and then got up. I could tell that the family of the woman who'd died was at the front; I'd seen people going up every so often to offer their condolences. But I wouldn't go; I felt it would be an intrusion.

As I got to the door, I noticed a large plastic bowl sitting on the table beside the pile of programs. There was a bit of money in it: mostly toonies and loonies, and a few five-dollar bills. I opened my wallet, started reaching for a twenty, then spotted a five, and a second one too. I pulled these out, put them in the bowl, and carried on through the door. Then I heard a voice from somewhere in the shadow behind the door, saying, "Thank you."

I looked in the direction from which the voice had come, saw an older woman sitting there. I looked at her and nodded. Then I left.

AS I MADE my supper, using the toaster oven the owner of the Airbnb had thoughtfully provided for my return visit, I remembered something Fred had said earlier, when he talked about growing up in the language and then being sent to school. It wasn't so much what he'd said, but how he'd phrased it: that he'd gone to school "in the English." Something came together as I remembered Bonnie having said that he'd grown up "in the language," meaning Ojibwe or Nishnaabemowin. This language was the norm of his world, the world and the territory he grew up in, and his having said "the English" instead of just "English" signalled that his mind was still embedded in its substructure. Or so it seemed to me.

I made a salad to go with the chicken legs I'd roasted, loaded my plate, and sat down to eat. What else had he said? That going to school was "the worst thing that happened to me."

I sat with that as I chewed and swallowed. Sat there as a sense of something surfaced: what it must have been like for Fred to be cut off from his native tongue, the language that was native to this place, all the living and storied legacy of that life embedded in it. What was it like to still be living in this familiar place, yet cut off from his normal way of understanding and experiencing that familiarity – the language that spoke of his belonging here, and through which he shared that belonging with others?

And what had I done when he'd told me that? Had I let in the pain he was sharing with me by saying that going to school in the English was the worst thing that had happened to him? No. I deflected it. I passed over the moment, paved it over, nullified it even. In a way, I had even colonized it with my question about whether it was a residential school he'd been sent to. As if the difference of venue mattered.

Then or now.

I washed the dishes, dried them, and put them away. I got ready for bed and turned off the light.

An image floated into my mind: Summer, Fred's granddaughter, standing beside her Poppa, holding his hand between the two of hers.

11

Witnessing Denial

Back home in BC, the winter dragged on into spring. I tried
to keep in touch with the occasional call, which I made on
Sundays, when my son and I had a weekly phone visit too. If
I wanted to learn what a treaty relationship with people like
Bonnie, Marcia, and Cully might mean, I had to keep working
the ground of it. I had to keep the conversation going. I had
to keep feeding this feeling of connection that had begun to
grow between us, or it would wither and die. It was hard
connecting with Cully because she used her son's cell phone.
When I called Marcia, she often wasn't feeling up to talking
and didn't even pick up the phone. So I concentrated on
Bonnie. Even then, every Sunday when I figured it was time
to call, I'd feel myself fade. I'd procrastinate, one hour to the
next, sometimes one Sunday to the next. I was still on such
thin ice here, and the passing of time kept making it thinner.
Once with Bonnie I got the answering machine, too, and
thought, she doesn't want to talk to me. I'd have to push myself to try the call again, telling myself, don't take it personally;
not everything's about you.

Whenever I did get through, she always seemed glad to hear from me. She regaled me with the latest news at home and down the road at Stoney. She asked how things were with me. We'd have a regular conversation, usually ending with her saying, "Take care."

I didn't want to kid myself, papering over and pretending away the centuries of barbed history between us. There was so much reckoning to do, acknowledging all the harm done and still being done; making the necessary reparations, the necessary changes. Still, these little things we could connect around as women – sharing the ache when tough things happen to our adult children, plus simple things like family meals we were making – these were real. They tilled a common ground between us, which gave me strength to face the stuff that stood between us. To let it in, let it become more familiar, less alien or "other."

One Sunday, Buck answered, and I heard him say, "It's Heather" as he called his mother to the phone. He'd used my name; neat. One weekday, Bonnie messaged me to say that Fred had been taken to hospital, and they gave him a double transfusion. "I knew you'd want to know," she wrote. I called, got the answering machine, left a message, and sent Fred a get-well card.

IT WAS MAY 2019 when I returned, repeating my routine of flying from BC to London, Ontario, and renting a car. This time, I stayed at a motel I'd noticed on Army Camp Road, directly opposite the former army camp itself, a motel with kitchenettes called the Pinewood. I'd resisted even the thought of staying there before because it was on land that had once been part of the reserve, and I wanted to respect that. But Bonnie said I should go ahead; some relatives from Australia had stayed there and it was clean enough.

I settled in, and headed over to Bonnie's to check in with her.

Everything looked the same, complete with Colleen's car parked by the fence, Beau outside the back door, wagging his tail, and the sound of the washing machine as I entered the back stoop and knocked on the inner door.

Some of my old awkwardness returned as I went inside. Something was up at Stoney, or had been. I'd been planning on returning a month earlier, but Bonnie had messaged me saying, "Don't come; they've blocked the gate at Stoney." Even in our phone conversations I hadn't learned much more, except that it was the Nishnaabe peacekeepers – she called them warriors – who were behind the blockade, and as a result the government had shut down the cleanup completely. I'd slowed down as I drove past the army camp entrance when heading to the motel, and noticed a camper parked by the gate, which hadn't been there before. Was this the blockade? Was it still going on? But it wasn't my business, not if Bonnie had wanted to keep me out of it.

Bonnie welcomed me as she always did, waving me toward the chair I'd kind of adopted as my own at one end of the wooden table. I pulled out the things I'd brought as gifts: something for Bonnie, for Fred, for Buck. I handed her hers.

"You shouldn't have," Bonnie admonished me, holding up the earrings I'd brought: Coast Salish silver with an Orca whale design. "It was the closest I could get to your totem," I said, then inwardly kicked myself: Why did I have to make sure she knew that I'd remembered her totem when I'd been shopping? Well, I knew the answer: I was feeling unsure of myself again because I'd been gone for a while. Plus I was showing off. I'd read up on the significance of totem animals and their role in binding people together through clan kinship ties to a shared place of origin in Nishnaabe territory.[1] In Nishnaabe origin stories, humans were created from the dead bodies of the First Ones, the animals created first in the regeneration of life after the great flood. Different animals, including fish, became clan totems, or *dodems*, derived from the Ojibwe word meaning original family residence, with this affiliation passed down through the father's side of the family.[2]

Bonnie beamed at me and set the earrings aside. She'd put them on later, she said.

I looked around, taking in all that had begun to be familiar: the clutter along the wall under the window, the stack of flyers on the chair by the woodstove, the ribbon-tied birch-bark log in the corner by the front door, the significance of which I now understood. It had come from an old medicine man and was meant to help protect the home. I scanned the display of framed photos on the sideboard, trying to guess if there were any new ones, but not wanting to ask.

I told Bonnie about the motel; nice and clean, and fully equipped for cooking, I said.

Bonnie nodded, that's good, that's good.

Then, I couldn't resist: I mentioned seeing the camper by the gatehouse.

"Oh yeah," she said. That's what she'd been messaging me about.

She sat forward in her chair, looked at me hard.

"They're clear-cutting at Stoney," she said.

Who? I asked, though inwardly I knew. The contractors, she said, looking for those UXOs (unexploded ordinances).

"That gets me so mad," she said, throwing back her head and raising one of her arthritis-crippled hands in the direction of Stoney Point just up the road.

All those old trees, Bonnie said, and she started listing off the different species. She'd known these trees all her life, first as a toddler, before the army took over the reserve and turned it into a training camp where soldiers learned to launch mortar shells and grenades, and then when she returned with her father, and took her own children and grandchildren there too.

"And you never clear-cut them," I said.

"No," she said. "We just used what we needed."

She reached for the onion and cutting board on the table in front of her.

"I went bitching in to Jason," she said. Jason Henry was the new band council chief. Bonnie had gone to Indian day school with his father; in fact, his father had been one of the school pranksters she and Fred had told me about. Plus, Bonnie had been band council chief herself at one point (the first woman to hold that position) and served for more than forty years as a band councillor.

I watched her trying to grab hold of the onion with one arthritic hand and the broad-bladed knife with the other. "Let me," I said, leaning forward. But she scoffed me away, got a better grip on the onion and sliced it in half. She looked up and continued telling me what she'd said to the new chief.

"'They've broken their own environmental law,' I told him. 'They've got that Species at Risk Act; we gotta use that.'"

I could follow what she was saying, though barely. It had to do with the Final Settlement Agreement that the Kettle and Stony Point chief and band council, Bonnie included, had signed with the federal government in 2016. From what little I knew, it laid out all the stages of the work to be done in cleaning up and "remediating" the land of the appropriated reserve. It also made everything subject to federal and provincial laws, like the Species at Risk Act, under which some of the ancient trees that were growing on the lands of the former reserve were now considered "endangered."

You had to be a band member to see the agreement. Still, as a federal undertaking, it would be a public document, and I had tried to find it online. But I didn't try terribly hard, I'd noticed. It was as though I didn't want to know, that I was afraid to take on what it meant. I told myself it was none of my business. It was also easier to stay focused on the past, on what I'd been invited to focus on: the particular events that took place between 1993 and 1995. That was responsibility enough to take on, as if the injustice going on was that containable.

Bonnie had pushed her chair away from the table and wheeled herself into the hallway. Colleen had been tending to the laundry; we'd heard the machine noise rise as she'd opened the door to the stoop. Now Bonnie told her what to put in the dryer first. She came back, headed to the kitchen, and started rummaging around behind the counter.

"Buck wants me to make corn soup," she said, "so I better get out my old soup pot."

Colleen followed her and tried to help. Sure enough, Bonnie shooed her away, told her to get herself a coffee. She called her Spark. Everyone with a nickname, I thought. But most of their official names had been imposed on them, so why not? It was a way of taking the power of naming back. And what nicknames! Dudley's was taken from a 1950s cartoon show about Dudley Do-Right, a slightly dimwitted but good-hearted RCMP officer. Cully's son Glen's nickname, J.R., came from the TV show *Dallas*.

Colleen had some photos of her grandchildren, she said, and pulled them out to show Bonnie. Then she brought them over to show me.

Buck came into the room. He was moving a lot faster than last time I'd been here, I noticed. I watched him lift two packages off the seat of the walker, one at a time, onto the counter. They were frozen Indian corn from the Walpole Island reserve. This was one of the only places you could safely grow the corn, someone had told me earlier. The reserve was located on a peninsula, and some islands and the water protected this traditional food from contamination from all the Monsanto-bred corn grown commercially through so much of southwestern Ontario.

Bonnie peered at both packages and chose one. Buck put the other back on the walker and started making his way toward the back stoop, where the big freezer was located. Bonnie called after him to bring some frozen celery.

Fred walked into the room and came toward me. I stood up, told him how glad I was to see him again. Told him he was looking good. He reached out and shook my hand. He said something in the language, then smiled and translated. It was a form of greeting and welcome.

He carried on, heading for the bathroom. I thought of mentioning the gift I'd brought but decided I'd leave it for Bonnie to draw his attention to it. All in good time.

Buck brought the package of frozen celery, hoisted it onto the counter, then went to where the coffee machine sat, seemingly with coffee permanently on. He said something to his mother, calling her "Ma." I watched her laugh, her face shining with pleasure. Then he turned toward me and told me about the time his mother ran out of her supply of frozen celery and had to go to the store. But when she discovered how expensive it was, she refused to buy any.

"She was on her celery boycott," Buck said, and he laughed.

Bonnie returned to the table and got back to dicing the onion. It was for the soup, she said, and explained how in the old days they grew and prepared their own corn. You used wood ash from the fire, she said. Hardwood burned in the woodstove.

"And no snot rags," Buck called out from across the room. Bonnie laughed and continued, "And you put that in the boiling water with the corn. Then you dump the corn into a frame with wire mesh at the bottom, and you rub it over the mesh. Like this," she said, raising her hands to demonstrate the rubbing action that got rid of that skin. I nodded as though I was learning how I might do it one day myself.

The back door opened, and two young women came in – more granddaughters, I soon learned. Bonnie introduced me. They said hi, then headed down the hall past the bathroom.

In a bit of a cul-de-sac at the end, there was a stack of cardboard boxes. Full of fabric and other sewing material, I now realized.

"I'm making them ribbon skirts," Bonnie said. I wondered if this was for a powwow but didn't ask. Bonnie pushed the cutting board away from herself, looked around, then looked at me.

"Get me that bowl, will ya?" I could see one on the upper counter and got up to fetch it. Good. She'd let me do one thing.

I could hear the two young women down the hall laughing and talking, sometimes dropping their voices to a whisper. I wondered if I could leave now; I wanted to get over to Stoney Point, see what was going on for myself. Maybe I'd find Kevin at the gate; he'd been one of the peacekeepers from the beginning.

I'd only seen him once since that meeting at Worm's place last October. This was after I'd taped a first conversation with Cully and was leaving. He was putting the lawnmowers into the maintenance garage for the winter, and it was easy to just walk over. I casually asked if he might have time to sit down with me, to record what he wanted in the book.

"What good would it serve?" he'd said. "Just get upset all over." And I couldn't help but agree. He'd told his story enough: first to the Special Investigation Unit of the Ontario Provincial Police, which belatedly – more than a week after the fact – had started to consider the police shooting death of Dudley George as a possible crime. A decade later, he'd had to go over it all again when he'd been called as a witness to the Ipperwash Inquiry. Reading the transcript of his testimony there, I also knew how badly Kevin had been treated. The lawyer representing the Ontario Provincial Police Association, Ian Roland, kept badgering him with questions about there being guns at the army camp, and trying to trick him into saying that someone in the camp was shooting at the helicopter that night in August 1993. At one point, Peter

Rosenthal, the lawyer representing the George family and the residents of Aazhoodena, challenged Roland's tone as "improper." Another time, the inquiry commissioner, Justice Sidney Linden, intervened to say, "You may have gone as far as you can with this witness."

Same with Marcia. She'd been summoned as a witness, but had had to wait and wait, day after day, only to have her appearance rescheduled. She'd lost her teaching job because of all the time she'd spent testifying, and waiting to testify, she'd told me when we'd sat down to record her memories. And for what? The Ipperwash Inquiry report had urged the government to immediately return the land to the Nishnaabeg, honouring their promise of 1995, honouring their treaty rights guaranteed under Section 35 of the Canadian Constitution, honouring the treaty of 1827.

"Have they honoured it?" Marcia had asked me, a contemptuous sneer in her voice.

No, I'd said. You're right. And by implication: Would telling the story yet again, for a book, make any difference, or just reawaken the trauma of that time? What was the point if the powers that be continued to refuse to listen and acknowledge what the treaty rights meant? Clearly many of the people here, even Marcia, who I was working with to pull the story together, were not convinced.

Now the two young women came back into the big front room, their arms full of fabric. Bonnie let me take the knife and cutting board away. She grabbed her dishtowel and wiped the table and then her hands.

"Here, show me," she told her granddaughters, pushing her chair back a little and facing them.

They unfolded the materials each of them had chosen, and draped them, hanging from their waists. Pretty fabric, I thought: one was a soft blue with miniature flowers in turquoise and pink. But my mind was already elsewhere, thinking about the clear-cutting at Stoney Point. Part of my childhood was spent on land that should never have been clear-cut but was. It was cleared to create a small family farm in eastern Ontario for settlers from Scotland, though not relatives of ours. My parents bought it after it was abandoned in the post-war period because my father, who'd been raised on the Menzies family farm in southwestern Ontario, longed for some connection with farmable land. But the land on the farm my parents bought had been left untended for so long that the soil had become leached and eroded. In the soil samples my father sent for testing to a government farm reforestation project, the land was categorized as "barren."

I'd spent spring after spring helping to plant government-subsidized seedlings to restore the land, and watched them struggle to survive with no larger trees around to protect them. So I could identify with how devastating this current clear-cutting would be. Maybe I could share some of my childhood experiences with Kevin.

I ended up not telling him any of this when I finally got there. Just that I'd heard about the clear-cutting, and that I was really sorry.

"Yeah," he said, looking down, shaking his head. "Jeez! There was no need. They said it was for the cleanup. They went in there with their magnetic equipment, and – it don't make sense to me. There's supposed to be consultation – and they say they've consulted."

He looked into the distance, in the direction of where the bush began, shook his head again.

"It's depressing as hell. They clear-cut the bush, and they made a mess of everything. They never cleaned anything up! You can't even go back there."

He tugged at his cap. His lean face looked tired. He was sixteen when he followed his grandparents in their efforts to reclaim their ancestral homeland; now he was on the verge of becoming a grandparent himself.

"I always say, if we are to be a community, we have to be self-dependent. We make things happen ourselves, as far as I'm concerned; DND can go git!"

He looked at me, then looked away into the distance again. "We need a voice for the community," he said. A quick shake of his shoulders, a nod, and he walked away.

12

Learning to Listen

I turned in at the army camp gate and stopped opposite the guardhouse window, my car window already rolled down.

"Hi. I'm going to see Cully."

A nod from the dimness beyond the half-open window, and the barrier went up, as if it was perfectly normal that I should enter. I smiled and looked around as I drove through. The camper was still here, though I couldn't see anyone inside. I nodded just in case, wanting to acknowledge the Nishnaabe peacekeepers' authority here, letting me in. I turned onto the little side road leading to the parade ground where the barracks were located. The parade ground was littered with rusted old abandoned cars and trucks, some tilting slightly over pancake-flat tires. The side road to Cully's place was cracked, the edges more broken down than the main road was.

I pulled up, gathered my stuff, locked the car door, went up the three steps to Cully's front door, and knocked.

"Come in!"

I breezed through the door and was immediately in her big front room. She looked up from where she always seemed to sit, at her Arborite and chrome kitchen table, facing both the door and the TV screen mounted on the far wall above a small window. It was turned on to a game show, like last time and the time before that. But it was late morning, the time she liked me to come. She smiled hello, told me to take a seat. I did, dropping my bag on the floor.

I glanced around, taking in the "Citizen Potawatomi Nation" sign beside the dartboard, the duct tape holding together some of the cork on which the dartboard was mounted, the tape itself multiply pierced by darts, too; and the postcards tacked to the wall in the corner, next to a collection of empty beer cans. She'd told me the story of all these things that day last fall when she'd first invited me in. We'd started with some awkward talk about the quilt she was working on and its design. Then she'd abruptly asked, "So, what brings you?"

I told her what I'd explained first to Bonnie and then to the others at that little meeting with Bonnie, Stewart, and the others: that I'd been learning about treaties and how her people considered them like a covenanted kinship relationship, and that responsibility to repair and renew that relationship was passed down generation after generation, starting with condolences for harm done. As in the other times, my voice had faltered when I got to that part. So, I'd said, I'd come to see how I might learn about my responsibility, and now I'd agreed to help pull together a book about what happened here, taping different people's stories.

She looked at me hard again, and said, "Sure, I'll talk to you." And that's when she took me into her workspace to show me some of her beaded moccasins, a miniature woven basket made from black ash, her plexiglass drawers full of sewing supplies, her sewing machine and work table criss-crossed with lines for laying out quilting pieces. We ended the tour in the far corner of her main living space, where she'd tacked up postcards from places like Miami, and filled a ledge with empty beer cans, including one with shamrocks. She keeps that one, she explained, to remember Dudley's birthday, which was close to St. Patrick's Day.

I noticed there was no kitchen sink, just a counter next to the stove; she does her dishes in the bathroom, she said, and shrugged.

"This isn't fixed up because I didn't expect to be livin' here that long," Cully had said as she watched me looking around.

Now I focused on her, asking her how she was. She pushed the quilt away from herself and reached for her cigarettes. My asthma's getting worse, she said. She thinks she got it from living where she is. She shrugged; it's just something she lives with. I asked about Pierre. Oh, he's around, she said. And J.R.? Her son worked nights in an auto-parts factory; he was still asleep down the hall.

I pulled out the package I'd brought. I'd left it in the simple brown paper bag from the store, not wanting to make a big deal of it. Cully opened the bag, pulled out the scarf, and held it up. It featured a Coast Salish motif rendered in red, black, and white. She loved it.

She jumped up. Come here, she said, and led the way over to her work table, where I could see angled bits of cloth laid out along its ingrained lines in a beautiful array of different colours. She was starting a new star blanket, she said. I could see the star emerging in what she'd sewn so far. With it still in progress, I could also see how intricate it was, and how much work was involved in bringing all the pieces together; how vital it was to cut and sew every angle right, each piece of the mosaic building on all the others. I stood there marvelling at the skill involved. And the colours! Did she work out her own colour combinations? She did. What about the design, I asked. Cully laughed, and rummaged under a pile of fabric ends and magazines at one end of the table, pulling out an old and tattered pattern book. It was dated 1991, but she'd added to it since. There were newspaper clippings of designs and other bits of paper bulging out from between the covers. She started with what's in the book, she said, but she likes to improvise.

"Once they took over here and got the barracks and stuff, I never went back to Kettle Point," she said. "I just got my sewing machine and my beads, my materials and leather. I figured I could use that to make me some money. At least I wouldn't starve!" She threw back her head and laughed.

How many quilts have you made, I asked. She didn't know. She shrugged and grinned: "They're all sold."

I'd seen one that I recognized as probably hers at the pot shop beside the highway. Hubert George's cramped camper operation that I'd been in when I first showed up here last July had been replaced by a bungalow-style building, complete with a wheelchair ramp and a bigger sign, though still hand-painted: Medicines of the Earth, with three marijuana leaves underneath.

Go sit down, Cully told me now, and headed toward the corner shelving unit. She picked up a big black binder, carried it to the kitchen table and set it down.

Want a pop? she asked as she went to the fridge. I opened the binder and started turning the pages, seeing photos of quilt after quilt after quilt. Beautiful, lovely, gorgeous, I kept saying as I turned the pages.

Cully was watching from her seat, nodding, offering explanations, stories, and smiling. I stopped at a photo of what looked like a white man holding a quilt. Cully reached for the binder, pulled it toward herself.

"That's John," Cully said. "He was from the Mennonites. He stayed with us for a full year. Kind of like a safety net, eh? So if the cops came, he was a non-native who could report."

"Sort of a peace witness?" I asked. I knew that the Mennonite Central Committee had sent volunteers, white people, to live in the community in the traumatic aftermath of September 6, 1995, when a phalanx of provincial police had opened fire on the unarmed Nishnaabe, Dudley among them.

"Yeah," Cully said. "And then he left. And then he got married and then he was gonna have a baby, so I gave him a baby quilt." She pushed the binder back in front of me. "See there. You can see all the extra detail I did in there."

"Exquisite," I said. I turned more pages, the quilts giving way to leatherwork: moccasins and whole outfits beaded in designs that danced across the leather, colour combinations that almost sang.

"That one was for a parade," Cully said, leaning toward me. "It only came in second because I didn't have time. My brother told me, there's a parade. Quick, make an outfit."

I turned the page. The photo showed a beautiful young woman in an absolutely stunning outfit. "That's my oldest granddaughter," Cully said when I turned the binder toward her. "She graduated from Windsor. Social work. And she's got another one, too, AutoCAD or something. "

"That's a switch," I said.

"Yeah, well, she got a job at Children's Aid, and she went down to Walpole Island and she tried to help out the people down there. She was really trying to help this young girl to not lose her kids, and she had her talked into this, and then Children's Aid wouldn't go along with it. She gave them her recommendation and they just told her no." She pushed the binder back my way.

"I wouldn't have stayed there either. What am I? The token Indian?" She laughed a short, harsh laugh.

"But to not have her advice respected," I said, outraged on her granddaughter's behalf. After all, Walpole Island was a First Nations reserve.

Cully looked at me surprised.

"There's still a lot of racism goin' on," she said.

"Yes," I said, and was immediately ashamed. I didn't want to deny or diminish the ongoing racism, but it looked like I did because I'd deflected away from seeing it or acknowledging it for what it was. I'd focused on the injustice done to

Cully's granddaughter in that individual instance, not the source of it ingrained in a system dating back well over a century. I'd kept my inner blinders in place, shielding me from what I didn't want to face. Hiding behind a faux innocence. And forcing Cully to spell it out for me.

"Yes," I repeated. "You're right. There's still a lot of racism going on."

I looked at her. She looked at me, gave a little nod and smiled.

When I left, she followed me out the door and showed me her rose bush, growing against the wall. It was just starting to show some buds. I admired it and continued toward my car.

A pickup drove by, then stopped. The man inside called out to someone else.

"That's Glenn," Cully said. Glenn George, Marcia's brother, was among those who'd come here that day in 1993, coming home with the elders, and he'd never left either. He was living in the old quartermaster's store.

I stopped and asked Cully if she could introduce me.

She laughed and shook her head.

"Go on," she said. "He won't bite." And I did. I also spotted Worm (Stewart George) a little distance down the road. He was hosing down a big pull-type lawnmower outside the maintenance building. I walked over and had a word with him too.

13

Witnessing Denial – and Possibility

Marcia stepped carefully down from her back stoop onto the cinder-block step and then onto the uneven ground. She was holding something wrapped in a pillowcase and peering over it to watch where she put her feet. I knew enough not to step forward to help her. I'd gone up to the back door when I'd first arrived, but she shooed me away, saying she'd be out in a minute. Now she placed the bundle carefully in the back seat, then buckled herself in beside me, her handbag with its stiff vinyl handles sitting upright in her lap. We were going to Stoney Point. She had the key to the chapel she still considered her home there tucked inside a pocket in her purse. She hadn't been back in years, she'd told me. Just too hard; it made her depressed. But now maybe she might move back. "We'll see," she said.

At the gatehouse, she made a sound, a sort of *tsk* of irritation at having to wait until they decided to raise the barrier. Once inside, I was about to turn right toward where I knew the chapel was.

"No, go this way," she said. We took a road that went the long way around the former parade ground with its array of rusted old trucks and cars – plus, I'd noticed when I'd first parked my car outside Cully's place, cartloads of garbage bags, sagging and split open in spots. Everything, including the garbage, looked as if it had been there for years.

"They've let the place go," Marcia said. I suspected she meant the Nishnaabeg, because for her this was home, and it was her people's job to look after it. Still, she wasn't the only one who'd left or had to leave. And the Nishnaabeg weren't in charge of looking after this place, except in cases like Kevin, where he had a contract through the band office with the Department of National Defence. The Canadian government was still in control.

She turned to me: "We used to do ceremonies in the parade ground."

I nodded, remembering what she and others had told me about the sacred fire, the sweat lodge, the language classes – all bringing Stoney Point, or, rather, Aazhoodena, back to life.

We neared the turn to the rifle ranges.

"Stop," she said, pointing to the left. We got out, crossed the ditch, and walked through tall grass and weeds.

"There," she said, pointing again. In among the weeds and small bushes, I could see the fading petals of a daffodil. There was only the single flower, the petals now shrivelled and turning brown. This was where her family's homestead had been, she told me. When she and her children came back in 1993, she'd transplanted some raspberry plants here too. We peered among the weeds and bushes, trying to spot the telltale leaves and canes, but couldn't see any.

She gave her head a shake, her lips tight together. "It's all grown up," she said.

I told her about the vegetable gardens I'd seen growing outside some of the barracks; many of the barracks were occupied by younger people who'd moved in later and weren't involved in the 1990s action. In one, the traditional Three Sisters, beans, squash, and corn; in another, silver-white sage.

"That was me that brought the sage in here," she said. "I got it from a friend in Toronto, and I told everybody: whoever wants, they can dig up some." She laughed. "Man, that stuff spreads." She looked at me and smiled. "So that was me."

"And you'd be harvesting that to use for smudging," I suggested.

Marcia shrugged. "Or just letting it go."

Yes, I thought. Sage has a right to grow just for itself.

We got back in the car, drove on and approached what I guessed had been the council hall. It was built in 1993 in one of the first work bees here. It was intended as a place to revive the Nishnaabe tradition of consensual self-governance, though it was mostly known as the Argument Hall. From what I'd been told, people weren't very good at listening for points of possible consensus anymore. Now bushes and small trees encroached on all sides, and a poplar tree was growing almost in front of the small plywood structure.

"Look," she said, "Even the door is open." I could tell she was shocked at the sight.

I pulled over, thinking we'd stop. I noticed bullet holes in the door, red-brown rings of rust around the edge of them. I made a move to turn off the ignition.

"No, go on," she said. She didn't want to stay.

She spotted her son Kevin outside the maintenance garage. He had the John Deere mower just outside the big doors, the side hood up.

"Stop here," Marcia said. "I've got some pictures I want to give him." She opened her purse and pulled out a Kodak envelope.

Kevin came up to the passenger side of my rental, nodded a quick hello to me across the interior space, then focused on his mother. She pulled out the photos: they were of Kevin's two stepchildren. He really cared about those children, she'd told me, encouraging them to stay in school, making sure there was special help for one of them who had a learning difficulty. Kevin took the photos from his mother, and they carried on talking about this and that.

I looked out the front windshield, seeing the billboard the Nishnaabeg had erected back in 1993: Stoney Point Aazhood-enaang, it said, reclaiming their own name for themselves as the people – the Aazhoodenaang – of this place, Aazhoodena.

I tried pronouncing the word in my head as Marcia had taught me, trying not to listen as she visited with her son, but of course hearing still. Pretty busy here, Kevin was saying; with Worm being sick, he was doing more of the maintenance work. Then: "You got that water heater fixed?" No, she said. She was still having to heat water on the stove.

A penny dropped. When I'd come to the back door earlier, I could see in because Marcia had opened the main wooden door, leaving just the storm door closed. Its window was smeared with dirt, but I could still see through it, and just to the left, I saw the kitchen sink. It was full, stacked high with dirty dishes.

Marcia was chuckling. "I sure miss having my bath," she said. She gave another quick laugh and shrugged. Then she asked Kevin something about his place. Did he finally get that new door?

Yes, I thought, everyone is carrying on here as best they can, dealing with immediate priorities like broken water heaters and broken doors. I gazed at the faded billboard, then looked at the lawnmower, half inside, half outside of the maintenance shed of this former army camp. And as I looked, I remembered the landmark 1997 Supreme Court of Canada Delgamuukw case in which an elder had sung a traditional song in court as evidence of his kinship ties to his ancestral land. He'd performed that song as evidence of his people's – the Gitxsan and Wet'suwet'en nations – land claim, the lineage of their long belonging to that place.

Maybe Kevin was doing the same thing here, I thought, testifying in the only way he's able: through his actions caring for this land, by cutting the grass.

I became aware of Kevin's voice becoming a little louder. He was talking to me through the open window. He'd taken off his ball cap and was running a hand through his hair.

"Tell you what," he said, leaning into the window beside his mother. "You drive me to Sarnia on Saturday. Go to Home Depot and look at water heaters. I'll talk to you then."

Great, thanks, I said. What time? He gave me his cell number and told me to give him a call. Not before ten, he said. He liked to sleep in on Saturdays.

He whacked the ball cap against his leg, put it back on his head, and stepped away.

Marcia and I drove off, heading for the army chapel, off in a little building of its own. The structure was completely engulfed in weeds. The shingles were curled at the edges and, in some spots, completely gone. But the concrete steps were solid enough, and the front door too.

She had the pillowcase-wrapped object in one arm. "I'll show you when we get inside," Marcia had said when she'd collected it from the back seat. There was a hint of excitement in her voice; whether it was coming back here after all this time or what she'd brought to show me, I couldn't tell.

I followed her up the steps, watched her insert the key, turn it, and push open the door. Then I heard her gasp.

"Look at the mess," she said. When I reached the top step and peered through the doorway, I could see it too. All down the length of the former chapel, ceiling panels had fallen onto the floor, spewing damp insulation and debris. The floor itself, once beautiful tongue-and-groove hardwood, was buckled upward in many places. And yet there was furniture down one side and at the far end.

All the elements of a lived-in space were clearly visible amidst the wreckage: A nicely upholstered chair with carved wooden arms sat in front of the woodstove. Beside it a standing lamp, and behind that a bookshelf full of books. There were pictures on the walls, a corkboard with faded newspaper clippings and baby photos tacked on it. It's as though life here had just been paused, but with the expectation of it continuing. Like it had been in 1942 when the federal government took over the reserve to run an army training camp, supposedly for the duration of the war only.

Marcia walked forward slowly, not saying a word. With me following, she stepped around ceiling panels and chunks of sodden insulation, plus slats that had held the ceiling panels in place. Clearly, the roof had been leaking. Marcia headed toward the back. This was where she and her mother, Melva, had lived, she said, from 1995 until Melva died in 2000. I could see a bedspread on a bed through a doorway. I could see a coat and a jacket hanging from a hook, but with that telltale droop that said they'd been hanging there for a very long time. Abruptly, Marcia turned away and started back across the floor. Then she stopped and pointed down. I looked at the blackened debris and the eruption of buckling floorboards. Marcia was pointing past all this to the strips of tape she and her mother had laid down on the floor for aligning quilt material. The pillowcase Marcia was still carrying contained a quilt Marcia had made here with her mom. She made no move to take it out of the safe packaging of the pillowcase, however. If anything, she held it tighter to her chest.

"It's finished," she said, her voice harsh with finality. The darkness of fatigue that I'd always noticed around her eyes looked darker, the lines running down from either side of her mouth were deeper. It was as though something inside her had broken; she'd given up.

"Let's get out of here," she said, and headed for the front door. But there she stopped, because there was a big, long cloth banner leaning against the wall in the shadow. She pulled one end of it forward so I could see it better: "Remember

Dudley George. Sept. 6, 1995" in big black letters stitched onto the off-white background. They'd carried this banner, she said, whenever they did a march somewhere or held a press conference trying to get the government to launch an inquiry into Dudley's shooting death. And they'd succeeded. An inquiry had been held. It had recommended that the government immediately return the land. And over ten years later, Marcia, Kevin, and the others were still waiting for the government to finish cleaning up its mess and leave.

I took a picture of it and some others to record the mess. Then we pushed the banner back into the shadows and left, Marcia carefully locking the door again and putting the key back into her purse.

I drove back down toward the barracks and the front gate. As we passed the little side road where Cully's place was, I could see her on the stoop having a cigarette. I slowed down, asked Marcia if she wanted to stop and say hello.

"No," she said. Cully had seen us, though, and waved. I waved back as I drove on. I'd go see her again tomorrow.

Did she want to go home now, I asked. "No. Go down that way," she said. She wanted to go to the burial grounds. I knew her father, Daniel George, was buried there, the first burial that had been permitted since 1942. I said something to the effect of her wanting to visit her father's grave.

"It's not his grave," she corrected me sharply. "I'm visiting my dad. That's still my dad that's buried there, you know."

"Yes," I said. Of course. And yet not really. I hadn't known this as Marcia did. I'd only known about it from something I'd read. A Nishnaabe legal historian, Darlene Johnston, had been commissioned by the Ipperwash Inquiry to do a research paper on the importance of burial grounds to the Nishnaabeg. In it, she'd referenced written records of some of the earliest French newcomers to the Great Lakes region, as they'd transcribed what they'd been told by their Nishnaabe hosts: that when a person dies, their spirit lives on in the burial grounds.

That's why burial grounds are so sacred, I realized now; they are inhabited. And that's why visiting them regularly is so important: to maintain that intergenerational connection to this place.

The burial grounds at the Stoney Point Reserve fill an upward slope of an ancient sand dune some distance inland from the current shoreline of Lake Huron. A narrow gravel road runs past it at the base of the slope. That's where I parked, next to what looked like a brand-new fence. There were heavy stone piers and, in between them, wrought-iron spikes sticking up from two parallel lengths of iron connecting them, all painted in glistening black enamel.

"They keep upsetting me, what they do," Marcia said as she got out. The fence had been organized by the band-office administrator in Kettle Point, in consultation with community elders, she said, though I could tell by the way she said it that she'd added air quotes to that phrase about consultation. She shook her head, pressed her lips together. Nobody consulted her, she said.

Because of the fence, we had to walk to where a gate had been set in the middle of the fenceline, and then back.

"I wish I had tobacco," Marcia muttered as she led the way up the slope.

Quietly, I fished in my satchel to find the baggie I'd packed, along with red cotton material for tobacco ties, before I'd come. She took the bag, pulled out some tobacco, and stepped forward.

I stood back quietly, doing nothing except gazing at the slight evidence of a grave here, a small grave marker there. Dudley George's grave was here, too, I knew. It was all pretty minimal; no upright gravestones calling attention to themselves. But I knew that many of the original headstones had been shot to pieces, used as target practice by young men learning to be soldiers.

I looked at Marcia's stooped back. Beyond her, I could see belled clusters of lily of the valley fading from white to beige among the whitened beach stones in the spot where Daniel George was buried. It was very quiet, not even a breeze whispering in the pines nearby. Time passed. I stood there, letting it pass through me. I was aware of my eyes prickling and an ache in my throat.

Spirits are alive here, I thought. I'd never felt this in a cemetery before. I'd never really thought of people's spirits being present, or let the possibility of their continuing presence – as something palpable – into my consciousness.

Marcia stood silently before the semicircle of stones that framed her father's internment site. At some point, she sprinkled her tobacco on the stones. Then she turned away. She was ready to go home.

As I pulled into her driveway behind her car, I could see Marlin under the trees in front of the house. He'd rigged up a fish-cleaning station there: a length of stainless-steel counter with a troughed ledge was set in a frame of bare two-by-fours. A garden hose hung down from where he'd strapped it to a tree bough.

His fishing waders were hanging from another tree branch, still glistening wet from the lake.

I asked if I could buy some fish.

Big smile. Sure, he said, how much? He packaged them up in one-pound bags, he said.

I'd take two, I thought.

Marcia asked if I did it up in batter. I said I never had. I didn't have any flour either, I said, so I'd probably just fry it in butter. Or poach it.

"I'll get you some," she said. "Stay here."

When she returned, I thanked her for her gift. Then, as she walked with me back to my car, I mentioned that my motel unit had a bathtub. She was welcome to come over and use it if she wanted a bath.

A smile touched her face briefly. "Thanks," she said. "I'll think about it."

I drove through Kettle Point and stopped at Bonnie's place to drop off one of the bags of fish.

"Stay for supper," Bonnie said, once she'd protested that I shouldn't have done this, once she'd relented and said miigwech. I thanked her and said no. I didn't really think Marcia would take up my offer, but I wanted to be back at my motel just in case.

"Okay," Bonnie said. "But you're comin' for supper on Sunday!" Big smile at her bossy tone.

I smiled back. Okay, I said. Thanks.

MARCIA DIDN'T SHOW UP that evening, but two days later she did, unannounced. She had everything she needed, she said as she came toward my door. "Right here," she said, hoisting the bag. I could even see the wooden handle of a back-scrub poking up from between the folds of a towel.

I made a space for her stuff, gave the tub a rinse, told her to help herself to extra towels, soap, whatever. Then I invited her to stay on for supper. I didn't have much, I said, but I could make us an omelette if she wanted to stay.

She did. And the omelette turned out fine; I had a stove to make it on, a proper frying pan and tools.

14

Surrendering Personally

It was June now. White clouds ballooned overhead; the air was soft against my face. I watched the clouds for a bit before getting into my car. I had some time to kill before I headed to Stewart, or Worm's, place. So I thought I'd drop in on Marcia, just as she'd done with me the previous evening – totally out of the blue. She wouldn't stay, though, she said. She'd brought something to show me: a buckskin outfit she'd made herself. It was in the back seat of her car.

She led the way back to the motel parking lot, then opened the back door, reached in, and pulled out a hip-length leather tunic. She held it up and draped it over her upper body so I could see how the front fringe of exquisitely tanned deer hide hung straight and true down the whole length of it. You had to cut the strips just right, she told me, and she fanned a bunch of them out across her hand, telling me how important it was to keep that line straight when you were cutting. I looked at the strips and marvelled: each one so thin and long and straight. And she'd done this herself?

Yes, Marcia said, and smiled. I looked at the garment with its beaded stitching around the neck. Marcia got out

the matching skirt and calf-height moccasins, and I marvelled at these as well: the knowledge and skill embedded
there, passed on from generation to generation, from one
woman's hands into the next. I marvelled, too, at the feeling
that had prompted Marcia to make this special trip over here,
to show me these things. I wanted her to stay and tell me
more about this and what it meant to her. Some part of me
recognized that this was her story, or her way of telling it. I
wanted to understand what this meant. And who had taught
her all this in the first place? Her mother, Melva, despite her
having been removed from the possibility of learning all these
things at home herself? Or had there been a grandmother
to teach her?

I offered to make her some tea. No, Marcia said, putting
the articles of clothing back in the car. She'd just wanted to
show me, that's all. As she got in the car herself, I repeated
my offer to help weed her flower garden sometime, and
that's what I had in mind as I pulled into the muddy yard that
morning.

Marlin had his Fish 4 Sale sign propped up on the side of
the road by the driveway again; maybe I'd buy some more
fish for supper. Pickerel; it was really good. I looked toward
the little camper on the right where I thought he might live;
the door was open, but there was no sign of him or anyone
else who could welcome me.

Should I honk my horn? No, I'd just go and knock on
Marcia's door. The dog had gotten to know me by now and
didn't bark. Still, I was glad he was chained to his doghouse
farther back in the yard.

I knocked a second time, and finally the door opened.
Marcia stood in the doorway, her face pale, frowning.

She'd been lying down, she said. She sighed. She takes
this medication, but it doesn't do much good. "Yeah," I said,
and listened as she went into more detail. Then I mentioned
about weeding.

"Oh," she said, "I don't think I have the energy today." Beyond her on the left, I could see that the sink was full of unwashed dishes, only now they were overflowing onto the counter. I wondered: If I gave her some money to help buy another water heater, would that be patronizing?

I asked Marcia if maybe I could just clear some of the stuff growing around the peony bush. I'd noticed a couple of buds pushing their way up through the weeds.

She shrugged, told me to go ahead. So I stepped aside, closed the storm door, and set to work. Weeding a garden was something I'd done all my life, and I was happy enough to work on my own. But soon the door opened, and Marcia came down the cinder-block step. She was carrying gardening gloves and insisted that I put them on. She sat on the picnic bench watching me for a while, then started pulling at the grass stems sticking up along the inside edge of the garden space. She said that she wanted to clear out some space in the house so she could bring stuff back from the chapel. She also had a dining table her father had made. "He was a really good carpenter," she said, and told me about the different projects he'd worked on – including the local United church. Oh, and he made a doghouse for her son Kevin too. She laughed.

I thought, yes, there isn't one set way of being Indigenous, tied up in traditional ceremonies and dress. I said something of this out loud, thinking I was being affirming.

Marcia scoffed. "I hate that word, *Indigenous*," she said. "It sounds like indigent or something."

Shit! I'd done it again. Said the wrong thing. Why did I keep doing this? Needing to interpret what was being shared with me; needing to categorize and conceptualize, as though this was what it meant to know something properly.

Really? And I realized that this wasn't just my personal insecurities at work either. Here I was, a settler trying to make amends, and I was locked into the ways of thinking that I'd grown up with and learned to practise at university. Compartmentalizing and labelling were so normal to me, just the way things are done if you want to communicate clearly.

Indigenous! Who decided that this was the right word? And who'd come up with this word in the first place? Not Marcia. Clearly, no one had consulted with her! And what power or authority had decided that there needed to be one all-encompassing label for people like Marcia and her father, all their unique differences diminished or even lost in that single word that presumed to say it all?

What arrogance caused me, a visitor on *her* land, at *her* home, and in *her* community to even think of interpreting back to Marcia my understanding of what she was telling me? And why did I need to categorize in the first place? This was taking control. More colonizing, really. I was doing it by interrupting the flow of our conversation, forcing what she was telling me into abstract boxes of meaning established in the public discourse of which I liked to see myself as a progressive part. But it wasn't meaning established or agreed to by Marcia, and that was the point!

I threw the weeds into the empty flower pot I was using to collect them. Quit trying to prove yourself all the time, I thought. Quit trying so hard.

Give up!

Yes, I thought: surrender. Let all those boxes in my mind fall apart.

I looked up at Marcia, taking in the lines of fatigue around her eyes and mouth. Maybe that's what she meant when she kept telling me to "just listen." Surrender the historical position I'd been raised and socialized to occupy, to be the one in the know, the one in charge of knowing, unconsciously colonial and superior.

If I concentrated on just listening, and only that, maybe I could start hearing what Marcia was actually saying. I could just let meanings emerge as I continued to listen, and stop burdening her with my preconceived ones, however progressive I thought they were.

"I'm sorry," I said.

She merely shrugged and carried on weeding. She continued with what she had been saying. She talked some more about her father, and then about other members of the family, and how all the different people of Aazhoodena were related. She had a binder of photographs she could show me sometime, she said. I said I'd like that and carried on with my weeding. After a comfortable silence, she said she wished I didn't live so far away; then we could keep visiting. I said we could talk on the phone. She brushed that off, told me that for one thing she didn't have long distance on her phone. I interrupted to say that I could call her.

She gave me one of her "just listen" looks and continued. "If you lived in Sarnia, even in London, then I could visit you. I like to just go when I feel like it. Like I did last night. I wanted you to see that buckskin dress, so I just jumped in the car and went."

Yes! I smiled at her. It was as if she was reminding me of something I hadn't even realized I'd forgotten: the capacity to live in present time, not just during meditation or on holidays, but all the time. We all do it when we're kids: everything is proximate, everything emerges moment to moment. It's the time of tides, and the warming of the soil in spring till it can incubate seeds into seedlings. It's how people relate to each other too.

This isn't an incidental thing, I thought as I drove away. Not if it's your way of life, not if it's fundamental to how you have always lived and governed your life, as a collectivity of ongoing relationships. It's letting life and the life of relationships take their own time, because that's the way life is.

Relationship time should really be at the centre of life, as it is in nature, I thought; not off in the margins.

I burst out laughing: here I was, heading back through the army camp gate in order to be on time to meet up with Stewart. He'd suggested I come at his lunch break, had said something about Barb probably being around by then. But she wasn't there; Worm didn't know when she'd be back. Still, he led the way inside.

Once again the gloom of the place engulfed me: a maintenance supplies building making do as a home. There was a bit of light coming through a small window in the far wall; for the rest of the space, what little light there was came from the rickety floor lamp and the squat one on the table beside a big-cushioned chair. I sat in it, and focused on what I'd come for. I got out the recorder and the microphone. I asked if I could set these up on the coffee table. He'd sat down in the big sofa chair at one end. Now he shrugged, okay, sure, whatever, and opened a package of sandwiches.

Why was I doing this? Part of me was recoiling: something about what I was doing wasn't right, plunging in like this, not even asking Stewart how he was, how his day had been so far. It was like I was on automatic pilot. This was his lunch break. I'd made a commitment to be here at this time. Worm, or Stewart, was one of the ones who wanted this done, or at least had lamented that no one knew the full story of all they'd been trying to accomplish back in the 1990s. And yet, in the moment of getting on with it, something pushed back.

Kevin had mentioned that Worm hadn't been well. Maybe that was it; maybe he wasn't up for this today, but was forcing himself just to accommodate me. Me, the white person in the room! Or maybe it was just being in this dark space again. It felt like ground zero, not just for the death of Dudley George but for all the violence that had been done to the Nishnaabeg here, mostly at the silent stroke of a pen. The violence was ongoing, and I was standing in the middle of it, tape recorder

in hand – as though with the stroke of a microphone I might
help to turn things around. Or, as the one directing the action
here, was I perpetuating it?

He took a bite of his sandwich. I plugged the microphone
into the recorder, placed it on the coffee table. Okay? A nod
as he kept chewing. No sign of Barb; maybe she was still involved with those kids who had needed fostering.

Ready? Another nod. I turned on the recorder and asked
Worm if he preferred to be called Stewart.

"My name is Stewart George," he said, his voice a rich,
deep baritone. He started to tell me about the maintenance
work he did, the perimeter patrol, which he'd been part of
since 1995 when the army and its military police had pulled
out. He was one of the warriors or peacekeepers.

He continued chewing on his sandwich, the white of the
bread almost glowing in the dim light of the room. I sat there
quietly, waiting for him to continue. I'd made a pact with
myself not to steer the conversation, or to try not to. If I was
going to help people like Stewart tell their story, all I could
do was hold the microphone. If I took the initiative, I'd disturb
the water. The currents carrying the truth would bring that
truth to the surface when the time was right. Still, I hoped
he'd talk more about back then. His father Abraham, or Abe,
was one of the elders who'd led the way that May morning in
1993. He'd helped others find where their parents' or grandparents' homesteads had been, helped locate the former
wells, encouraged people to dig them out and get them running again. Abe had helped restore traditions like the sacred
fire and the sweat lodge. And when the young men organized
themselves in the tradition of warrior societies, he gave them
the name Etwaagnikejig, meaning Nation Builders.

Stewart hadn't played a leadership role like his father had,
but he was there; he'd taken a beating that night when Dudley
George was fatally shot.

Now he put his sandwich back down on the coffee table. "Can we do this another time?" he said. "I'm not feeling so good."

Of course, I said, reaching to turn off the recorder. As quickly as possible, I pulled all that I had scattered on the coffee table toward me, disconnected the microphone, bundled up its cord, put that away, stuffed everything into my bag. Trying to minimize the space I occupied but feeling like the elephant in the room again; very big, and destructive too.

Who did I think I was? I thought as I drove back to my motel. How could I possibly level the playing field when there were two hundred years of inequality between us? Not by presuming to call it level by switching my nameplate from "colonial settler" to would-be treaty kin! In fact, I was proving how unequal things were by presuming to do just that – to think it was okay for me, a white person, to help these Nishnaabe tell their story.

I wasn't appropriating their story in an obvious colonial sense. I wasn't stealing it, trying to repackage it under my name. But even as I was recording this story, I was framing it in my own familiar terms, using my own familiar tools. I was focusing on words too, not on hats made of finely split ash wood, or beaded deerskin tunics and animal totems sewn into the fabric of quilts.

There was appropriation going on, and I was doing it.

I drove back to the motel, got my stuff out of my shiny rental car and locked the door.

Forget it, I thought; quit and go home before you do more damage.

I unlocked my motel room door, dumped my bag of stuff on the table, and grabbed the kettle to make myself a tea.

I knew that I was starting to change – to decolonize, if I wanted to use that big, abstract word. I was getting somewhere; I could give myself that much, I thought as I pulled the mess of cords out of my bag and started winding them up properly. I'd shown up here blithely assuming that I'd done pretty well all the decolonizing I needed to do, when I'd barely scratched the surface. What biases I had were buried, or stitched in, so deep that I wasn't even aware of them, and thought no one else would be either.

Nor did I think they were doing any harm – until I came here. And that's when it started. Usually with something small, a shift in the energy between us, maybe a tightening of the lips at something I'd said, a pulling back. Sometimes, as with Marcia, a flash of anger. It knocked me sideways, knocked me off my pedestal, and forced me to notice my hidden assumptions, my colonized ways of thinking. But at a cost to them, I thought now. It took up their time. It taxed their patience, their energy. And for what? Would pulling off this book make it all worthwhile? And who was I to judge?

I reached for my work bag again and pulled out my notebook with its list of people whose stories I either had recorded already or hoped to. And it hit me: This wasn't colonial thinking lying there like an old seam in the cloth of my mind needing to be unstitched. This was active: active colonizing or recolonizing. I looked at the tools of my trade laid out on the table: I'd brought my sewing machine with me.

I picked up my voice recorder as though examining a piece of evidence. Being digital these days, such devices were so small they were hardly noticeable. Well, to me at least; I'd been using these things since I was in my twenties. I picked up my notebook and looked at where I'd inscribed my name on the front, as I always did when starting any new writing project. Yes, I thought, with these in hand, I had turned a few moments of possibility into the whole plan of a book project. Well, that wasn't entirely true, but partly so. I'd gone back to that same maintenance building today because, with these things and my daybook, I was presuming to set times for people to sit down with me and let me tape their stories.

Meanwhile, there was Stewart, living inside that dark space day in, day out. He'd been living there since 1995, and with who knows what kinds of toxins around him. Sure, he might want the story of what happened here to come out finally. But he might have other priorities at the moment. Priorities change.

I shouldn't be here. I wasn't attuned to the priorities here, priorities that shift and change for the sake of day-to-day survival! With my notebook, daybook, and digital recorder, I had been rearranging the priorities for action here, instead of paying attention to the action that was actually going on, whatever it was at any particular time, and respecting that.

The kettle had long since turned itself off. I turned it back on.

Sure, Cully had told me I was "the first person to come in here wanting to listen to us." But maybe it was enough just to listen and, in that listening, to be challenged to change – personally. Maybe that was the story that mattered here: me changing the one thing I *could* change: myself.

I thought of Kevin. I'd promised to take him to Sarnia tomorrow to see about a new water heater for his mom. I'd stay on and do that. The least I could do was give Kevin a ride.

15

Living a Land Claim

I texted Kevin at ten as he'd asked me to. He answered right away and was standing outside when I drove around the side of the barracks. He lived in what had once been a sergeants' quarters in the former army training camp. The roof, I knew, now leaked in spots.

Kevin told me to take the big highway. It was longer, he said, but faster. And soon we were at a mall on the south edge of Sarnia, a gigantic Home Depot on one side of it.

"I won't be long," Kevin said as he got out.

"No rush," I said. I'd already decided to let taping a conversation with him go. If it happened, fine; I just wasn't going to push it. It was enough for me to have realized what he seemed to be doing as he faithfully cut the grass around the barracks, there in his ancestral homeland. As the lawnmower inscribed line after line in the grass, he was spelling out his rightful claim to the land, the place of his belonging.

I followed Kevin into the store and to the back, where there were rows of water tanks, toilets, shower stalls. I deliberately hung back, but still sales staff approached me. No, I said, I didn't need help, and I nodded toward Kevin, saying I was with him. I watched them seeming to ignore him and fumed inwardly on his behalf. Still, he didn't seem to notice; just carried on looking, checking one model against another. He didn't seem to expect or need any help. Finally someone did come up. Kevin asked for a printout, had a question about attachment options, and then we were off.

There was a Dairy Queen on the edge of the parking lot near the exit, and he asked me to stop there. His wife, Lacey, liked the chicken salads they made, he said, and got out of the car. When he returned, he had two coffees as well, creamers bulging from between his fingers as he clutched everything together. I reached over and opened his door. He settled himself, laughing, and pulled some sugar packets out of his pocket. No, I didn't take sugar, I said, but thanked him for thinking of getting both. And for the coffee, I said.

I started heading back home the way we'd come.

No, Kevin said, turn here. He thought we'd take the road along the lake; there was a spot where he often stopped when he wanted a bit of time for himself. It was a conservation area, right on the water. When we arrived, I drove to the far end of the parking lot, as he suggested, and pulled into a spot facing the vastness of Lake Huron, near a dock. It was a beautiful sunny day, though there was a haziness in the air and low-slung clouds in the distance.

Kevin took the lid off his coffee, said something like "So?" and I guessed we were on after all. I got my recorder out of the bag I'd left on the floor in the back seat, conveniently within reach. I asked Kevin if he was okay with this, recording what we talked about. Sure, he said, sipping his coffee and looking out over the water. Then he pointed; there was a great blue heron fishing in the weeds nearby.

I plugged in the microphone and asked Kevin about putting it in the cup holder. Sure, he said, and watched as I pressed Record.

"So," he said as soon as I'd done this, "You wanna hear about my growing up?" I started to say something, but he'd already continued. "You wanna hear about my grandfather and what you'd call his drinkin' buddies? One of them was a war veteran. His name was Pudd." This was his grandfather Daniel George's brother, who'd been missing in action and reported as killed in the Second World War.

"I was raised by them to be proud of who I am and where I'm from and never to forget that!" He glanced at me, quick smile. He took another swallow from his coffee, chuckled. "I got into trouble at school for that. I got put out of class in high school for arguing with the teacher about Potawatomis being extinct – knowing full well that we aren't." He glanced at me again. "My grandfather and grandmother were one of the ones that fought to have the Potawatomis in Canada recognized," he said.

I couldn't look at him. There were tears in my eyes, and I didn't want him to see them and feel obliged to take them on. They were my tears, my shame and deep, deep sorrow, because what he'd said kind of summed it all up, the story of his life, and his mother, Marcia's, and his grandparents' lives – denied. Denied not just their treaty rights but their very existence as a people. Nullified. Terra nullius over and over and over again. I was just beginning to uncover what had been officially disappeared, what had been in front of my eyes and under my feet all along. I was beginning to feel it stir inside me.

I blinked hard and sipped my coffee, looking out the front window at the lake. Kevin carried on talking about the Potawatomis and how they'd rallied behind Tecumseh – on the side of the British, on the side of Canada, not the United States, Kevin emphasized – in the War of 1812. He went on to say that many descendants of these people had been involved in what they were doing back in the 1990s. Some had come from places like Walpole Island to support them. I glanced at him.

"Tell me more," I said, and he talked about how, at age sixteen, he'd followed the elders, including his grandmother Melva, into the still-functioning cadet training camp, how they'd settled in near where their family homesteads had once been, though this meant being near the rifle range, too, but at least it was near the bush. He described how everyone pitched in with various things to create a cooking area, to build their own Nishnaabe council hall, to revive their culture and rebuild the community around it.

"Everybody did what they could. Everybody was happy. We were proud of what we were accomplishing like that – goin' back home!"

He broke off, pointing over the water. "Look! Look at that! There's an eagle." He looked at me as I spotted it, too, and let out a laugh.

"They're comin' home just like us! I remember stories about them when I was growing up, but I never saw one till I moved to Stoney," he continued.

Still, he'd had a dream of an eagle before his grandfather died. And there'd been one in the sky overhead when they drove the hearse around the army camp to the burial grounds that fall day in 1990, he told me, giving his grandfather a last ride around his home reserve as they took him home. Daniel George was the first Nishnaabe to be buried there since 1942, and that was only because Kevin's uncle Graham had lobbied army officials to make this small concession to the man who had spent so much time over the years protesting outside the army camp gates, asking that his right – his treaty right – to live in his ancestral home be honoured. He and his wife, Melva, kept coming to the gates to stage protests, even when his emphysema got so bad he had to bring a folding lawn chair to sit on while holding his sign.

I carried on looking out the window as I listened; the clouds had advanced across the lake and were looming close.

One of his stories, Kevin continued, was about Mandoka, their Potawatomi ancestor, also known as Manidoka, who fled with his family to Canada after US president Andrew Jackson had passed the Indian Removal Act in 1830. "He said Manidoka means spirit of the Manitou. The 'ka' means that you're doing it; you're spirit people."

He laughed. "I don't know if it's in your DNA or it's just we like to pat ourselves on the back and tell ourselves stories." He went on, saying that in the legacy of the Three Fires Confederacy, the Potawatomis are responsible for the sacred fire. Kevin helped tend the one they started when they claimed the army camp as their rightful homeland in 1993.

"People usually keep a sacred fire going for a few days, but this was over nine months that we kept it going, I guess because we all knew that what we were doing was special. I mean, it's not only land that's been taken illegally. What's happening here is happening all across Turtle Island – actually, all around the world! Colonials went everywhere! Took land, lied, cheated, and stole." He laughed.

"No argument with me there," I said. It had started to rain. The clouds were so thick and close around us that it was noticeably dark. Kevin wasn't bothered, though; he carried on as though the oncoming storm was nothing.

"When we started to think about what we were trying to do there, it was more than just ourselves, I guess. But on the other hand, what we were there for was our home and those elders. We promised them that we were home to stay; we weren't gonna leave."

Ah! It was like pieces of a puzzle falling into place. Something settled in my mind at hearing this, the why of his and the others carrying on their land-reclamation action. It was another inkling, too, of how different Kevin's perspective was from mine. It was something about being embedded in a shared place, generation after generation; still being an individual but simultaneously and indivisibly also being part of this larger whole. It was the indivisibility of it that was different. It was non-negotiable, undebatable; it just was. All these people he talked about, he was related to them all, through kinship and shared multigenerational experience. He was indivisibly part of them, and the land they'd shared through all this time.

Now he was saying that even having to deal with all those criminal charges that were laid against them after Dudley George was killed – mostly minor things like unlawful use of property and mischief – helped them in a way. He wasn't charged with anything himself, but that was largely because the police had never succeeded in identifying him by name. But he made it his business to help others who didn't have a ride to court to get there on time.

"Everyone would show up at the courthouse at the same time, and there was a togetherness there. We'd have time to talk, what was goin' on. If it was wintertime and you needed help with plowin', somebody would say, 'All right.'"

The rain was coming down faster now; it was hard to hear Kevin above its drumming on the car roof. He kept on talking. I leaned in close.

"And we had different social clubs that we started – loosely based around the ceremonies when we started them, but really it was just social clubs, a lot of them. We got stuff done, though!" In the former Ipperwash Provincial Park, land that had originally been part of the reserve, "We had this thing called the Jamboree. We built a stage – a gazebo basically. Wired it. For the stage, I tore apart one section of a barrack. Every board, you had to pound, pull one nail out at a time, because it was old, dried-out wood. Any other way, it would just crack, make it useless. It was cedar, so it was gonna last." The gazebo was the centre of the Jamboree action, and more bands kept coming, drawing in more and more people.

Kevin took a deep breath. "Well, part of the Ontario–Kettle Point deal on returning the land was to clear it of everything.

[The government people] told me to my face, 'No, no. We're just here to take the government's buildings, the government's mess – as environmental cleanup.' When I went back down there the next morning, the gazebo was gone! Park outhouses are still there. You can go there today. There's sewage weeping tiles; all that's still in the ground."

A huge clap of thunder, and the rain began falling in sheets, obscuring even the dock right in front of us. Everyone else had gone. We were the only ones in the parking lot, and it was now flooded with water. My rental car was like a little island in the middle of it.

"Are we safe here?" I asked. Kevin shrugged and laughed. Of course: This was his territory, including the territory of his consciousness. The thunder that's so famous from storms rolling in off the Great Lakes is sacred in legends of the Thunderbird.[1]

While rain pounded on the car roof, Kevin carried on talking.

"I think the reason why they did it is because we were building not just our community but our nation. We had people from Walpole Island, Sarnia, Muncey, Chippewa on the Thames [all reserves], all of those youth that had talent in the arts would come down once a year. We called it the Aazhoodena Jamboree. We did it for three – no, four – years. They'd go there, sing their songs."

"Drum?" I asked.

"Yup."

"Ceremonial songs? Traditional dances?" Sheesh! There I was, off again in my own way of thinking: wanting to see it as some re-enacted past. As though, to be authentic, real Nishnaabe culture, it had to be something *I'd* recognize as their culture, preferably a freeze-frame replay of a museum piece.

Kevin was gracious. "Not so much. Mostly modern stuff," he said. There was a continuity I'd missed out on because I hadn't been aware of it going on all around me over the years. Kevin was good enough to not spell this out.

We sat and watched the rain, and I continued to nurse my coffee as one hour slipped into a second. I asked about the present, and he shook his head at how bad things were, the cleanup of the former reserve barely begun.

He looked up again; the rain was letting up, the sky lightening a bit.

"Right now, I see it in the youth, the same look I had when I moved in in 1993. I mean, it's sellin' weed and that, but they're proud of what they're accomplishing. What's wrong with that? And it's legal."

I asked him what his vision was for Stoney Point.

"That *is* my vision," he said. "To see our youth have their own source of income. To make a living and be proud of it. I hate the idea of welfare. I see the need for it, but there's other ways."

He gave a quick nod and looked out at the lake, visible once again.

"My vision – it's not just for our community; it's for our nation. Because our community is just one small corner of our nation. When you talk about those original agreements between us, the Nishnaabe, when we had the Two Row Wampum belt, the [Royal] Proclamation, talkin' about those two boats travelling side by side – we'll stay in ours, you stay in yours, sharing the land – we never gave up this land; we agreed to share it. We set aside small parcels where we weren't goin' to share it. That's why they're so small."

He gestured. "That lake out here, we agreed to share it."

I sat beside him, listening hard, feeling hard, his words sinking into me, taking hold. Yes, I thought. It's that big: the challenge of real reconciliation.

"I don't know how it's gonna come about," Kevin continued, still looking out the window. "But I know there is gonna be a change."

I nodded, an ache in my throat so huge I couldn't speak. His faith was so strong.

"The stepchildren I'm raising, the looks on their faces every time they hear something's moving forward – the excitement in them. It's incredible to see, to witness."

He glanced at me. I nodded, smiling at his fervour. He shook his head. "I dunno. They have three lineages to Stoney Point: their mother's side, their father's side, and my side. So they're Stoney Point through and through." He laughed. "I try to build them up as much as I can, because they've been through *so* much growin' up."

I nodded. Yes, I could imagine. I listened as he shared some of what they'd endured, the struggle life continues to be.

When he fell silent, we sat like that, comfortable in the quiet, the sky clearing and the sun glistening on all the wet surfaces outside. I felt the need to ask something I didn't want to ask. What was it like having the government still in control of everything, especially the timelines on when the cleanup would be done and the land fully back to being theirs? Kevin sat there saying nothing for a bit, just shaking his head.

"It sucks," he said finally. "There's so much that needs to get done in there, and our lives are short. I'm in my forties now, and life's way too short for what we want to get done. Because we're talking about building a nation, or a community. Little things like getting food or growing an orchard. It takes years and years for those trees to grow." (The women had planted some apple trees back in the 1990s when the social clubs were still active. One got driven over by someone who was drunk. One split because it hadn't been pruned right. One's still going, he said.)

I admired his steadfast commitment, his capacity to sustain it all these years. But what if his efforts and his faith weren't enough? If all this effort, since 1946, really, to restore Stoney Point as Nishnaabe territory came to nothing? Did he ever think about giving up?

"Yeah, sometimes." He glanced at me and away again. "But just for a second. I know our people; it's more than just – I mean, it's part of us. It's who we are. It's in our DNA. You can't deny it." Again he gave me a quick look. I returned it, nodded. Yes, I hear you, I thought, and hear the challenge: to recognize this reality as reality, and act on it.

He leaned forward. "You could be raised in Timbuktu and told that you're somebody else, and it's still gonna come out. Whether it's in your dreams or something. Something in your head tells you there's more. There's something in you."

Tears welled up in my eyes. This deep, inalienable connection to his ancestral land. It was like an umbilical cord anchoring him to the earth in a way I could never know myself, not like that; in a way that is simply lived, an ineluctable part of your identity. My ancestors had it, and it has been lost over time. And yet perhaps some vestige of its memory had lingered and been passed on to me. Kevin's words, and his passion, had moved me so deeply. It was as though something was stirring awake inside me. As though what he'd been talking about was answering a call I'd never been consciously aware of. Meanwhile, here he was, acting on that connection, living it with quiet dignity despite two hundred years of official denial. Yes, I thought. Yes!

Now he was reaching for the door handle.

"Smoke break," he said and laughed.

I pressed pause on the recorder and watched him run across the still-wet parking lot, leaping the biggest puddles. He stopped at the porta-potty, then headed down to the dock and the water. He hunched over, then straightened up, smoke drifting up over his shoulder. I watched him smoke his cigarette and thought, giving up that lived connection to the land, giving up on trying to live out the meaning of that connection, is not an option for him. He might be a "spiritual exile" on the land, as Tecumseh had warned back at the turn of the nineteenth century, when settler colonizers were using

treaties to displace Kevin's ancestors from their home territory.[2] But he's also refusing to be one, as he's quietly, insistently, and in his own way living his own truth, that he will
not be exiled, that he is home. Aazhoodena is alive under his
feet and through the actions of his hands tending that land
every day. The challenge for me was to keep letting that truth
permeate my consciousness – and take on what it means.

Kevin got back in the car. He'd gotten some texts from
Lacey.

Jeez, he said, though he was chuckling, he hadn't realized
how long we'd been sitting here talking. Me neither, I said,
though an entire thunderstorm had gathered itself across
Lake Huron, unleashed its fury, and dissolved away during
the time that we'd talked.

"Best be getting back," he said.

As I drove, he talked some more about his step-kids; the
oldest was graduating from high school this year. And, he
said, he was taking the family on a vacation this summer.
"I'm being paid to take a vacation! First time," he said, grin-
ning. Then he started talking about movies, his favourites
being ones with Chief Dan George in them. Had I seen *The
Outlaw Josey Wales*? he asked. No, I said. He started quoting
his grandfather's namesake: "I never surrendered. But they
surrendered my horse; he's pullin' a wagon up north somewhere." We both chuckled.

"There's a movie *Little Big Man*, with Dustin Hoffman,"
he continued. I nodded. I'd seen it. Kevin nodded. "But there's
an Ojibwe version of *Little Big Man*. That's one story I used
to hear when I was young." He sketched the plot: When the
Ojibwe were going into battle against the Sioux, everyone
scoffed and said he was too little to fight. But he went anyway, "And he continued fightin' even after losing his head.
His body kept fightin' when his head was singing his death
song," Kevin said. And this was a turning point, rallying the

other Ojibwe and spooking the enemy. Kevin laughed. "That's one of the legends that I heard – Little Big Man."

He was quiet for a bit. I kept driving, put on my signal for turning onto Army Camp Road.

"There's lots of history that you hear that makes you proud of who you are, that you would never, ever learn in school." Still, things have begun to change, he said. They're teaching more Nishnaabe history in the schools, even the language. But there was none of that when he was growing up. "It was all, send them to Forest. Forest knows best. Let them teach our kids. And you see the results of that: a lot of people who are embarrassed at who they are. It's kind of hard to live a productive life if you're embarrassed about yourself just existing. That's not right."

I nodded and watched the barrier go up at the army camp gate. I drove along the cracked and potholed road, past an old car with vapour barrier for a window, turned the corner and stopped outside the army barrack that Kevin had made into a home for himself and his family.

I told Kevin that I'd like to meet Lacey someday, and his children too. Maybe I could have them over to my place for supper, or we could all go out somewhere. Kevin smiled, said he'd talk to Lacey about the idea. He got out of the car, gave me a little nod, and disappeared around the corner.

16

Connective Cadences

The next day was Sunday and Bonnie had insisted I come for supper; I wondered why. But I had the afternoon free, so I arrived early.

One car was in the laneway when I got there. It belonged to Bonnie's sister Janice, if I was remembering right about whose car was whose. I pulled in close behind it, in case others came. I noticed pansies blooming in the front border, a cleared patch of dirt by the old wicker table where I knew Bonnie wanted to plant more flowers. Someone had been busy. And there was Buck over by the big walnut tree, walking with just a cane. Walking slowly, his right foot dragging a bit, but still managing without his walker.

I breezed through the back door, though I still knocked before entering and calling out "hello, hello" as I opened the inside door. Yes, it was Janice. She was in her usual chair at the far end of the table; she was just leaving, she said, which I knew didn't necessarily mean a thing. She and Bonnie had been going through a pile of stuff on the table.

"It's from when me and my husband went on these trips," Janice explained. She'd finally started clearing out the trailer and had found all the brochures where they stored their sheets and other bedding.

I nodded and acted on Bonnie's gesture for me to sit down. A young woman walked in through the back door, one of the granddaughters I'd met last fall. Bonnie picked up a seed packet from the table, turned her wheelchair and wheeled it forward.

"Here," she said. The young woman took the package, smiling, then followed as her grandmother wheeled back to the table. Bonnie pointed out the window.

"I want you to plant them morning glories right in front there. So I can *see* them." She turned, a big smile on her face.

"Sure, Nana," the granddaughter said, and headed out the back door again.

I was tempted to ask if she'd ever got that back pay she was owed, just to show that I cared enough to remember. I listened instead as Janice talked about how she was going to empty out her shed next, so she could put all her gardening tools away properly.

Bonnie laughed and told her she'd never get it cleared out. She turned to me.

"She's a hoarder," she said in a loud whisper. Then she turned her chair and headed into the kitchen area. I had smelled onions frying when I came in. I followed her over and poured myself a coffee, wanting to tell her about meeting the minister at the local United church.

Bonnie had wheeled herself to the stove, then heaved herself forward, up and out of the chair, grabbing the side of the stove with one hand, reaching for a spatula with the other. She looked around.

"Can I get you something?" I asked.

"Yeah, that salt there," and she nodded toward where a big salt shaker sat on the other side of the sink.

She shook it over the pan, then picked up the spatula again, stirred and turned over the meat, saying something about buffalo meat, which told me that this was what she was frying. Then she plunked herself back into her chair, wheeled herself toward and past me as I stepped back. She gestured toward the countertop, where there were two squashes and a long English cucumber.

"Give me that, will you?" she said, and I reached for the vegetables, offering to carry them over myself.

No, she said, she'd take those. See those knives, the bowl, and a cutting board? I could bring those.

I set everything down in front of Bonnie's place at the table, took my own seat and watched her try to grab one of the squashes in her left hand and peel it with her right.

"Please," I said. "Let me."

Bonnie gave me a look, then relented. "But go get me that other cutting board first," she said.

We settled in, Janice talking about who'd been at bingo last night and what food there'd been to eat after.

I peeled carefully, then stopped and showed Bonnie what I was doing, how thin the peelings were. My mother had taught me: don't waste a thing.

"Yeah, that's good," she said, then pulled the second cutting board into her lap, grabbed the cucumber and the big knife, and started slicing it up.

"I'm gonna make pickles for tonight," she said. "And venison. *And* I got some pork tenderloin."

It sounds like a feast, I said, wondering if she could possibly be doing this to honour me. Thinking, surely not – though smiling inwardly.

The back door opened. A tall young man strode in, put a bag on the counter, and said something to Bonnie. She answered back, something so terse I couldn't catch it as she pushed the cutting board back onto the table, turned and wheeled herself away down the hall, disappearing into a small room opposite the bathroom. She returned, handed something to the young man. They exchanged another few words, and he left.

It wasn't coded communication, I thought as I sat watching and listening to it all. It was simply talk so stripped down and minimal, because so much of the context was known and mutually understood, that it seemed like code. I continued to peel the squash.

There was something in the web and weave of everything that was going on around here, everything that was said and done. It flowed in and out, so fluid. As though the back door was a heart valve, with family and the community flowing through it. Life blood. Blood memory. Affiliation. Kinship.

My eyes were learning to see and my ears learning to hear all that I had missed before, or considered irrelevant, merely background noise. Now it felt like I was starting to sense and follow the undertone, the connective cadence of all the storylines moving through this space. There was almost a different reality at play, or a different way of living it. I was starting to tune in to it, or at least become aware of it.

Bonnie wheeled herself back to the table. "That was Adam," she said. "He's gonna see about fixing that lawnmower out there, but he wants to take the warranty, just in case." Buck wants to get mowing, she said.

I offered to dump the cucumbers she'd sliced into the bowl; I'd thought of going ahead and doing it when she was busy, but had learned enough to hold myself back.

No, she said, that's for the squash. She's got a big jar she makes the pickles in; she'll put the cucumber straight into that. She gestured with her hand, and I saw the jar sitting on the counter. But Janice was already up and fetching it.

She had to go now, she said as she grabbed her big purse. But she might come over later, to see Summer. Oh, good, I thought: Summer's coming.

The last time we'd talked, Summer had told me more about the work she was doing for a large archive, gathering some of the elders' stories, recording them to add to the archive's holdings. Summer was taking her time, which meant following what she'd been taught. On a first visit, she told me, she just took gifts and listened, maybe explaining what she'd been tasked with asking but that's all. Maybe on the next visit, they might tell her one thing, she said. That's how it went, the slow gifting of this story and then that one into Summer's hands. It was hard, though, Summer had said, because she'd been hired on a contract, which was due to expire in three months, and already her boss was asking for what she had collected.

I had been mulling this over since that visit, recalling Summer's soft voice as she'd told me this – but also her anxiety. As what she'd shared with me sank in, composting in my mind, it occurred to me that Summer wasn't going through the motions of some protocol. She was establishing a relationship with the elders, showing her respect through her gifts. In the act of selecting them and giving them at just the right moment, she was cultivating respectful, attentive presence. The gifts and other rituals of approach were a sort of medium for tuning in, I imagined, becoming attuned, one to the other. Showing respect was only the tip of the iceberg. Or rather, I was beginning to appreciate why this concept of respect, of seeing again, seeing fully, was so essential to effective communications. No wonder it was among the seven grandmother/grandfather teachings.[1]

I could envisage the elder starting to share what had been entrusted to her or him, when they felt they could trust Summer to hear them right. Right relations as right listening. Yes!

This was happening a lot. As I sat on the things that had caught my attention in different conversations, turning them over in my mind, if I was patient and just waited, a door would open in my mind. It was as though I was crossing some inner threshold. And here it was again: my imagination was moving around in a space my mind had opened up, where before, my stitched-in assumptions, my filters and blinkers – call them settler-colonial or just how I'd been schooled to think, in institutions moulded in the colonial mindset – had stood in the way. They'd blocked my ability to fully see and hear, to take in and grasp the integrity of what people like Summer were saying. It wasn't that I chose to disrespect by not seeing, not hearing it fully. The mindset operating within me did the work, shaving or cutting it down to fit my conditioned way of thinking, boxing me in, and boxing the fullness of this other reality out. It was up to me to disrupt this.

I wasn't starting to think in new ways. But I was starting to see that there was a completely different way of thinking. In conversations with people like Summer, I was starting to feel the presence, the existence, of that difference and to respect it. I hoped Summer and I might get another chance to talk later.

I finished peeling the second squash, then volunteered to cut them up.

"Okay," Bonnie said. She'd finished cutting up the cucumber and was dumping the slices into the big glass jar. She'd add a mixture of vinegar water and some sugar, and they'd soon be ready to eat, she said.

I picked up the big knife ready to cut up the squash. "How thick?" I asked Bonnie. She spread two fingers to show me. I did some cutting, knowing she was watching me. I looked up.

"Yeah. Good," she said, nodding.

Now seemed a good time to tell her about what had happened when I'd gone to the local United church at Grand Bend for the morning service. I'd gone because the United Church of Canada had run the Mount Elgin Residential School near London, Ontario, where so many Nishnaabe from here had been forcibly sent – Bonnie's mother, Hilda, included.

They had a right-relations group at the local church, I said. Apparently someone had photos of kids from the Mount Elgin Residential School, taken by one of the former teachers.

Bonnie stopped midway through sweeping up her mess. "I heard about that. They had them on the wall there, I heard." I looked at her, startled. It was as though her whole being had come to a full stop, her attention was so riveted.

Yes, I said. I'd asked about them too. The minister was going to see where they went, or who had them.

Right away, Bonnie said she'd like to get copies of them. A group on the reserve had put together a registry of all the kids who'd been sent to the residential school. But there's lots of names, lots of children, that are missing, Bonnie told me.

I told Bonnie I'd keep her posted.

"I'd like to meet that person," Bonnie said. "And I'll pay for those pictures too!"

She pulled the jar of sliced cucumbers into her lap, foot-paddled her way over to the counter, got the sugar bowl, then disappeared behind the counter looking for the vinegar.

Fred came in, coffee mug in hand, stopped to pour himself some more, then crossed the room and took the seat at the end of the table, where Janice had been sitting. He smiled at me, nodded hello. I asked him how he was.

"Pretty good," he said. He smiled, then pointed out the window, saying that the oriole was back, in her usual nest high up in the birch tree. I looked out at the big old birch tree on one side of the front lawn. I remembered watching for the return of an oriole to the elm tree outside the farmhouse where I partly grew up, the satisfaction my mother always got at seeing it.

We both watched Bonnie as she wheeled herself back to the table with her fresh provisions. She plunked them onto the table, then turned to me.

"Mush Hole," Bonnie said, her voice hard with anger. "You know why they called it that? Because the food there was so bad!" She poured vinegar into the big jar, looked at me again.

"Did I tell you they didn't sew pockets in their clothes there? It was so the kids couldn't steal food." Bonnie knew this because her mother, Hilda, had been so good at sewing that they held her back at the school during the summer to sew. She'd had to help make all those uniforms without the pockets too. I paused in my cutting: the cruelty of being forced to do that.

The back door opened. It was another granddaughter, holding a daughter of her own in her arms. Bonnie wheeled herself over, her face radiating joy as she greeted her great-granddaughter. The little girl was wearing a pink plastic-coated jacket with a unicorn hood, complete with a horn bouncing at the back of her head.

"I bought it myself," the young mother said, heading to the counter to check out the food. She picked up a couple of slices of cucumber off the cutting board Bonnie had left on the counter. She popped one in her mouth and handed one to her daughter, then set the little girl down on the floor.

"Come over here and give Nana a hug," Bonnie said, leaning her body over one side of her chair. Then, "Come here, I've got something for you." Bonnie headed to the back room where she had her sewing stuff and, I guessed, a stash of candies.

Bonnie had let me peel some potatoes next, and when I carried the pot of cut-up potatoes to the counter, I felt the need for some air.

"Yeah, sure," Bonnie said when she got back. "Go for a walk. Anywhere along the lake here is fine."

I wandered out onto a spit of land where someone had cleared away the tall phragmites. I gazed out over the ancient lake, the wave action as timeless as time itself. I stood there for a while, taking in the rhythm of the water rising and falling as it approached the shore, splashed against the rocks, and receded. Suddenly I laughed, remembering when I was learning to swim. It was in a lake somewhat like this one, a little murky from the wave action near the shore. When I took the test to prove I could swim so I could get my first badge, I cheated. I dropped a foot down in the water, using the stones on the bottom to hold me up. Now I thought, I'm learning to swim all over again, but not groping around for familiar stones anymore. I hadn't learned to move through the water yet, but at least I was learning to float. I was learning to trust the water to hold me up.

I looked out over the lake some more and said an inward thank you, miigwech, for that gift of insight. Then I turned and headed back.

SUMMER WAS SITTING on a stool beside her grandfather when I came back inside; she was holding one of his hands between both of hers like she had before. She got up and came over, big smile on her face. She put her arms around me. "It's good to see you again," she said.

I smiled back. "You too," I said. She'd had her hair cut and some streaks added.

"Nice hair," I dared to say. She touched it briefly, then introduced a young man, a non-native, a zhaganash like me. Ian, she said. They were engaged to be married. Ah, I thought, a penny dropping in my mind about this feast I'd been allowed to help prepare.

Bonnie was starting to dish up the food. She'd put on the silver earrings I'd given her, I noticed. Someone had already pulled the table out from the wall, cleared off its normal clutter and set places all around. Now Summer and I carried bowls of vegetables and platters of meat to the table. People gathered around. One of Bonnie's daughters was there, two granddaughters, and a great-granddaughter. Janice was also back. Bonnie told me to go sit beside Summer. "I'm gonna eavesdrop on what you two are talkin' about," she said, smiling her wicked smile.

Summer and I took seats near a space that had been left for Bonnie's wheelchair. Everyone started filling up their plates, Bonnie watching the progress of the dishes doing the rounds, encouraging everyone to eat. Buck came in, took a plate off the counter and came to the table. But he wouldn't sit down. Instead, he loaded up and headed back down the hall to the family room. Ian was sitting next to Fred, listening to whatever story Fred was telling him. Bonnie pushed the bowl of pickled beets down the table toward Summer and me. Had I got some of the buffalo too? I said I had, thanks. I told her what a fine feast this was.

"Thank you," I said, looking at her smiling face. I forked some mashed potato into the gravy and ate the last of the venison stew on my plate.

Summer was talking about the people with whom she was working, the trouble she was having getting them to listen to her. Partly, she knew it was because they were full time, in a union, and she was only on contract. Plus, they all had degrees in library science and museology, and hers was in education. But it was more than that.

"I'm having this ethical dilemma," she told me, laughing softly as though at herself for putting it this way. She doesn't know if the people at the archive will treat the elders' stories she's been gathering the right way. She's already keeping one of the stories back because it contains sacred knowledge. Even with the other stories she's collecting, she said, she wants the archive staff to make it a point to always invite in an elder when these stories will be shared with the public. She was thinking of including this as part of her report. She looked at me as though interested in what I thought.

I agree, I told Summer, nodding and smiling, then dared to add, "It's not just 'holdings,' but 'holding.' Relationships of holding."

Yes, I thought, as I heard myself say this, though it had only just come to me, this breakthrough in my *own* thinking so that I could grasp what Summer was saying: that the relations around the telling and receiving of stories were as important as the stories themselves. The context of right telling, right listening; the ecology of engagement. In fact, it struck me that these might be inseparable from the stories themselves. If the integrity of the elders' stories was to remain intact, they had to be understood and respected as more than just "holdings," which is how most people associated with archives, museums, and libraries think. They had to include the relationships in which stories are held and made available to be shared with others.

I'd told Summer earlier about the work I was doing, representing writers and other creators on the steering committee of the National Heritage Digitization Strategy, headed up by Library and Archives Canada. All the other members of the steering committee were "holdings" people associated with the major museums, archives, and libraries across the country, and all the books, papers, artifacts, and so on were held by them. They needed someone like Summer on the steering committee, I'd thought earlier, to help them understand. Now I thought, yes, they do, but they also need to do their own homework and not expect someone like Summer to lead them by the hand.

As we finished eating, Summer told me a bit more about what she had in mind. I nodded, smiling, and said that I would be happy to support her in any way I could.

She smiled in the way I noticed that her mother smiled, her eyes almost shutting as the smile took possession of her whole face. She was starting a teaching contract with a

Nishnaabe college in the fall, she told me. Even if the archive offered her another contract, she might not take it.

I nodded. Yes, I said, I could see the wisdom of that choice. She needed to feel there was a welcoming space for what she had to contribute. Right now, her status there was marginal, only a short-term contract. Precarious for her, and no real commitment from the institution to make the changes that would be needed to truly accommodate what she was bringing to it in her work.

I was aware of a sadness inside me as I returned to the motel. I lit a candle and sat for a while, letting moments from the day wash over me. A memory surfaced from when I'd told Bonnie about those photos of children from the local residential school. I'd been jolted by her reaction, taken aback by her fierceness. I'd thought the photos would be of interest to her, as they had been to me. But this wasn't just of interest to Bonnie. This was her life, her mother's, her aunties' and uncles' lives. Their identities had been stolen from them, and she wanted those identities back, every scrap of them. Even if some of the remaining scraps were photographs taken by one of the hated teachers.

It went beyond that, too. Bonnie had mentioned missing names; she wanted the photos to help remember the missing.

I'd read in the Truth and Reconciliation Commission report that a lot of kids died at those residential "schools" – five times the national average.[2] I'd also read that a lot of the deaths hadn't been fully recorded. Not only no cause of death listed in half the cases, but no names either.[3] The children had disappeared without a trace. But not here, I realized now, the jolt I'd felt hitting home. Those children hadn't disappeared from the minds and hearts of the people back home. They were still missing, still unaccounted for, their homecoming suspended indefinitely.

Bonnie's reality was so different from mine. Even though I'd read about all these children's deaths, the reality of them, as lived lives and part of an indivisible webwork of lived lives, had remained remote – until now. I stared into the candle flame, aching at that remoteness, aware, too, that in a way it echoed the indifference of those school officials who would do such things. Leaning toward the candle flame, I sat with that indifference, and the racism in its shadow. I sat, too, with what Bonnie had said, the emotion of her response bursting in on me, her fierce desire to get copies of those photos. I sat there as the candle burned lower, feeling that urgency, identifying with it, making a connection. I was starting to make Bonnie's reality part of my reality. Sharing it.

I kept gazing at the candle flame as it flickered and held steady, flickered again and steadied itself. The boxes in my head kept us at a distance, I realized. That jolt had been a sign of it: the difference in our perspectives, our sense of reality and what was important. But the sadness, if I dwelt on it, also signalled a crack. Every crack was helping me break out of my inner boxes, opening the space between us, filling it with empathy – and the capacity for love.

I had been thinking a lot about that treaty phrase *cede and surrender,* and sensing parallels between the external territory of land and the internal territory of mind and heart. Now I found myself considering its double meaning, at least in terms of what I was experiencing here. It wasn't just surrendering in the sense of giving up – no longer resisting, denying, and keeping a hard truth at bay. I was surrendering in another way, too: letting in, genuinely surrendering to, whatever was being revealed to me, shared with me. I was opening myself to it, wanting to know more, willing to be moved – even as some part of me knew I'd have to face the consequences of that, and was afraid.

The journey I'd begun when I'd leaned against that rusty old barbed-wire fence on that hot July day nearly a year earlier was going on inside me. I'd chosen not just to lower my defences in whatever I was doing here. I'd chosen to let myself be open, permeable even, to another person's truth. And here it was: what had been of interest to me before had now become urgent to me, because it was urgent to Bonnie. From *her* point of view. I was ceding space in my imagination partly because I was ceding space in my heart.

I thought of Fred and Summer, and Kevin, Cully, Marcia, and the others, and all that I was learning from listening to them.

This journey I was on – of unlearning what I thought to be true, and of new learning, even transformation – seemed to be happening. It was happening on a small scale – unstitching old patterns, opening up the cloth, spreading it out, making space within me. And yet it didn't stop there, I knew; it's not just surrendering personal head space.

I sat back and thought of what Summer and I had talked about as we ate our buffalo meat, venison, and pork tenderloin. I gazed into the steady heart of the candle flame.

Yes, I thought, it's ceding and surrendering space everywhere, including institutional spaces like archives and museums, how they are structured and run. Unlearning has to go on there too; undoing too.[4] Unstitching old patterns in the mind and also in institutional systems. Dismantling institutional structures to genuinely share space. That's what the treaty meant, and what reconciliation means now. It's huge.

17

Colonialism Ongoing

It was late October again, 2019, and I was heading back to Stoney Point, plus Kettle Point, where Bonnie lived with her vast extended family. By now I was looking forward to these trips as visits: a chance to keep getting to know Bonnie, Marcia, Cully, Kevin, and others. Maybe I was laying the groundwork for a treaty relationship, maybe not.

I was having more and more misgivings about the book project. Not with having shown up as I had, in the place where the treaty had been broken – the treaty which, in my way of thinking at least, had sanctioned my ancestors' having settled in Nishnaabe territory in the early 1800s. Not in having chosen to implicate myself, trying to honour Indigenous understandings that treaties are relationships that need to be renewed and, where damaged, need to be repaired – and that everyone is responsible, not just government authorities. My doubts were around how I'd let that responsibility be framed. I'd told myself that helping to pull everyone's stories into a book was a way of expressing condolences and possibly starting to repair the treaty relationship. But that seemed like an alibi now. It had been a way of deflecting away from confronting the colonial thinking that still occupied my mind. The more aware I was becoming of this, the more I realized that it got in the way of my being able to work on this book project with any integrity, especially since I was still so unconscious of how steeped in that thinking I still was. The world they lived in was so different from mine, even in the same geographic space; their lived reality still so remote from mine. The more aware of this I became, the more I worried I became that I could sabotage a true telling of the story.

The repair work to be done, I'd come to realize, wasn't in helping to write a book. The repair was in me, rewriting me. And it was happening, too; I knew that. But it wasn't happening in isolation, not when I was on my own. It was happening in the course of all these visits. I kept going back and forth in my mind about this even as I prepared to board my flight. Maybe I could keep showing up without the book project as an excuse. Because the relationships that had developed between us, not just with Bonnie and her family but also with Cully, Marcia, Kevin, and others, were real. They were my path, or my compass along the path, and what I focused on. They were my map, too; these relationships were mapping me into a whole new world. Still, this book had become real in their minds; I'd raised expectations about completing it. If I did follow through, this visit would be my last before I had enough material with which to start writing a first draft; I was that close.

When I landed in Toronto and turned on my phone, there was an email alerting me to a Facebook message from Bonnie. Immediately, I thought of Bonnie's husband, Fred, worried that something had happened to him. When I'd seen him in the summer, it looked like that double blood transfusion had done the trick. Still, the doctors didn't know the underlying source of the problem. But I couldn't open Facebook on my cell phone; it was an old model and out of sync with lots of new systems.

I texted Bonnie's daughter Barb as I waited to deplane. Kept it light, just asking if she'd heard of anything happening with her folks. I also said that I was thinking of her too. Worm had finally gone for tests; he wasn't getting any better. She texted back, no, nothing she knew of.

As I waited to board my flight for London, I turned on my laptop and found Bonnie's message. "Postpone your trip," Bonnie had written; that's all. I had an hour before my flight, so I called her and said, I'm sorry, but I got the message too late. I'm nearly there.

"That's okay," she replied. "Come on over when you get here." Fred was okay, she said. "There's more trouble over at Stoney."

I DROVE ONTO the reserve with a sense of familiarity. The leaves were once again gone from the trees. Puddles had again taken up residence on the road. I parked in my usual spot in the lane by the fence, behind what I knew to be Colleen's car. I went in, knocking and calling out hello as I came.

"Hi, Colleen," I said as she turned toward me, smiling. "Good to see you again." And it was.

Bonnie was over by the table, talking with someone on the phone. I shook my head at Colleen's offer of coffee, but stayed back and away from the table. Whatever was going on, Bonnie was obviously talking about it with someone on the phone just now. But it was their business, not mine. Bonnie and the others would share it with me if they wanted to. I wasn't going to ask.

Bonnie pushed her chair back from the table, stopped in the middle of the room. She looked at me fiercely. "The government seems to feel they can still dictate. It's kind of like, 'Well, do you want us to turn the land back?'" I knew that she was referring to the Final Settlement Agreement between Ottawa and the Kettle and Stony Point First Nation, signed in 2016, but I'd never read the document or seen a copy of it, so I didn't really know what she was talking about. She turned, wheeled forward and lifted her coffee mug up toward the countertop. She had to heave herself out of the wheelchair to do it, but she brushed aside Colleen's gesture to take the mug. She worked her feet to wheel herself back to the table.

"I've always felt bad about myself because I didn't go over there and stay," she said. But all those dozens of others, like Worm and Marcia, Kevin and Dudley, they went there in good faith in 1993, to get the land back, "and look at what happened to that good faith. Look what happened to Worm and all those others. Same thing with the cleanup. They call it decommissioning and they're in charge, and they'll drag ass all they can. That's not good faith!"

I said something vague, trying to be supportive but not having a clue what was going on. Bonnie looked at me, exhaled noisily in disgust, then shook her head and laughed.

"I'm so pissed off at the federal government dictating to me," she said. There was this land-use plan the community had to develop, and it had to be approved by the government people before they'd get on with the clearance and remediation work. Apparently, that too was part of the Final Settlement Agreement that the community had supposedly agreed to back in 2016.

"We got the money to rebuild Stoney Point. What the hell right have they got telling us how to do it when it's our business?"

Now Bonnie was off to an elders' meeting. Should I go over to Stoney Point? Bonnie hadn't been clear whether the Nishnaabe peacekeepers were back to stopping people from going in, or just adding their own level of vetting as a way to register their claim that this was Nishnaabe territory, Nishnaabe jurisdiction. And if she hadn't wanted me to come back right now, maybe she didn't want me involved in whatever crisis was going on now.

Cully's birthday was coming up. I'd go get her a card, I thought. Then maybe I'd drop in on Marcia. I wondered if she was using the fleece hand warmers I'd brought her in the summer, thinking especially of her hand where she'd had a bone graft and her wrist continued to ache in cold weather.

No. I had to face this *now*. The Final Settlement Agreement had become an elephant in my living room, or it felt like that in how I shied away from knowing too much about it. I knew that it had been nearly ten years in the making, that most of the negotiations had gone on in Ottawa, and that the chief and band council at Kettle Point – the ones who were officially representing the Nishnaabeg – had relied on an Ottawa consulting firm to advise them on all the legalese and bureaucratese involved in its negotiation. I knew, too, that only a summary of the nearly hundred–page agreement had been distributed through the community before it was put to a vote, and that a lot of people didn't vote. Still, a majority of those who did had voted to approve it.

It was a done deal, therefore, and none of my business. If I did have any business being here, it was the book project. Or that's what I'd kept telling myself. Part of me still resisted seeing beyond the tidy confines of this commitment. I'd inwardly drawn a line around it, wanting to keep myself outside that line. It was almost a con game I was playing with myself. I was aware of the other stuff: the overdose deaths, Children's Aid swooping in on families, people not getting paid or just for short-term bits of work. I'd kept all this in my peripheral vision, at first anyway, along with the glaring fact that people like Kevin still hadn't regained control of their home reserve. Over time, though, these things had gradually seeped into my field of perception, and my feelings too. The seepage had begun because I'd gotten to know people like Kevin and Bonnie, and had come to care about what was happening in their lives.

As with the realities of the residential schools, this was still my colonial heritage at work. I couldn't box it away. I needed to let myself feel implicated. I needed to know what was going on *now*, and to acknowledge it fully.

By now I'd come to understand that colonialism was not an event neatly contained in the past. It wasn't even just an isolated process or a system, though it was those things too. It was also an active dynamic, almost a gravitational force field, pulling everything a certain way unless it was actively resisted. There was a lot of psychology – including the psychology of social identity – tied up in its politics.

As I drove to the motel, it occurred to me that I was in another gravitational field and being acted upon by it. I'd been challenged by people like Bonnie and Marcia, Kevin and Cully, and I had begun to change in response. At some level, my identity, or its orientation, had started to change as well. It was as simple and subtle as changing a relationship, which had begun when I learned to just shut up and listen.

Back in my room, I turned on my computer and went online. Bonnie was upset. Maybe Marcia was, too, and Kevin and Cully. I needed to know why. I was implicated. It wasn't political; it was personal. Or it was both.

It had been convenient that the settlement agreement was hard to get hold of. The deal was you had to go into the band office to read a printed copy, which was single-spaced and long. Or, if you had a computer and internet access plus access as a band member, you could download a copy. None of the people I'd come to know had a computer. But there was someone else I'd met who did, a band member who now responded and would send me a copy.

I phoned Marcia while I waited. No answer. I put on the kettle, made a coffee. I texted Cully on her son's cell phone; she generally had the use of it when he was sleeping, before his late shift at the car-parts factory where he worked, and he'd likely still be sleeping now.

I heard an incoming email, sat down, and there it was. The *Ipperwash Final Settlement Agreement* was on the screen in front of me, an easy-to-read PDF. I clicked it open, reading that this was an agreement between "The Chippewas of Kettle and Stony Point and Her Majesty the Queen, in Right of Canada." I scanned the table of contents and began scrolling down.

Page 34 dealt with setting up an Implementation Team to support the Implementation Directors; a Project Manager (a government appointee) plus a Project Engineer (First Nation) who "may be present to observe the work of the Independent Contractor," although any access to the site must be "coordinated through the Implementation Team to ensure the necessary health and safety protocols are understood and followed ... and no undue interference." That was on page 40. It was hard to piece together what it all meant; I had to jump from a sub-clause in one section to a sub-clause in another. I had to keep reminding myself that this was all about land that had been nominally turned back to the Nishnaabe First Nation – because it sure didn't look as though control was being returned to them.

I reached for my phone. No text back from Cully. I called Marcia again and got her answering machine again. This time I left a message that I might drop by later.

I got up, went to the window, and looked out. The long-closed army camp, the still-existing Stoney Point Reserve beneath the army's distinctive debris, was directly across the road. I could see some of the bush and even some of the very old trees. And, directly opposite my window, the barbed-wire fence still carried the skull-and-crossbones signs warning about UXOs (unexploded ordinances) on the land beyond. The fence had been there, and whatever unexploded bombs there were had been there, since before I was born – and I was seventy years old.

I warmed up my coffee and took the mug back to the table I used as a desk. I faced the screen again, forcing myself to read the document chapter by chapter, page by page, clause by clause and sub-clause. This was the present and future for people like Bonnie, Marcia, Cully, and their children and grandchildren: the government's rules and regulations by which they'd have to live if they wanted to live once again in their homeland.

There was a whole chapter on species at risk, outlining how species would come under that designation, how conservation measures would be developed and permits issued for their implementation. Article 9.01 began: "A. Canada and the First Nation will, as appropriate, negotiate agreements on conservation ... B. Canada will consult with the First Nation prior to recommending to the Governor in Council that a species be added to Schedule 1 of the Species at Risk Act ... D. Canada will consider traditional knowledge ... "

Article 10 covered "Archaeological and Cultural Considerations," including burial grounds. Article 10.02 began, "A. The First Nation will develop an Archaeological and Cultural Resource Protocol ... D. The First Nation will provide Canada with a draft protocol for review and comment. The Parties, through the Implementation Team (as described in Section 11.03) or their delegates, will negotiate the terms of the final Archaeological and Cultural Resource Protocol ... "

Article 13 dealt with "First Nation Land Use Plan." Ah, I thought, this was what Bonnie had been talking about. Section A stated, "The First Nation will develop a Land Use Plan for the Settlement Lands that identifies the First Nation's intended uses of the Settlement Lands, subject to the following terms and conditions." It also mentioned that "completion of the Land Use Plan is a pre-condition to the development of the Clearance and Remediation Plan by Canada." Maybe this was the problem behind whatever was going on now.

How had Bonnie put it? Something like, "Well, do you want your land back? Submit to our authority." Things were coming into focus; sharp focus.

I continued reading, going back and forth as I followed a subsection in one article when it referred to a subsection or subparagraph of another. I finished my coffee, got up and washed out the mug, and returned to my reading. I kept getting lost in all the cross-referencing. Still, a connecting theme was emerging: virtually everything, including "land-use management," seemed to be subject to government policies and procedures – existing government policies – and any difference in thinking was subject not to negotiation but to the government's dispute-settlement mechanisms. In other words, on government-defined terms.

I stared out the window at the sagging barbed-wire fence with its death-warning signs on the old fence posts. This wasn't historical colonial thinking that hadn't been fully weeded out to make way for renewed nation-to-nation thinking, in keeping with Section 35 of the Canadian Constitution and the United Nations Declaration on the Rights of Indigenous Peoples. This was *renewed* colonial thinking, in the form of policies that would tie the Nishnaabeg's hands and minds in perpetuity.

Then it hit me. The document referred to the Stoney Point Reserve as "Settlement Lands." The Huron Tract treaty wasn't mentioned once, and the word *treaty* was used only as a descriptor. I checked Article II, in which key terms in the agreement were defined. There was only *Settlement Lands,* duly defined as "that parcel of land consisting of Part I on Plan 25R-3072, Municipality of Lambton Shores, County of Lambton in the Province of Ontario." I stared at this entry in the seemingly innocuous list of key word definitions. This ancient piece of Nishnaabe territory that predated the formation of Canada and the province of Ontario had been mapped into exclusively contemporary Ontario and Canadian government terms. And this neologism, *Settlement Lands,* had been inserted into what was supposed to be an exercise in historical reparation. A simple word substitution cancelled out any link of responsibility back to the 1827 treaty, which had promised to honour the Stoney Point Reserve as Nishnaabe territory in perpetuity. This document simply wrote right over it. Nullified it.

Terra nullius at last.

I closed my laptop, grabbed my jacket, and headed out for a walk down to the lake. The waves were continuing to pound the shore, almost a week after there'd been a big windstorm. There was still no beach to walk on, and the water's edge was littered with bushes and even whole trees that had been washed away by the extreme high waters the storm had set in motion. I tried picking my way around the mess, but it was too dangerous. Plus, I needed to walk hard and fast to work off what I was feeling: rage, responsibility, and the urge to do something! Despite the new Trudeau government – Justin, not his father Pierre[1] – boasting of its embrace of the UN Declaration on the Rights of Indigenous Peoples as self-determining peoples, and with Section 35 of the Constitution explicitly honouring treaties and recognizing treaty rights, this was happening. Here, on this very ground, clause after now-being-acted-upon clause was laying down fresh colonial cement, and people like Bonnie were expected to step into it.

I walked back up Army Camp Road again, past where the sand dunes give way to sumac trees and then to the spread of old-growth trees. I looked at them, a big white pine here, a massive old beech there. There'd been a sign tacked high up on one of the trees closer to the beach when I'd first started walking here in the summer of 2018. "Ancient Native Land," it said. But the sign wasn't there anymore; someone had taken it down. I looked at the trees, at their enduring presence, and I wondered what I could do about all this, what my role might be.

I kept walking, calmer now, and it came to me. Keep showing up, bearing witness even if you can't be of service. You're still responsible. But you're not in charge, not responsible for everything, either as colonizer or as decolonizer.

MARCIA'S CAR WAS there when I arrived at her place; no Fish 4 Sale sign, though. I got out of my car, uncertain whether to go up to the door and knock. Then Marlin appeared from around the back of the house. He was wheeling something that looked like a cross between a wheelbarrow and a lawnmower, full of firewood. The wood was sitting in the scooped bin of what had been a wheelbarrow. And this was secured to the chassis of an old gas lawnmower, the handles of it in Marlin's big, capable hands. I asked about getting some fish.

No fish, he said. That big windstorm last week? It took the whole beach out, he said. I asked if he'd lost any equipment. No, he said, he'd known enough to bring all his stuff in before the storm. Still, he was waiting for the water to settle back down before he went out again; it was still all churned up, the waves still coming in really high.

I asked if his mom was around.

He flashed a smile. "I'll go have a look-see," he said, and went inside.

I talked to the dog as I stood waiting. It stood at the end of its chain looking my way. Not barking, but not wagging its tail either.

The door opened. I looked up and Marcia was standing on the doorsill. She was wearing faded red sweatpants and a matching faded top. I stepped onto the cinder-block step as she pushed open the storm door. I said hello and asked how she was. She just stood there and gave her head a little shake.

Her face was pale, the lines in it cut inward, downward more deeply than I'd seen since that day in the old chapel. Her hair hung unevenly around her face. She said she didn't feel up to visiting.

"I'm burned out," she said. I looked at her, struggling to find words to both acknowledge this and somehow make things better. She shook her head, as if to cut me off from even trying.

"Just do the best you can without me," she said. She stepped back, letting go of the storm door, which silently swung into the space between us.

I stood there on the cinder block, continuing to look at her, now through the glass. It was clouded, fogged over with dust, soot, mud, pollen, and whatever else had piled up over time, fusing into a grey veil of opaqueness. I could barely make out the features of Marcia's face on the other side. And while it was still just a time-weathered storm door, in that moment it seemed to embody all that stood irrevocably between us. Then Marcia stepped back further and closed the inner wooden door. I stepped away.

I went back to my motel, self-doubt crashing in again. Who was I to come swooping in here with my good health and buoyant good intentions? I came here seeking to express condolences and to do what I could in the spirit of reparation. I thought that helping them tell their stories might be a form of reparation. Maybe I was wrong. Maybe the book project was pointless, though Marcia's last words had been telling me to carry on.

I took off my wet shoes, thinking of Marcia's lined face on the far side of that old storm door, her eyes looking at me before she closed the other door. I took off my damp socks, found a fresh pair and pulled them over my chilled feet. Then I went to my work table, thinking of what Marcia's son Kevin had told me about the Two Row Wampum: its two rows of shells representing separate, equal peoples and the sets of three shells connecting them. One shell represented respect, the second friendship, and the third peace.

I turned on my computer and pulled up the image of the Two Row Wampum that I'd downloaded some months ago. It had stopped being merely a historical artifact to me now; it had become a thinking aid or tool. I didn't think of it as part of my heritage, not really or not yet; though I was starting to call it by its Indigenous name, Guswentha. My heritage or not, it was part of a heritage that intersected with mine. It could teach me about that interconnection and maybe my responsibilities toward it.

I focused on those three shells and what they meant. I felt I had begun to learn how the shell of respect could be stitched back into place, at least a little. Each encounter here, renewed in the next visit, helped; each time some laughter rose between us, some warmth of fellow feeling helped too. And shared sadness. All of this pulled the thread tighter. Same thing with the shell of friendship. Something worthy of that name was being stitched into place. Bonnie even used the word sometimes at the end of our phone visits: Take care, my friend, she'd said more than once. Even Marcia, I thought, remembering what she'd said that day when we'd been weeding. It was at least a beginning.

It was the peace shell that was missing. I thought of how Martin Luther King Jr. had defined it, saying that peace wasn't just the absence of violence. It was the presence of justice. For the Nishnaabeg of Aazhoodena, this whole long, dragged-out wait to get their ancestral homeland back had been a denial of justice. And now this Final Settlement Agreement stood in the way. I remembered Bonnie throwing up her arms in disgust, saying the government wasn't negotiating in good faith. Not now, not then; maybe never. The shell of peace wasn't just broken, I thought. It was missing altogether and maybe had been all along, with the thinking associated with the Doctrine of Discovery as an excuse.

I remembered that shabby old storm door swinging shut between Marcia and me. There could be no genuine treaty relationship, let alone reconciliation, with the mindset associated with that agreement standing in the way. Me changing my mindset was not enough, though it was a beginning. I had to believe that.

18

Preparing to Leave

Cully greeted me with a grin, raising an arm and half getting up from her chair.

"You should have come to the party," she said as I came in. "I should have *invited* you." I'd dropped by the previous afternoon and left a plastic bag with the card I'd bought plus two cans of a beer she liked hanging from her doorknob. She'd texted the next morning, thanking me for the card. I saw it now, tacked to the wall next to her collection of postcards.

"Come here," she said, getting up. She wanted me to see how the new quilt was getting on. We walked over to her work table, and I gazed down at the emerging star. All those single sequences of colour – yellow, orange, red – that, earlier, she'd been sewing together individually were now all assembled into a starburst at the centre of what would be the finished quilt. Different shades of blue, some patterned, some not, were sewn into position to fan out from this centre, continuing the starburst pattern all the way to the border.

Was the way she was working the design outward like this her idea, I asked?

"Yup," she said, smoothing it flat with her hands.

I said it would be great to see all of her quilts in an exhibit. She snorted.

"Like I told you, they're all sold!" But she smiled at me, seeming to accept this affirmation. Then she laughed, saying that I could help organize a display at her funeral.

She headed back to her kitchen table.

"Want a pop?" she asked, going to the fridge first to get one, and the jug of cold water for me. There were smoke detectors on the table; three of them, all in shiny plastic packages.

"That's from DND," she said. She smirked. "They promised them last year," she said, and they'd only just brought them. A whole crew of them had come through the other day, with someone from the band office. One guy had a clipboard and was writing things down – what they were going to fix up, Cully said.

She laughed, gesturing to a row of large plastic water jugs. "I got them to go get me my water." She laughed again, blew smoke up at the hanging stained-glass lamp. "Might as well get some use out of them while they're here."

I asked if Pierre was around. I suspected not. There was a stillness about his place across from Cully's. I'd noticed it as I got out of my car. Plus, the faded brown grass growing among the broken patio stones of his walkway was splayed over top of the stones, suggesting that no one had walked that way for a while. But I knew from Cully that he wanted to talk to me, to tell his story for the book. And I wanted to seize any chance I got before I left.

No, Cully told me. "They took him away in an ambulance again." He'd fallen against the wood stove and burned himself badly. He was staying with a friend in Sarnia, and a nurse was coming every day to change the dressings.

I had met him briefly. Once when I was leaving Cully's, he was coming out of his place across the road; it was little more than a shed really, next door to the firehall where he had been living until the roof leaked too much. I remembered our brief conversation that day I ran into him; how skinny he was, his straightforward "I'm thirsty." He was hoping I'd give him a lift into town.

I reached over and touched Cully's arm. "I'm so sorry," I said. She looked at me again, shook her head, and pushed her hair back behind an ear. It reminded her too much of her mother. She hated it, she said, that there was nothing she could do.

I nodded. "Yes." That's all I could say; just acknowledge what she'd said. She looked up again. Our eyes met, then we each looked away. For want of something better to focus on, I looked at the smoke detectors in their shiny hard plastic casings. Somehow they reminded me of a line in Timothy Findley's novel about the First World War. It's a scene where Toronto matrons are handing out chocolate bars to soldiers boarding the troop train at Union Station, sending them off to the trenches. "Chocolate mitigating bullets," Findley had written.[1]

I got out the money I'd brought to buy a pair of Cully's moccasins. A member of my family was expecting a baby, and the tiny set Cully had shown me would be a perfect gift. Cully got talking about the community centre that had been promised as part of rebuilding Stoney. There was going to be a museum inside, and she was collecting things for it already. She'd found an old wooden bucket made from split black ash. It was kind of worn, she said, but she figured that was okay. I agreed. She had it stored in the back.

I put the baggie with the moccasins into my bag and reached for my jacket. I might not see her again till I came back next time, maybe not till next spring, I told her. I thought I had enough stories, enough material people had given me, that I could start pulling things together, maybe into a first draft of the book. Cully looked over at me and grinned.

Then she got up, came around the table, put her arms around me, and gave me a fierce, warm hug.

"I trust you," she said, her dark brown eyes looking at me fiercely. Tears welled up in mine as I hugged her back.

I SAT IN MY CAR outside, trying to decide what to do next. I still hadn't heard from Kevin, and there was no sign of him or his truck. I could see the maintenance shed from here, but I didn't want to go over; if Kevin was there, he'd be working. Plus, I didn't want to barge in when Worm might be around, too; I wanted to give him space for whatever he was dealing with. I brought up Marcia's number on my phone again and pressed connect. I'd called yesterday and left a message saying that I'd be leaving in two days. I'd like to at least say goodbye, maybe take her for a coffee, too, if she'd let me.

I heard the phone ringing and ringing at her end, and then she picked up. Yes, she could come for a coffee with me if I liked. And sure enough, she was standing on the stoop when I arrived, her purse and that old plastic shopping bag in her hands. A Tim Horton's coffee and a muffin each, we settled at a window table, one that Marcia had chosen far from the door so she wouldn't feel the cold draft. She said that she'd tried out those hand warmers I'd given her; they helped a little. She told me about the new medication she was on for her arthritis; she was still in a lot of pain, but it was better today.

Had she seen Kevin lately? I asked. She pressed her lips into a downward frown, gave her head that disgusted shake I'd come to know. No, she said. It depressed her too much to go back there. I still didn't know what the latest upsetting thing was, only guessed that it had to do with the government's ongoing control. If it had upset Bonnie, it might well have upset the others too. I asked if Marlin was back out fishing again. No, she said, that storm had been it for the season. She buttered the top half of her muffin and took a bite.

"I got that new water heater," she told me, and smiled. "Oh, that feels good, having a bath again."

Yes, I said, smiling too. She sipped her coffee, looked across at me.

"There should be a genealogy chart," she said emphatically, "because everyone who was involved is related."

Okay, I said, trying not to smile too much. Good. She was back – and telling me what to do.

She'd help me, she said.

I looked at her, noticed the little smile, and grinned.

"Thank you."

I said that I could start with what family information was in the documents she'd given me; we could work from there when I came back. How would that be?

She nodded; that would be fine. She took another bite of muffin and sipped her coffee. I told her that I'd found some material about burial grounds and why they were so central to Nishnaabe life. I thought some of that should go into the first chapter, too, to help set the scene. Along with the origin of the Three Fires Confederacy, the Royal Proclamation, the Treaty of Niagara, and Tecumseh with his dream of securing a substantial Nishnaabe homeland. And then the Huron Tract treaty, negotiations for which had begun not long after the War of 1812, when Tecumseh was killed.

"That treaty was really for you," Marcia said. "For the settlers."

I looked at her surprised, confused even. She raised her eyebrows, gave a little shrug. "We had the land before the treaty."

Yes, of course! In my mind I'd always seen that treaty as simply a historical fact, and it was. But it was a colonial fact. The colonial authorities had used the treaty as a tool to legalize taking land for themselves. The colonial authorities might have chosen to call the land "the Huron Tract," but it was Nishnaabe territory.

I pulled out my notebook and scribbled down what Marcia had just said. I'd have to double-check everything that I wrote by way of background, I thought. Not fact-check it; check it for bias. Hopefully there'd be more checking along the way, too, as I sent copies of every draft to Marcia and the others.

"Thank you," I said and picked up my coffee. Marcia reached for the butter packet, saw it was empty, and asked me to go see if they'd give her another one. I went to the counter, brought back two, sat back down and watched as she buttered the other half of her muffin. I sipped my coffee and looked out the window, letting the silence just be.

Marcia started talking about the language classes her mother, Melva, had given when they were both back living at Stoney Point. It had meant so much to her mother to relearn her language, Marcia had told me when I taped her stories. She'd all but lost it at residential school, where it was derided as backward, and speaking it was punished. Once Melva had had to watch and do nothing as her little brother was knocked right off his chair because the teacher hit him so hard, just for speaking Ojibwe.

Such a beautiful language, Melva always said, and Marcia had shared this joy as she too began to learn the language, and then to teach it. And the stories too. The stories kept the language alive, Marcia had told me, and the language kept the stories alive. All this was tied, in turn, into genealogy, the kinship connections with each other, with the ancestors and with this place. You couldn't separate one from the other, she'd said.

She looked up from her coffee. Had she told me about the hand puppet she'd made for teaching kindergarten children the language?

No, I said. She smiled. "Crazy Horse," she said. She called the puppet Crazy Horse, though in class she used the Ojibwe word.

"And the old people in the community were so happy," she said, "that I could pronounce that word, *bezhgoognzhii*, for horse." She took another sip of coffee, then folded the muffin paper together on her plate. I watched her as she continued to fold it into quarters and then smaller still.

"You know how when you get older, you remember what you learned as a child and you forget what you learned later on?" She looked out the window. "That's what's happening to me; I'm losing it." She looked at me as if to see whether I got it.

Yes, I understood. She's losing what should have been her mother tongue: her ancestral language, despite all she's done trying to keep it alive.

"I'm so sorry," I said, returning her look.

She nodded and looked out the window. Then she gave her shoulders a shrug I'd come to recognize as the decision to change the subject. She looked back at me, a little smile on her face.

"I've got something for you," she said, reaching down to the old shopping bag at her feet. It was the same bag she'd used to bring her copy of the Ipperwash Inquiry report the first time she'd come out with me for coffee. Of course, I'd wondered what was in the bag when I'd come to pick her up but knew this woman enough not to ask; she'd tell me or show me what was in there when she was good and ready.

Now she pulled a big green hardcover book out of the bag and held it out to me in both hands. It was a dictionary. I took it, with both hands too; it was heavy. I read the title: *Eastern Ojibwa-Chippewa-Ottawa Dictionary*.

Marcia had bought it for me at a bookstore in Sarnia.

"Look inside," she said. It showed how to pronounce the different vowels. It explained how the spelling of words varied from one local dialect to another, depending on how people were used to saying things in a particular place. In other words, I thought, the written word keeping faith with the oral, which was that much more embedded in the local.

I looked up at her, stunned that she would buy this book for me. I should pay you back, I said; the receipt was tucked inside, and I could see that it was more than a hundred dollars.

"No, this is my treat," she said, smiling in a way that was almost smug, certainly mischievous.

I pushed the dictionary across the table, asking if she'd write something in it.

She opened her purse and took out a pen, then opened the book to the inside title page.

She wrote "To Heather Menzies" and then the date. Under that, she wrote: "Best wishes with your writing," and signed her name.

She watched as I read what she'd written. "Do you like that?" she asked.

Tears came to my eyes. I looked up, nodded. "Yes," I said.

I felt that I'd just been blessed. Or my involvement in this book project had.

Marcia put the lid on her coffee and picked up her cup. She'd take the rest home, she said.

How about I get one for Marlin too, I asked.

She smiled. "He'd like that," she said. "Large triple triple."

19

The Poignant Blessings of
Relationship Building

Last stop. I recognized Janice's car, parked behind Colleen's in the laneway outside Bonnie's home in Kettle Point, and tucked mine in behind it.

As I came past the end of the fence into the yard, I saw a deer hanging from a big branch of the maple tree. The same block-and-tackle arrangement as I'd seen outside Glenn George's place. I wondered who'd shot it and brought it here. Maybe I'd find out, maybe I wouldn't. I knew that Fred had been a good hunter in his day. He also shared the work of skinning and butchering his kill with ones too old to hunt, sending each one home with an equal portion of meat. Bonnie had told me about this, too, the easy dignity of it, the inter-generational sharing.

I knocked, came in, and there was Colleen, just inside the kitchen, mop in hand.

"Hi, Spark," I said, daring to use her nickname. Big smile in response, as she offered to pour me a coffee. No, no; I was fine.

I put the carton of cream I'd brought on the counter and took my usual seat at the table. Bonnie and Janice had been to see their sister, who was in a home, sometimes strapped into a wheelchair by the staff to keep her from trying to get up.

"She has Alzheimer's real bad," Bonnie explained. But still she could recognize Bonnie.

"'Sister,'" Bonnie recalled Sue having said, the smile on her face speaking her joy at the connection still there between them. Sue had talked about the little people coming to help her, Bonnie said.

Janice made a fussing sound at her end of the table.

"She doesn't like to talk about this sort of thing," Bonnie explained. She continued telling me the story, how she'd asked Sue, "How many?" Bonnie held up her right hand, raised what looked like three fingers.

"Ah," I said, moved that she would tell me this, though not having a clue what three might mean, only that it meant a lot to Bonnie, who believed what her sister was seeing. I believed it too.

Buck came out of the bathroom, his hair wet from the shower. He still used his cane, but was leaning on it less, I noticed, as he moved his right foot forward.

"Great party, Ma," he said when he got opposite where we were sitting. He laughed. "Got nice and loud."

I'd known that something was in the works last time I'd dropped by. Bonnie had talked about getting the turkey into the oven. Summer had shown up, and Buck had stayed in the room to visit. Summer used to call him Uncle Godzilla, she'd told me; he'd carry her around on his shoulders, calling her "Baby Godzilla." Buck had got out his cell phone, pulled up some photos and handed the phone to me; these were his children, he said. One was coming over later.

Now, the day after his birthday party, Buck wanted to cut up the carcass and make turkey broth. "For Barb," he said, for Worm. Worm had started chemotherapy for cancer of the esophagus, and Barb was having trouble getting him to eat.

"So now I gotta get out my big soup pot again," Bonnie grumbled with a grin.

One of Shelly's daughters came in, bringing the latest news and gossip from the band office, where she worked. A big Pentecostal church was going to be built at Kettle Point, and rumour had it that the band council was helping to fund it.

"A helluva lot," Fred offered when everyone was speculating how much money the council might be contributing. He'd come into the room and now made his way toward the bathroom. Bonnie spoke to me quietly: "It makes it harder for Shelly's daughters doing their strawberry fasts."[1]

Yes, I said, guessing that she was referring to the power the Christian churches on the reserve still exerted, able to police Nishnaabe spirituality even here, still. In the quiet after the girls had left, I filled Bonnie in on my attempts to get those residential school photos from the United church in Grand Bend. The minister thought she'd found them. They were in a photo album that belonged to an aunt of the person who'd taken the pictures. But the album had been lent to a nephew, and she had no contact information for him.

I'd emailed the minister prior to coming on this visit, gently reminding her of her promise to try to get the album back. And she'd emailed back, sorry, until it comes back nothing can be done. I'd been angry when I'd read the email, this casual letting the matter drop. I'd put off answering for a few days, waiting to get past my initial righteous indignation, knowing that a lot of this reaction was me playing catch-up with my new awareness. Then I'd asked the minister gently what she "might be moved to consider as a next step."

I wanted to keep the sense of accountability alive in her, as it had come to be so vitally alive in me. But I couldn't guilt her. She had to feel it as I did now for it to be actionable – in concrete actions of reparation. Otherwise it would just be lip service, going through the expected motions. I ended the email by asking if she'd like to meet Bonnie sometime.

Now I asked Bonnie if she'd be willing to meet with this minister.

Yes, Bonnie said right away. She wanted me there too, she said. Then she headed to the kitchen counter, making sure Colleen was cutting up the turkey carcass right.

The back door opened, and a man I'd never seen before stepped inside. Bonnie looked up.

"Oh, yeah, hang on a minute," she said, and scooted her wheelchair back to the table where I'd noticed a file folder sitting when I arrived. She picked it up.

"Customary care," she said to me. "They want to know how we define it." She handed the file to the man, who'd stayed by the door, then came back to the table when he left.

"It's the word we came up with," she said, when they created Mnaasged Child and Family Services, the Nishnaabe version of the Children's Aid Society, in 2006. "We called it 'customary care.' It's just the way we usually do it – you know, take care of our kids. And now we've got these government people in head office in Toronto trying to define it: exactly what is customary care?" She shook her head and laughed.

I smiled, hearing what she was telling me. From the bits and pieces I'd picked up in various conversations, I also gathered that the woman whose children were being fostered within the community was doing better. She was spending more and more time with her children and might soon have them back again full-time. They hoped that this would become the normal way of doing things when families were in crisis, now that the Ontario government was finally recognizing Mnaasged Child and Family Services. Bonnie wasn't on the board anymore, although she's still one of its elders.

As usual, I was letting myself drift along in the time zone that seemed to prevail in this place: an endlessly evolving, intricately interconnected present. But surrendering to it was an ongoing process. It was an ongoing struggle, too: giving up being in control, removing my perspective, my

priorities, from the centre of things. It was almost like breaking the habits of an addiction, I thought. The compulsion is
so strong and needs to be resisted again and again and again.
It's like they say in Alcoholics Anonymous: one day at a time,
one moment of temptation resisted, and a new pattern laid
down more clearly, more believably, one day at a time.

It wasn't about removing myself completely from the
picture, or not implicating myself in the circumstances in
which I had found myself. It was about removing myself
from the centre of gravity here and opening myself to how
this changed everything I saw and came to grasp as real. This
was also where my unlearning got murky, and not easy to
stay with. This was where the disorientation, the sense of
being lost, got more intense. Because my sense of what was
real and relevant was in a twilight zone of change. It was evolving as I opened myself to the reality here: the people flowing
through Bonnie and Fred's kitchen, and all the others with
whom I had started to form relationships. These relationships
were the reality, or the medium out of which reality and its
meaning emerged.

They were a medium in an almost physical sense, too, just
like the medium in a petri dish where a bacterial culture is
grown, and also in the sense that Marshall McLuhan had
meant when he rephrased his famous "the medium is the message" as "the medium is the massage."[2] I had to stay immersed
in this medium, letting it massage the muscles of my mind.
I had to keep myself present, learning to attune my attention
to the patterns of how all these people in Bonnie's kitchen
and elsewhere related to each other in the simplest ways and
the smallest moments. I had to let the minutia in the flow of
moments seep and sink into me, becoming a whole new ge-
stalt as I let them be.

I remembered something Fred had said to me when word
of the latest crisis in the community came bursting in through
the back door. "What can you do," he told me, shaking his

head, his lips pressed tight together, and yet a slight smile on his face as he looked at me.

Yes, what can you do, I thought as I sat there, trying hard to just let things be, because on this particular day, it was hard. I hadn't checked in for my flights the next day, and there was freezing rain in the forecast, a possibility of snow. Plus, I had a purpose and agenda for this last visit. I had told Bonnie that it might be good to have a few more stories about what daily life at Stoney Point was like before the army came in 1942. I was suggesting we put this in the opening chapter so non-native readers would get a sense of the life – a whole, rich way of life – that had been interrupted when the army took over the reserve. She'd agreed and promised that we'd make time to record a bit more today. My digital recorder and microphone were still in my bag at my feet as I waited for when it seemed the right moment to get them out. Meanwhile, I sat there telling myself to let things be what they will be, and accepting one more coffee refill. I was glad that Fred generally made it so weak.

Another man came in the back door. He stepped into the kitchen and looked around. I recognized him from before but couldn't remember the circumstances, and we had never been introduced.

Bonnie gestured with her head. "He's up there with Buck," she said, and the man headed into the hall, to the family room. I wondered if they were watching more YouTube videos on hunting, like they'd been doing on Buck's birthday; Buck had laughed and said: "I'm a YouTube hunter!"

Bonnie looked at me, tilted her head again. "He's the one that shot that deer out there," she said. Now one of the granddaughters wanted to help skin it, and Fred was going to teach her.

BONNIE WHEELED HERSELF back into the kitchen area and heaved herself out of the wheelchair to check the water level in the soup pot. I heard her inhaling noisily, then "Yuh," as she lowered herself back into the chair, satisfied by the smell.

"That's good," she told Colleen, who was checking in now that she was done for the day. Colleen put on her jacket, and I went over to say goodbye.

Finally, it was quiet. It was also three o'clock in the afternoon; I'd been there since well before noon.

"Okay," Bonnie said. "Set that thing up." I got out my recorder and positioned the high-quality microphone I'd bought as an attachment. I noticed Fred as he came and sat down at the far end of the table. Bonnie looked as surprised as I was. He usually left the room if I was going to record anything. Maybe it was a coincidence, his coming into the room just now. No matter; I was glad of it, because he knew so much. Partly this was because knowing the language had allowed him to listen to the older ones who had all the knowledge and stories, and partly it was his own experience in the bush. He knew a lot.

Bonnie and Fred now told me about the root cellars every family on the reserve used to have, how they were built half underground, the snug smell of food security inside them. They talked about the outhouses and what they used to clean them, Bonnie regularly asking Fred, "What was that ... ?" and Fred usually having the answer. They talked about all the work bees through the year, the ice-hauling bees, the wood-cutting bees, the maple syrup time in the spring, the ice-fishing in the winter – all kinds of different work shared. And they talked about the medicines they got from the land, and the teachings they got from their animal relations as they observed what medicines different animals used themselves.

Fred mentioned something that sounded like *weekon*. It means rat root, or muskrat root, in English, he said.

"Looks like a cattail only smaller. You get the root of it, eh? Some people, they'll go get it out of the muskrat house too," Fred said. He chuckled. "But they don't take it all on him; it's his medicine, too, eh? They only take what they need.

"The moose, he goes for that, uh, like a water lily; the bottom of it." He laughed. "You don't hear moose goin' around sneezing. He keeps himself clean."

In the spring, there's medicine in the buds of the birch tree. "You chew on that, it cleans out all the toxins in your system," Fred said. "But only in the early spring."

He leaned forward and looked out the window at the old birch tree standing on one side of the front yard. He watches for the birds every spring, he said, coming to drink the sap water from the opening buds. "They come right in that old birch there," he said. "That's why they're up there, getting that medicine."

He turned and smiled at me, and in that instant when our eyes met, something happened. It could have been how Fred had tilted his head so he could look out the window, connecting with a spot high up in that beautiful old birch tree where he watches for the birds returning every spring. Or it could have been the joy that seemed to radiate off his face as he evoked this seasonal ritual, this moment of kinship with a bird seeking the sap's healing power after having endured a long winter too. A bird sharing its knowledge of this with human beings. It could also have been the fact that he was sharing this with me, letting me in on this and all it meant to him. It was as though he was inviting me in, not just into this circle of shared knowledge but into a kinship circle of sharing that included muskrats and birds too.

I felt as though I had crossed a bridge, as though I had caught a glimpse of the other shells on the wampum belt. Not just the purple shells representing the Nishnaabe canoes going their way, separate from the white people's sailing ships, but the white shells in which these purple lines were embedded: the cosmos that held them. I got a sense of what it was like to be stitched into that bed of white shells: a land shared with trees and birds and the relations between them too.

As I thought about this later, it occurred to me that there wasn't just a different narrative going on here – the colonial story of sovereignty and identity systematically denied, and the steadfast, dogged story of persistence in the face of this. There was a different narrative space. After all these visits over the past year and a half, I was becoming conscious of it. In that moment at Bonnie and Fred's kitchen table, I had entered it in my imagination, or it had entered me. It was surfacing in my consciousness – or at least an awareness of its existence was surfacing. It wasn't just a lived-in space either, though it was that. It was a lived and living space. It lived. It had integrity, as it was created every day, created and recreated through all the relationships that extended through it – including to the trees outside and the land beyond. Right here in this room I was immersed in it. I could feel it, sense it as alive: all the never-to-be-severed, loving, rooted connections.

Tears welled up in my eyes, and an ache bloomed in my chest. I looked at Fred, looked at Bonnie. I thanked them and thanked them again as I packed away my recording equipment. I was so touched, so moved, so grateful not only for what they'd gifted to me, these precious insights, but also for the fact that they had offered them to me. They had honoured me with their trust, and something more.

There was something else amidst my gratitude. "You've taught me to listen to my own ancestors," I blurted, more tears rising. I didn't know what I meant by what I'd just said, only that it was huge. It felt as though something had broken through that had been rising and surfacing for a long time within me.

But it was time for me to go. Fred came over and, as he had begun to do on recent visits, shook my hand goodbye. But this time he put his other hand on top of mine.

"G'waabmin Minwah," he said; he'd been teaching me a bit of the language, including this phrase for "see you in a little while." I said the words back to him, stumbled, tried again, and almost got it right. Fred just smiled and nodded.

Bonnie had wheeled herself off to her storeroom, and now she came back. She handed me a gift: a candle in a glass. There was an eagle head and some words: "Humility is to know yourself as a sacred part of Creation."

I crouched down and wrapped my arms around her. "Miigwech," I said. "Miigwech."

All words – even Ojibwe ones – seemed inadequate. I looked at Bonnie and she at me. Her eyes looked shiny with tears too. I'll be back in the spring, I said; I'll be in touch.

"Take care," Bonnie called as I left. "You too," I called back.

I WOKE UP at four o'clock the next morning with tears trickling across my nose and onto the pillow. I was aching both with sadness – at leaving – but also with joy and gratitude at the gift of learning I'd received here. I turned on the light, grabbed my journal, and wrote, "I haven't just learned about the way of life that prevailed and still prevails here. I've been brought into it, welcomed into its presence and given a sense of what it is like to live inside it – thanks to the generosity of Bonnie and Fred, and the others."

When I woke up again, it was daylight. It had snowed during the night, plastering everything in white. The clouds were breaking up, the sun coming out. And I knew what I had to do: I had to put more tobacco down.

I walked down the road toward the beach, my eyes as usual roving among the trees, which were covered with snow and, in the case of the towering white pine, weighed down with it. As I walked, I gazed deeply into the now-familiar space, my eye lighting on this tree and that, saying goodbye. I walked through the road-allowance parking area, past the spot where Dudley George had fallen when he'd been shot, and down to the beach: whitecaps as far as my eye could see, the water still carrying the burden of the storm.

I took out my tobacco, wanting to thank this beach and these waters, too, for all they had given me, even taught me. I had walked up and down this crescent stretch of fine sand at the end of almost every day of my time here each visit, especially this last one. I knew its sounds by heart, understood the curvature of its waves and wavelets, an eternity of call and response, water to land, land to water. It had helped to soothe me, calm me; helped me to think.

I gave myself permission to step over the small railing that marked the boundary of the Stoney Point Reserve; it ran all the way down from the dunes and across the beach into the water, in at least a symbolic attempt to keep tourists and summer campers out. I walked a few paces along the strip of beachfront that had re-emerged after the big storm. I watched the water come up toward my running shoes and recede, the sand shifting from shiny wet to matte. I watched this pattern repeat itself until I knew when to put my tobacco down.

Now!

I watched the shredded bits of tobacco move into the ebbing water, some of it returning, some drifting away.

I turned around. I didn't climb up the dune onto the land itself, continuing to respect it as Nishnaabe territory on which I could come only as a guest when visiting someone like Cully, or with someone like Marcia. Instead, I waited on the wind to help me. And sure enough, it did. My hand came up with an incoming gust. I opened my fist into its crescendo, and up and over it went, my handful of tobacco. As it rose, scattering in the wind, the morning sun caught it from behind, burnishing its brown into gold. And then it was gone, carried inland where I had hoped it might go, even to those big trees, conveying my thanks for their blessing.

As I drove through Forest on my way to the airport on the outskirts of London, I was tempted to stop at that rickety little Airbnb where I'd stayed on my first two trips here. I should put some tobacco down there, I thought, because it had served me well. It was so clearly *not* my space, and it wasn't *their* space either. It was nobody's space, sort of a transit zone of reckoning with necessary change.

I arrived at the airport, returned my rental car, checked in, and made my way to the boarding lounge. There was a text from Kevin. I'd felt his absence in my parting rounds the day before. I'd texted him several times since seeing him when I'd first arrived two weeks earlier. He hadn't replied once, and I had to leave it at that. I'd tried not to take it personally, but still feared that he'd written me off. Now here he was, apologizing that he didn't have the energy to meet up with me.

"I did my best to get this land back and justice for Dudley. Now I'm just trying to find some of what I missed in this life before it's over. Because that is one thing that is guaranteed: this life is far too short! So I apologize for not being of any more help to you, and hope you can understand why ... Your friend from along the road, Kevin Simon."

I boarded my flight and flew home to BC. I'd held the microphone so that people like Kevin could tell their story. Now I would transcribe those stories, piece them together with as much integrity as I could into the manuscript of a possible book. I'd bring a first, second, third draft back here and we'd work on changing it, making it the story they wanted to tell, and how they wanted to tell it. Maybe I could help them find a publisher or an agent who could take it from there. And maybe the book would be published, so that the truth – their truth of what had happened here, what they've been trying to achieve and why – would finally be known.

20

Surrendering Professionally

Self-doubt returned as I prepared to start writing. The longer
I sat with the voices of those who had entrusted me with their
stories, the more inadequate and unqualified I felt. My need
for defensiveness had gone, or perhaps my willingness to tol-
erate it had gone. It had taken me a long time to realize how
much my posture, my choice of words, my patterns of thinking and even of listening had stood in the way of serving the
Nishnaabeg with integrity. Now I realized that they still could
– as long as I left them unexamined and unchallenged. There
was more surrendering to do, I realized, especially now that
I was starting to embrace this as something positive rather
than resisting it as criticism and blame, becoming defensive,
taking it all personally. It had taken a while, but now I could
at least see how much I was part of the problem I'd shown up
thinking I could help to solve. I could acknowledge that, at
least, and almost laugh at myself about it.

How blind I'd been at the beginning. Yet, looking back, it
was so obvious– how I almost epitomized the problem in the
way I had arrived! Introducing myself, presenting myself as
ready to step into a treaty relationship, was like a magic trick

I performed: Presto and there I was, gone. Showing up to be accountable as a colonial settler and disappearing myself in the same breath – into this cover-up. The arrogance of it: the colonial power of naming slipping out of my mouth, disguised as an act of humble rapprochement. It wasn't for me to define myself in these terms; I had to earn them, grow into them, if that was even possible. Maybe it wasn't. And it certainly wasn't for me to say that it was.

I doubt I fooled my Nishnaabe hosts. But I initially fooled myself with my self-cloaking act. I was the invisible woman; or rather, the colonial mindset I'd grown up with and lived most of my life moulded by and perpetuating was invisible to me – until I began this project. Over the past nearly two years I had been forced to realize that my seemingly innocuous ignorance – innocuous to me, at any rate – had also been a convenient one because it allowed the status quo of systemic colonial injustice toward Canada's First Peoples to carry on. I had encountered a microcosm of this at work at the site of the former cadet training camp still occupying the Stoney Point Reserve. And I had learned to connect the dots between my ignorance and the convenient ease with which a colonial status quo can be perpetuated – there and elsewhere.

I really only started connecting the dots between this on-going injustice and my own behaviour as I got to know people like Bonnie, Cully, Marcia, and Kevin, taking in the realities of their lives. My awareness only surfaced and took hold inside of me as I worked with their stories, listening again and again to the recorded conversations. As I spotted my gaffes, sometimes indicated just by an awkward pause, I began to see what was so problematic, not just in what I said but in how I talked and took up space. I had kept turning that shared conversation into a conversational space familiar to me as I interrupted with a clarifying question or whatever.

I'd started to change the relationship, to truly listen and hear them, while I was there. But now I was alone in front of my computer screen in my home office. Could I pull this off, this proof of a changed relationship in book form? It would be an oral history, with large chunks of direct quotes drawn from the stories I'd recorded and the Ipperwash Inquiry witness transcripts, the voices of many others as well as the core dozen or so I'd met. That much was easy, or relatively so. But it was up to me to frame these storied voices with historical background and connective narrative lines. Could I stay true to the voices as I wrote those pieces of text?

It's hard to admit it now, but at first I took for granted that I could speak for them, the Nishnaabeg of Aazhoodena, simply because I was a professional writer with many books and a couple of awards to my name. That I was a settler-colonizer didn't affect my professionalism or my integrity as a writer. I knew how to frame their stories into a book, how to line up their words on the page. Or so I told myself.

I realize now that I'd internalized the effects of their having been spoken for, their speaking on their own terms having been denied, their words having been downgraded to the status of mere quotes in historical and anthropological texts, in realms like the libraries and archives where I took my cultural bearings. In fact, and this has been the hardest to admit, at first I was almost treating their stories as raw material, input to a process I would manage, professionally, on their behalf. I'd done this all my writing life.

The circle could well have remained closed, and I could have perpetuated it with my nullifying assumptions – the unexamined assumptions I brought to my work as a writer – because initially I still regarded these as neutral. I wanted to assume they were neutral, because they'd served me so well, helping me gain the success I had. I didn't want anything to challenge that. These were simply professional norms with universal applicability, not at all tainted by colonial/settler thinking. Surely not! And so I had resisted.

But as I kept listening to the taped voices and stories, I began to acknowledge the patterns at work in my mind and take responsibility for them, the internalized blinkers and filters that blocked my ability to truly hear what people like Marcia and Cully were saying to me. And I didn't want that; I'd come to care for them and to feel personally accountable to them. If I wanted a genuine relationship with the Nishnaabe I had met and even begun to love, I had to keep confronting the colonized-colonizing self within me that blocked and corrupted my ability to see and hear the Nishnaabe in the fullness of their humanity – that is, on their own terms. Perhaps the fullness of my own humanity was at stake here, too; though this thought only came later.

I started to write, full of self-doubt still, but carrying on. And the writing project I'd taken on as a big, lofty historical reparation project out there in the larger world shifted once again inside me. It became both intimate and personal *and* public and professional. It was a reparation project personally and professionally. I had to repair[1] myself, not just as a settler with an inherited colonial mindset but as a seasoned "know-it-all" professional writer. Decolonizing my mind was not just a good intention anymore. It was the work I needed to do on myself professionally if I wanted to fulfill the commitment I'd made to these people in 2018, when I accepted their invitation to help them tell their story. In other words, the book itself had to reflect this reparation; the proof would be there. It was only as I sat there writing, day after day, that the immensity of this hit me.

WHILE THE WRITING continued through weeks and into months, the news was tracking the spread of a possible epidemic called COVID-19, first as mysterious satellite images out of China, then mass illness and death across Italy, and from there through Europe and then across North America.

One Sunday when I called Bonnie, one of her granddaughters was really sick with it. Cully texted me to say that Pierre had it and was in hospital. ICU, she thought when we talked on the phone; no visitors allowed, she said, clearly distressed.

When I went shopping for food, people were wearing masks and gloves, stocking up on disinfectants and wiping down everything they touched. It was a relief to be in my own little bubble of isolation, home alone with my trusted and familiar writing tools.

In late winter, I finished a first draft, made copies for the four people I'd found myself working with the most, and sent them off. But I couldn't go there to review it with them in person. The reserve was in lockdown. On the phone, Bonnie said that at least once a week there'd be a hearse and parade of cars going by, taking someone on a last ride through the reserve before the burial. When I texted Kevin, he was in quarantine because someone he worked with had COVID. No, he hadn't started reading what I'd sent yet; busy, he said, but he'd try. When I finally got through to Marcia, she was upset because the police had impounded her car for forty-five days. Marlin had been driving, she told me, going into Forest to get her medication, and the cops had pulled him over; something about a ticket not having been paid. But the cost, Marcia said! I asked, and just the cumulative daily charge at the car pound would be over five hundred dollars. I sent her a card with a cheque inside: a small contribution to help out, I said.

In the end, no feedback. Was it everything else that was going on, or were they not identifying the book enough as theirs? I'd put my name on the cover page, but had put theirs first, in a form I hoped would honour the collective authorship they wanted, with none of their names on the cover. I'd put: "the people of Aazhoodena/the Stoney Point Reserve and Heather Menzies." I asked a couple of friends if they could read the draft. My friend Dona Harvey, who'd been a newspaper editor, offered many helpful comments. Another, a former book publisher, worried about my name being on the title page, identifying me as the one doing the writing. Clearly this was a problem. I was a problem, if not *the* problem.

Sure, I was the one with the computer. I was the one with the skill set they said they needed. And I'd been invited to help. But I wasn't one of them. Moreover, I was on the side of Canadian history that had suppressed their voices for centuries, the side that had written and spoken for them.

I found myself remembering something I'd written in the late 1980s amidst the controversy that erupted when Women's Press in Toronto rescinded publishing contracts with two white writers on the grounds of "structural racism." While the media debate focused on censorship and freedom of expression, I wanted writers to reflect on authorial voice and its limitations, and the ethics writers needed to bring to this issue in recognizing those limitations – especially in this historical time. I ended my piece, published in the Writers' Union of Canada newsletter, by saying, "Nor do I construe it as a form of censorship of the creative process as much as a corrective for the prior censorship implicit in the established representations of humankind through a voice which has been overwhelmingly white, middle class, heterosexual and male."[2]

As I reread the piece, I noticed that I'd quoted a line by the character M. Butterfly in an award-winning play by that name, in which he explains his confidence in daring to impersonate a woman: "Only a man knows how a woman is supposed to act."[3] Exactly, I thought.

I was clearly in the wrong now, at least structurally. And yet here I was, still in these relationships, ethically committed to this handful of people who had entrusted me with the task of writing their stories into a book, twenty-five years after Dudley George's death. It was also a story that a historian, Donald Smith at the University of Calgary, had identified as a gap in the historical narrative.[4] But filling that gap with integrity meant ensuring that the book told the Nishnaabe story from their point of view, and I couldn't guarantee that I could do this.

So: Continue with this collaboration or step away? Then I thought of what Nishnaabe scholar and author Lindsay Keegitah Borrows had said in a webinar I watched when I was trying to write. First, "We have more in common than we have differences," and, later, urging settlers and settler organizations not to be afraid of "amplifying [Indigenous] voices."[5]

But what if I distorted those voices in the process? That was the risk, and also the responsibility. It depended (to a certain extent anyway) on my ability to respond to the Nishnaabe who had entrusted me with this task; that seemed to be what accountability meant here. Their response to me would be my guide. I might be able to address the ethics involved if I treated this not as abstract absolutes but as relational. The relationships, even friendships, I had begun to form with Bonnie, Marcia, Cully, and Kevin mattered to me. I hoped they'd keep me honest, and that this might be enough.

The struggle continued, or perhaps I should say continues. I finished a second draft, sat on it, reworked it into a third and then a fourth draft, repositioning myself on the cover page to "assistant," and sent it off. It was summer by now, July 2020, and I took the risk of returning to Ontario to meet with them. This was also because, through an e-introduction from a senior writer friend, I had sent the manuscript to a big publishing conglomerate, where the receiving editor was initially so enthusiastic that a contract offer seemed imminent. Wearing a facemask and a plastic visor, I flew east, quarantined for five days, had myself tested and, with a clean bill of health, finally headed to Aazhoodena/Stoney Point. Whether it was the prospect of the book actually having a chance of being published or that I'd finally delivered something they could embrace as theirs, everyone was ready to talk when I arrived. Kevin showed up with a copy of a family history that traced the four main families associated with Aazhoodena back to Tecumseh's sister Tecumbeesh, and Manidoka; Waapagance, who'd been chief at Aazhoodena at the time the Huron Tract treaty was negotiated; and Oshawanoo, who married the daughter of one of the earliest chiefs at Kettle Point.

As we sat in his truck with a Tim Horton's coffee each, Kevin also broached the subject of how I'd written about the Peace Tree being planted in May 1993 as part of a burying-the-hatchet ceremony. I'd quoted from the Ipperwash Inquiry witness testimony of Clifford George in recreating that moment, where he'd talked about their throwing plastic toy hatchets into the hole they'd dug for the small tree.

"My auntie Cheryl, she married Darryl Stonefish – he's from Moraviantown, down by the Thames," Kevin began, staring out the truck windshield toward the lake. "I believe they were involved in the burying of the hatchet," he continued. "They were the ones that got the hatchet." Made of black stone, it was a combination of pipe plus hatchet. "It was the real deal ... The war pipe was what that was ..." I listened in awe, both at what Kevin told me, and how. It was all so respectfully done: not so much correcting what Clifford George – one of the elders who'd led the way home that day in 1993, and who had died during the course of the inquiry – had said as a witness at the inquiry, just adding to it.

At Marcia's place, we went over the first draft of a genealogy chart I'd sent. She'd already added some names before I got there. Now, with her son Marlin helping out, we fleshed it out further. I showed it to Bonnie, who corrected the birth order in her own family line. I took it over to Cully, who added the name of her brother Michael, who died of pneumonia at six months of age. We started working on a map too. And every day I checked my email for something from the publisher. I'd been expecting something any day, for almost a month by now. Finally the editor wrote, apologizing but saying there was a problem. He didn't say it in so many words, but my being a white person was clearly the problem. End of story, I thought as I shared this hard news with the four Nishnaabe with whom I was collaborating. I was so sorry, I said, feeling that I'd let them down. Bonnie put her hand on my shoulder. Cully said, "Don't give up on us." If need be, Bonnie said, we'll self-publish.

So I carried on, asking them about revisions. But instead of just asking them what I'd gotten wrong or was missing and then falling silent so they could have their say, I'd notice myself saying things like, "You might want to consider." Saying it politely, of course. Being politely pushy, but still pushy; still taking up space with my thinking, not theirs.

I paid attention to the response I got: seldom overt push-back; more often a quiet, dignified, stubborn silence. Nothing said, and yet. I learned to consider it more an absence of presence, perhaps even a withholding of presence. I wasn't yet deemed ready or able to receive. I had more learning to do, more distance to close, before they would fully recognize their story in what I was writing and claim it.

I leaned into the silence and what it could teach me. Was there more inadvertent colonial thinking – even racism – at work in this or that instance? It wasn't that I considered their thinking to be less worthy than mine. Mostly I just kept anticipating what a publisher would expect. I tried to tell myself that this was a technical matter, really, just strategic thinking to get the book published, because secretly I hadn't given up on finding a publisher that would bring this story to the larger world. I also kept catching myself needing to be the one with suggestions. It was almost compulsive, I noticed: a need to do this not so much to assert superiority as simply to justify my presence and my role. It was strange; as though the superiority trap I kept triggering myself into was a two-sided coin, with an inferiority complex as its shadow, flip side. And being a writer was my cover, allowing me to flip the coin and regain some measure of clarity and certainty by being the one on top of things, the one in the know.

It was a paradox. I had to be confidently and fully present as just me with the people I was working with and getting to know in order to genuinely become their writing *assistant*, no longer the "professional writer." The hardest learning lay here, confronting this contradiction: just being – being uncertain even – versus playing a definite role. I was pretty sure that wrestling with something as simple as my need for certainty was a way of wrestling with the privilege and power of colonialism. Seeking certainty[6] was a cover for this. I also felt sure that staying in the uncomfortable realm of uncertainty and the powerlessness of not knowing was crucial if I wanted to at least mitigate the appropriation of their voices.

I've always felt that imagination isn't about making things up. It's about making room to let the full experience of experience in. Now I thought, it's a variation on the notion of surrender: letting go of resistance and letting in what's out there, on its terms.

I had to keep challenging myself, and the more I did this, the more I could see how unexamined things like "professional" status helped perpetuate the larger status quo. And it opened my mind, to see more possibilities in the notion of "surrendering." I could see the continuity from "surrendering space" on a personal level, in one's own mind, to surrendering space on a more institutional level, where professional roles are played, and one's status in those institutions is maintained, or not.

As I kept writing, and draft 4 of the oral history became drafts 5 and 6, I realized the uniqueness of the journey I've been on, and the challenge. I kept catching myself on seemingly innocuous things: my mind so eager to come up with a metaphor or simile – it's like this or that. No! This was more taking control, I realized; using my familiar interpretive lenses to make the unfamiliar familiar. I had to keep telling myself, just listen to them and let them in. Letting a sense of what's being said emerge and, with that, the word most appropriate for linking this quoted excerpt to the next one.

As George Orwell, who so acutely understood the colonizing power of language, put it once, "Let the meaning choose the word, and not the other way about."[7]

I submerged myself more and more, going deeper into the unknown, the unfamiliar behind the words and stories, and into the possibility of learning to know differently, letting the "getting to know you" ways of knowing get me there. It was uncomfortable, like becoming a cub reporter all over again, a neophyte writer. But as I simply let go, let in, and let be, I relaxed, trusting the listening process, because I wanted to fully hear and respect what Bonnie, Marcia, and the others were confiding in me. I kept going back to this as my compass; back to the recordings and the transcripts, re-immersing myself in the original voices, waiting for insights and the sense of what they were saying to surface in their own time.

The process required patience and sitting through a lot of fear and temptation because I am so used to translating the unknown into the known or knowable, using the knowledge and thinking tools I have. They're handy hinges and hooks for linking the new to established, so-called universal, frames of meaning. All these tools of my trade had served me well. The habits were hard to give up.

When I first reflected on this, I thought of it in fishing terms, the right word or image likened to a fish slipping off the hook back into the depths of its own realm if I wasn't patient, if I pulled on the rod too soon. Then it occurred to me that I should forget about fishing, lines, and hooks. I had to keep my thinking submerged. I had to stay in the medium, tune in to its rhythms and flow. That was the message. The fish and the living water were one. It was a whole different approach to story and to knowing how to know. All immersed in relationships.

The self-doubt continued. It even got worse later on when first one and then a second book contract offer eventually emerged. I had been squeezed in what some have called the culture wars of recent decades, and I learned how helpless one can be when the powers that be exercise that power and control. I had learned to be afraid.

Many nights I woke up at three o'clock filled with dread, afraid of where all this might lead. I even wrote in my journal one wakeful night, "I don't need the trolls coming at me through social media feeds. They're under the bridge in my mind. Go back, go back, they shriek. Try crossing this bridge and we'll eat you! My uncertain mind turns to mush."

Yet I was *trying* to cross the bridge, trying to establish a meaningful relationship – if not a treaty one, then at least one that would lay the groundwork for reconciliation. I didn't want to censor or self-censor that. I wanted to cross a bridge, or maybe help build one, using those three connecting shells of the Two Row Wampum: respect, friendship, and peace/justice. I wanted to believe that there was a way to share our humanity by respecting difference, if I could "amplify" the voices representing some of that difference honourably. And so I carried on, living with the risk and the responsibility, sleep-fractured night after sleep-fractured night.

21

Helping Prepare a Spirit Plate

It was July 2021 when I returned to Kettle and Stoney Point – or, as I was starting to think of it, Nishnaabe territory – ready to review a seventh draft of the manuscript. As usual, I'd made copies for everyone and sent these in the mail for all the collaborators to read. I checked into the Pinewood Motel, and started on my rounds.

Marcia was ready when I arrived, her copy of the manuscript all marked up with pencil. She had it in her arms, still in the Express Post cardboard envelope it had come in, and was standing on the side-door stoop when I pulled in and parked.

We'll sit out here, she said, indicating the picnic table with Marlin's work tools and some machine parts on top. I cleared these to one end. This was fine, Marcia nodded, then came round and sat down, her back to the road. She had a zippered pencil case full of pens and pencils, a sharpener and eraser, plus a ruler so we could go through her copy line by line. She'd circled everything she wasn't happy about, including several references to "occupation." This was something we'd talked about before. Many of these circled words were in quote marks, and the quotes were the words of the Nishnaabe themselves, including her own son. Marcia had circled that one too. She was angry and wanted them all changed. Sure, that's the word the media used, and everyone had more or less accepted.

"But for us, it wasn't an occupation," Marcia insisted, "not like you do an occupation and then go home. We *were* home."

As we sat side by side at the picnic table outside her house, on cushions that Marlin had brought out so we would be comfortable, I used my pencil to jot down the essence of the clarification that was needed. The importance of shifting the paradigm in how the media and other people think. I'd find a spot where we could insert this, I said, and show it to her later. We carried on, with Marcia using her ruler to keep our eyes focused on each line as she read it out loud.

She stopped at the reference to the Huron Tract treaty; she'd crossed that out. But that's what it's known as, I said, as gently as I could. She sat back and looked at me hard.

"Not by us," she said.

Yes, I said, not by you, and I realized the enormity of the insult. The colonial authorities had called this part of Nishnaabe territory a "tract" and named it after a nation whose territory was mainly to the north, around Georgian Bay and Lake Simcoe – a nation that they called "Huron," derived from the French word *hure*, referring to the bristly hair on a boar's head,[1] not as the Wendat identified themselves.

But if I delete it and just leave the date, I said, readers are going to wonder whether this is the treaty being referred to. You use existing knowledge as a bridge to new knowledge.

Marcia shook her head impatiently. She didn't want to go along with that. She closed the manuscript and crossed her arms over the top of it. Were we finished for the day? I hoped not. Eventually Marcia relented, and we got back to work. Sometimes I would get impatient with her. Sometimes she would get impatient with me. And we carried on.

A week or more later, we were done. And then things started falling into place fast. The same editor who'd been unable to persuade his superiors in the big publishing house to take a chance on the book had reached out to a friend, a Nishnaabe literary agent. She read the manuscript, liked its oral history approach, decided that my forebears' connection to the treaty legitimized my involvement, and took on representing the Nishnaabe storytellers informally. One of the contract offers was from UBC Press. Moreover, Justice Sidney B. Linden, who'd chaired the Ipperwash Inquiry and had been cordially responsive to email queries I'd sent to him as I'd worked on the book, sent an email introducing me to a friend with whom he'd worked to establish Pro Bono Ontario. The staff there, in turn, persuaded two partners in the Toronto office of a major law firm to represent the Nishnaabe in contract negotiations.

I outlined all this as I visited around with the manuscript, but held off detailing the contract offers until we could all meet together, if we could. We met at Cully's place, all but Bonnie present. Cully offered Marcia her padded black office chair with a lever underneath for adjusting the height. Marcia sat down in it with a smile and almost immediately suggested a way of characterizing their collective authorship on the front cover. Aazhoodenaang Enjibaajig, she said. That's how the elders, including her own parents, had started referring to themselves during their long years of protest leading up to the decision to stop waiting for the government's permission and simply go back home.

What does it mean? Cully asked. "The ones who come from Aazhoodena," Marcia said. Kevin nodded, and at a nod from Cully, I wrote that down. I would run it past Bonnie when I took everything over to her.

I'd anticipated that they would ask my advice on which contract offer to accept, so I'd canvassed friends who'd had careers in publishing and had either retired or moved on to other things. I relayed the advice I'd gotten from them, and despite UBC Press offering a smaller advance, the group decided to go with them. Then came the signing. Though the collective authorship was meant to include everyone whose story and voice was in the book, there had to be individual people behind it on the contract. I suggested that it be the four of them who'd been working with me the most. One after another, they signed the contract, and others signed as witnesses. Then we talked about the foundation they wanted to set up to receive the royalties so they could use them to revitalize Aazhoodena. But the pro bono lawyers advised postponing this until the book made enough money to warrant this. Until then, they suggested that the Nishnaabe co-authors just agree informally among themselves on how to disburse the royalties.

I wanted to honour the moment with a feast, copying some of what I'd learned from Bonnie, plus what I'd read about feasts and ceremony in books. Marlin sold me a bunch of pickerel he'd gotten up early that day in order to bring in fresh. Marcia gave me her recipe for bannock. Cully would have us all come to her house; she wanted a spirit plate made up for Dudley.

I drove to Grand Bend, to the home of two members of the right-relations group at the local United church, Virginia and John Scott. The minister was still away on leave, taking care of her aging parents during COVID. But these two were happy to stand in for her. They gave me full access to their kitchen so I could prepare the fish, plus a potato salad and the bannock mixture, and they lent me bowls and pans in which to carry all the elements of the feast to the gathering.

I had bought paper plates and plastic cutlery at the local dollar store. We passed these around and everyone helped themselves to food. Kevin showed me how much of everything to put on the plate that was to be the spirit plate, and

I did as he directed. At his nod, I put it down beside me. Then he got out his lighter and reached for the fresh braid of sweetgrass he had ready. He opened up one end of it with his fingers, lit the grass, then blew out the flames so a nice smudging smoke would remain. He wafted this over the spirit plate and spoke a prayer to the Creator giving thanks for this food, for this gathering, and for this book coming together at last.

After we ate, Marcia said we should take the spirit plate to the burial grounds. We drove there in my rental car, with Kevin's stepson, Isaiah, in the back seat and Marcia beside me holding the paper plate of food carefully in her lap.

We'd take it to her father's burial place too, Marcia said, because the spirit plate was for them all, all the ones who'd struggled to reclaim their homeland, Daniel and Dudley included. We walked up the slope in silence, came to the burial sites, and stood there. Marcia said something about never having done this before, and then she stepped forward, said a few words of prayer in a voice so low I couldn't make out the words, and set the plate down on the ground.

We all had tobacco and put that down. And then, while Isaiah wandered off, Marcia and I carried on standing there in silence. I found myself offering my own inward prayer of thanks, and also a word of greeting to the spirit of Dudley in this place. I looked around, idly watching Isaiah, and remembered something I'd read about ceremony shifting or even raising "consciousness,"[2] and what someone had said about a ceremony of reparations around a former residential school she'd been part of: how it "gives you a sense of belonging and that's a whole opposite to abandonment."[3] Isaiah had noticed that a branch had fallen into the burial grounds, and had gone to pick it up. Now I watched him carry it to the old back fence and heave it over into the bush. And then we drove back.

IT WASN'T ENTIRELY happily ever after from then on; there was still more learning to do. When Bonnie, Marcia, and the other two had signed the contract, they also signed a document the pro bono lawyers had approved, deputizing me to act as their go-between with UBC Press as production moved forward. I was determined to be just that and only that – a go-between. I wasn't going to presume to speak for them; I didn't want to assume a thing.

And so when the copy-edited manuscript arrived, I flew back to Ontario to review it with them. They didn't like what the copy editor had done in many instances, such as changing all their *won'ts* to *will nots*. They didn't, or did not, care if this was what the style guide said, either; they didn't think all those contractions needed to be "corrected." This was an oral history, told in their way of talking, and they wanted it to be true to that. So in all the instances where I'd written "can't" and the copy editor had rewritten it as "cannot," they wanted them changed back. This is how we talk, sitting around the table here, Cully told me. "The other way it's like being in an English class."

In round one of my feedback to the editor, some of the changes back to the original were accepted. More in round two.

And then there was the press's policy to use the term *Indigenous,* not *Indian* or *Native.* The co-authors didn't like that either. Bonnie, Marcia, Cully – they were all used to saying *native* and *non-native,* and that's how I'd originally put it in the manuscript. But the manuscript came back with everything changed to *Indigenous.* And the problem was that this was based on a book called *Elements of Indigenous Style,* published in 2018 and written by an Indigenous man, Gregory Younging, long-time managing editor of Theytus Books. They'd never heard of this guide, and in the end I thought that wasn't the problem or even the issue. The power dynamic of colonialism was (and still is) the imposition of control from an imperial centre, often from a distance. Unilaterally using terms like *Indigenous* seemed like replacing one form of control with another.

When I got home, I pulled Younging's book off my shelf and reread the foreword by Warren Cariou, Canada Research Chair in Narrative, Community, and Indigenous Cultures at the University of Manitoba. Cariou notes that the guide is written in a style "that puts readers at ease and positions them ... in a conversation."[4] The book's ethos, he writes, "is contained in the advice that there is no substitute for engaging in a relationship with the Indigenous Peoples who are represented in a text. This book foregrounds the Indigenous methodology of working from the basis of relationships, and thus it is an excellent example of decolonial scholarship."[5]

Well, I thought, the publisher was now part of the relationship I had begun to form with the Nishnaabe co-authors. If the editors at the press wanted this to be a respectful relationship, and I knew they did, this meant respecting how the Nishnaabeg wanted to self-identify. It meant being responsive to them, not rigid. I approached a more senior staff person, the production editor, about adding a couple of sentences to the introduction to contextualize this choice. Agreed. And so we continued.

The winter dragged on, with minor corrections and edits before the manuscript was ready for typesetting. Then there were page proofs to read and an index to review. But there'd been another COVID-19 outbreak on the reserve, and it was in lockdown. So I couldn't go back, and it was hard to get people on the phone. Still, I thought, I could handle this on my own; an index is just an index. Then I caught myself: Was that another assumption about what's "normal"?

I printed it off and flipped through the pages, all seventeen of them, single-spaced. It looked so clean and neat, so well thought out, and so complete. There was only one query from the indexer, and that was minor. How to know if something's missing? I thought. I owed it to the Nishnaabe co-authors to check, thoroughly. It had never occurred to me that there might be colonial bias in an index, but maybe there was.

Clan. That was the first word I thought of as missing as I read the page proofs for typos, the first absence I detected in the index. But what about *dodem,* the Ojibwe word for clan? I put both words into the index and inserted all the page references where the word came up.

Doctrine of Discovery? That concept still loomed large in how the Nishnaabeg individuals in the book had experienced history, and it was certainly mentioned in the book. It should be referenced in the index too.

What about the word for nation builders? *Nation builders* was in the index. But the term that the elder Abraham George had come up with was Etwaagnikejig. The Ojibwe word should be in there, maybe even as the primary reference, I thought; the index entry for nation builders could have "see *etwaagnikejig*" beside it.

The more I worked on this, the more gaps I could see and the ineluctable bias behind them. There was an entry for 'Great Lakes Region.' But why not add *Gichi-gaming,* the Ojibwe word for the great waters and waterways of their territory? There was an entry for Tecumseh, but not for Obwandiac, or Pontiac, a less-remembered historical figure. Here was a chance to reverse that historical forgetting, so I added him as two entries: both as he's remembered by Indigenous peoples in stories passed down about what prompted King George III to issue his Royal Proclamation in 1763, and as he's been named (as Pontiac) in English textbooks.

The indexer was responsive and even ran with this, suggesting more cross-references; more little bridges in the mind.

By this point I was tired. I'd been working on this book for longer than I'd worked on any other. I also knew that it was the most important writing I'd ever undertaken. Not just for the challenge to listen, to look, and to really hear and see, but also for the responsibility and the uncertainty of whether I could fulfill it. I lost a lot of sleep worrying, and spent a lot of time rewriting.

I'm fortunate to have a wood stove with a glass front door, and I often spent my evenings just sitting in front of the fire, my eyes on the dancing, shape-shifting flames, letting my thoughts drift as the fire subsided, becoming a smouldering bed of embers pulsing with heat and residual luminosity. Some evenings, especially during the COVID lockdown when I couldn't get back to see the Nishnaabe men and women who were becoming my friends, it was as though they visited me. Memories of moments would surface, snatches from the conversations we'd had without the recorder on, little things they'd spontaneously shared. These flickered in and out of my mind, much like the last flickering tongues of fire itself: some brought home the deficit of justice I kept witnessing, others the possibilities I'd glimpsed on the other side of denial, beyond the walls of colonial thinking.

In a Sunday phone visit with Bonnie, she told me that she'd just been diagnosed with spinal cancer. She told me not to worry, but of course I did, and many evenings I found myself remembering visits with her, including the last recording, when she and Fred had shared so many stories with me so generously. I remembered how raptly I'd paid attention when listening to them talk, especially about the medicines they learned from the animals, and how they'd learned this. They learned simply by living side by side with them in ways akin to theirs, attuned to the patterns of their behaviour. They didn't just live *in* a network of relationships with all kinds of beings – the more-than-human as well as human beings. Their lives were the mesh of that network. They lived it. That was their map of the world and how to thrive in it.

I remembered being hungry to hear these stories, voraciously hungry! It was as though I was starved or sick, as though these stories themselves were medicine. Again and again I recalled Fred's face as he looked out the window to the spot high in the old birch tree where the birds came to get the rising sap in the early spring, then his looking at me to see if I got it. And the hugeness of the Yes! that I'd felt. I remembered that too.

It was as though my capacity for knowing had grown, or some part of it had been missing, or had gone missing and was back, had been reawakened. How had I put it? "You've taught me how to listen to my ancestors."

I still didn't know why I'd said that or what it meant; but as I sat there gazing into the glowing embers of the dying fire, it occurred to me that my journey wasn't over. I wasn't an outsider anymore. I wasn't an insider to something different either, but implicated. I was starting to orient myself to its gravitational field, starting to get my bearings from its possibilities, and this gave me hope.

22

Continuing the Journey
Toward a Possible Settler Counter-Narrative

The book was published, finally. It had the title *Our Long Struggle for Home: The Ipperwash Story*, which the Nishnaabe co-authors had chosen. And the photo on the cover was one that Cully had pulled off a shelf full of quilting and sewing stuff. It showed her grandchildren Jana and Aidan (Dudley's great-niece and -nephew) wearing Nishnaabe regalia made and beaded by Cully; they are walking away from the camera along a path near the water in their traditional territory.

The book launch was held in the territory itself, at Aazhoodena/Stoney Point. It was a blustery but partially sunny day in mid-October 2022. Kevin rented a canopy and a portapotty, someone from Kettle Point catered some food, and Cully's daughter Claudette made tobacco ties.

It was strange not being there myself, yet also appropriate. I had played my part in helping to pull their stories together into a book and had acted as their bridge to the publishing world. I had gone back at the end of August, carrying advance copies of the book, plus posters I'd had printed up of the front cover. I'd spent two weeks visiting around and, one night, playing rez bingo. I'd also helped them prep for media interviews and explained what a book launch involves. Near the end, we celebrated with a barbecue, and everyone signed a card for me. "Chi-miigwech for all your work and all the time invested. Most of all – the visits." A message to treasure.

Now the book was in their hands, and they were taking it forward, hoping it would promote healing at least in their own community.

I was glad that the first review to come out, in the *Anishinabek News*, endorsed the collaborative role that I'd played. Maurice Switzer ended by saying, "Heather Menzies might not feel that her cultural background gives her the right to tell the stories of the Aazhoodenaang Enjibaajig, but treaty partners have responsibilities, and she has done well in trying to fulfill hers by giving them voice."[1]

Maybe it took that affirmation to give me the courage, the strength of heart I needed, because at that point I was able to acknowledge the truth of what Mohawk poet and essayist Beth Brant had said in the early 1990s: "No one can speak for us but us."[2] The last of my defences fell and I finally admitted to myself that this book could never be fully, authentically, an Indigenous story. It's not a fully "inside job,"[3] emerging from an Indigenous sensibility.

Still, I didn't consider myself fully in the wrong in what I'd done; just not fully in the right and above reproach. The people whose stories the book preserved were aging and dying. They'd invited me to help them, using my skills and connections as a writer, and I'd done the best I could in a complicated, messy situation. Real life is like that, complicated and messy. So is reconciliation.

I don't think of what I've done as reconciliation, but as laying the groundwork, and possibly modelling this in the context of a treaty relationship, which is about people, and peoples, trying to relate to each other as equals in a shared space. I didn't think of it as modelling at the time either. I was just there on that hot July day in 2018, leaning over a rusty barbed-wire fence. I was trying to find a way into a particular space that was supposed to be exclusively Nishnaabe territory but was littered, still, with elements of occupation by the Canadian military. My way in began with my wanting to express condolences, apologize for the injustice still at work in that space, and state my willingness to acknowledge a broken treaty relationship and my desire to learn how to make amends. I undertook the work I did, paying my own way for every trip, with no thought of receiving any payment then or in the future. To me it was an act of historical reparation but played out personally on behalf of my forebears, who had come here in the early nineteenth century. I was changing the relationship on their behalf as well as my own: from a colonial one to one based more on mutual respect and recognition – the values the Nishnaabeg had brought to the treaty council fires of the time.

As I reflect back, it was significant, and crucially important, that this encounter, and the relationship building that ensued over the next four years, took place in Nishnaabe space, albeit often in the dilapidated architecture of army barracks and maintenance buildings. It was a necessary historical corrective to be on their turf, immersing myself in native mind space as well as living space. It was there that I learned to listen and to change. I learned to collaborate on their terms, not mine. Sometimes there was compromise between theirs and mine, and this emerged from dialogue, dialogue in good faith, in which they listened to me, too, and came to trust me as a collaborator.

Could I have stayed the course of this journey if I hadn't had a project, a committed action to fulfill? If it had just been good-intention relationship building for itself? I doubt it. My good intentions would have faded in procrastination. More than that, though, if I hadn't had a project that forced me to challenge myself as a professional and part of the institutions of culture, the transformation might have remained personal and private. The book project took me from the personal and private into the public and more overtly political realm, and this gave me some insight into the decolonizing that has to happen there. It also implicated me in those changes when I continued to work with the Nishnaabeg as the publisher edited and packaged their oral history. I kept representing their perspective and at times pushed hard to ensure that it was heard and honoured throughout this professionally adjudicated process.

I think it's important for every person and every institution seeking to unsettle themselves and decolonize their ways of both thinking and operating to find and negotiate their own way in, with their own appropriate action. There are many examples, too: a pilot project in a school,[4] and a memorandum of understanding creating a frame for recognizing Indigenous authority in a museum, nature preserve, or park.[5] But for real change to emerge, any project has to be undertaken as a learning exercise to which the whole institution is committed, for decolonization and change. The change, in turn, has to move from changing relationships in the pilot-project phase to changing structures and systems throughout the institution – be that policing, medicine, or the care of children and the elderly or of the environment.

Such actions signify a good beginning. But for reconciliation to achieve its full meaning, it must include the land as the living earth. As Justice Murray Sinclair and the other commissioners wrote in the final report of the Truth and Reconciliation Commission in 2015, "Reconciliation between Aboriginal and non-Aboriginal Canadians, from an Aboriginal perspective, also requires reconciliation with the natural world. If human beings resolve problems between themselves but continue to destroy the natural world, then reconciliation remains incomplete."[6]

And so, even as I packed the files I had created for the book project into a box, even as I knew that my work here was done, I also knew that the journey I'd begun was ongoing. For one thing, I had yet to deliver on those photos of children forced to attend the Mount Elgin Residential School. The minister of the Grand Bend United church who had taken a leave during COVID was eventually replaced. I had yet to broach the subject with the new minister. But there was something larger nudging me on too. I had learned so much. Now I sensed the opportunity to take what I'd learned further, especially around what I'd told Bonnie and Fred that last day of recording their stories, about their having helped me connect with my ancestors.

In fact, I'd been trying to connect with and listen to my ancestors for some time, the idea that there were ancestral spirits to connect with having been gifted to me by another Nishhaabe, a friend I'd made in Ottawa many years earlier, Bev Lubuk. When I was preparing to make my first trip to Scotland in 2010, she'd smiled and said, "Oh, you're going to welcome your ancestors back."

At the time, I'd thought this was an intriguing idea, a way of seeding the imagination. Yet I'd learned, from walking the land of my ancestors in the Scottish Highlands and opening myself to the possibility of their presence, that a conversation with them, offering further insight into their way of life, was still waiting there, ready to be renewed. It was an intergenerational conversation that had been cut off by the enclosure of their commonly shared lands through the eighteenth and into the nineteenth centuries, and their forced choice to emigrate. From those earlier trips, I'd learned enough about how they had related to the land they'd inhabited since before recorded time that it helped me to hear what Nishnaabe people like Bonnie and Fred were telling me in the stories that they shared. It was the subject of my last book, *Reclaiming the Commons for the Common Good*.

I made myself a cup of tea, went to my bookshelves and found the *Commons* book. I sat by the window in the late October sun and flipped through its pages, stopping at some of the Gaelic words I'd discovered in my research. Words like *dùthchas,* or ancestral homeland, which referred to the traditional Scottish land tenure system of heritable trusteeship[7]; *dualchas,* which means one's heritage; *dual,* which means one's due. They're all linked to the proto-Celtic, Indo-European word for earth, or soil, which is *du.* I reread the phrase *Tir mo dhuthchais,* which one author I'd read had translated as "land to which I belong," adding that this included all the stories associated with that land. And then there was how someone who's been cut off from their land was described: as "a broken person."[8]

Maybe there was more listening to do, and more healing too. Because by now the journey I was on had become a healing one, if it hadn't been all along: a journey of both decolonization leading to the possibility of reconciliation, and also healing a broken treaty relationship. I didn't think of colonialism as a wound as such, though the disconnection of people from land that had long sustained them and their cultural identity could, I think, be likened to a wound, and this disconnection has been central to the colonization process. Still, I had come to believe, in keeping with the Truth and Reconciliation commissioners' assertion, that perhaps the biggest healing of all was healing our relations with the earth. This was the bed of shells on which the two rows of the wampum belt were stitched. The earth itself was part of the treaty relationship, and why the treaty, from an Indigenous standpoint, was made with the Creator.

Perhaps I could contribute to a settler counter-narrative, I thought. I'd helped prepare myself with the Aazhoodena book project, surrendering space in my mind and in my practices as I tried to disrupt and deconstruct colonial patterns. But a genuine counter-narrative has to be grounded in a different mindset and sensibility. My precolonial, premodern – even pre-feudal – heritage seemed to offer me such a grounding place – and a historical space-time, too, in which the mainstay institutions of the economy were centred in the home and the earth, not in financial markets. I needed to check this out. I would return to Scotland with what I'd said to Bonnie and Fred in the back of my mind as a guide and a boost of confidence. I would go back actively seeking that connection, connecting with the land as I walked it, renewing that relationship and opening myself to what it had to teach me.

Who knows whether another book might come from it. At least the journey would help me better respect the mindset behind what Indigenous people like Bonnie and Fred's children and grandchildren were bringing to the table of treaty renewal and reconciliation. That might be enough.

Are we living in end times? Certainly we're living in a time of crisis and choice. There is the crisis of an almost total-surveillance society, a fully realized online world in which most aspects of daily life are enclosed, and on which people have become dependent for most aspects of their lives, including information on what's happening outside their windows and what it all means. Then, outside the digital world and seemingly unconnected with it, there is the crisis of climate breakdown, with fires and storms, melting ice caps, rising sea levels, and breathtaking heat waves threatening lives, livelihoods, and millions of homes. There's the related crisis of social breakdown as global inequalities intensify, along with the competitive pressures to get jobs and keep up, and, for those left on the margins, racist scapegoating, anger, and division. Then there's the COVID pandemic, a crisis in its own right and perhaps, too, a symptom of an almost universal dis-ease.

It had once been thought that necessity would force radical change: peak oil and, later, rising CO_2 emissions driving global temperatures past the breaking point. One or other of these would prompt a policy pushback to regulate the global economy to function within the carrying capacity of the earth and human society. But corporate leadership, which has largely eclipsed democratic leadership in recent decades, seems to be putting its money elsewhere. Billionaires are investing in space stations and the possibility of colonizing other planets. If nothing else, these are a distraction, allowing the status quo to continue and diffusing the urgency of transformative change.

For me, allowing the status quo to continue is not an option: I've not only come to a deeper appreciation of how lethally toxic it is, but I have encountered an alternative path as I've begun to learn what being in a treaty relationship with Canada's First Peoples means, personally and politically. I choose this path because, for me, its centrality of respectful relations, including with the earth, offers the best hope for seriously addressing these larger challenges. Healing and transforming the relationships can lead to transforming the larger systems that have brought us to this point of crisis.

I will continue to be inspired by the Nishnaabe people I have met, and their lived sense of place in the kinship networks of this earth. I will continue to act on that inspiration, sharing it with settler fellow travellers who are also committed to healing and to change, and modelling it. I can at least help to keep hope alive: for me, for them, for my son and grandsons, for all my relations that constitute this beautiful but troubled earth.

I've learned that decolonization is a two-part journey. It's not just about reckoning with colonialism's legacy both in the past and in the ongoing present, and actively disrupting it. It's also opening a space of renewal and reconstitutionalization to honour the founding treaties of this country and what it means to share this space, this land, now.

Our treaty heritage here in Canada and the possibilities associated with the precolonial heritage that settlers and others have brought to this country offer a way back *and* forward. Together, they hold the promise of genuine reconciliation, including with the earth.

Epilogue
Lighting the Eighth Fire?

Someday perhaps my son and grandchildren, my great-nieces and -nephews might accept an invitation from the children and grandchildren of Bonnie Bressette, Marcia Simon, Cully George, and Kevin Simon to join them around a treaty council fire. A fire that enacts the prophecy of the Eighth Fire, heralding a time of peace and equilibrium around the world, when all people will be free to flourish in all their difference, and the earth will be free and healthy once again.

If this happens, I'd like to think that I and other settlers have helped prepare the way. I'd like to think we've done the work of reckoning: acknowledging the injustice of a colonization that's been imposed and is still being imposed on this land and the people who've lived here since before recorded time, trying to annihilate their ways – vested in their languages and rituals – and their means of maintaining good relations with the land and with their neighbours.

I'd like to think that we've committed ourselves to the necessary work of restitution: outwardly in terms of repairing the damage done and restructuring systems, institutions, and relationships so they function and flourish on both European-informed and Nishnaabe-informed terms; and also inwardly, unstitching the privileged hold that colonial thinking has in ourselves. Slowly, painfully, we'll have learned to repudiate white, settler privilege in our behaviour and in the structures of our social institutions. We'll have learned to listen to the Nishnaabeg and other First Nations of this land and, in that respectful listening, opened ourselves to change and trans-formation – both to accommodate their self-determination and to embrace what that has to offer for revisioning and reconstituting all of Canadian society. Through an expanding settler counter-narrative, we might have begun some of this change.

Settlers like me in the thousands will have supported the Nishnaabeg and other Indigenous peoples as they've gath-ered wood for the Eighth Fire treaty council fire. Sometimes this will be through restorative funding for language revival and other measures, and sometimes simply by getting out of the way so that the Nishnaabeg and other Indigenous na-tions can gather the elements of the fire themselves: lan-guage, laws, teachings, rites, rituals, and ceremonies.[1]

Is there a place at the fire for others' premodern, precol-onial languages and teachings? Some accounts of the Eighth Fire prophecy allude to it being the responsibility of all peoples to remember their past, to retrieve the wisdom from when the people who were their ancestors might have lived in direct, if not right, relations with the earth. It's said that the wisdom of all Indigenous knowledge systems is needed for the Eighth Fire to take hold.[2]

I'd like to think that the legacy of my ancestors, with their land-centred form of local self-governance based on sharing a common territory and living within its means, has some things to offer. However, if I can bring only one small stick to the fire, or one stone to the council-fire circle, it would be the old Celtic-Gaelic concept of *dùthchas,* which referred to a people's collective claim or tie to the land that they in-habited. *Dùthchas* was the equivalent of a land title but wasn't set down in an abstract, static legal deed, nor did it need to be. Its existence was vested in the lived-out relationships between the kin-connected people and the land they shared. It existed as long as it was respected, its language remem-bered in remembered stories, ceremonies, and songs.

Learning to listen to the Nishnaabeg of Aazhoodena, the Stoney Point reserve, over the past few years has helped me better understand concepts like *dùthchas*, and prompted me to research it more – not just for myself but also to share. It's like a dialogue with the past, or a dialogue with the an-cient roots informing it. Learning to better understand the history around this piece of my pre-settler heritage, in turn, helps me in my ongoing efforts to honour the spirit of the historical treaties, and to stand ready to support those Indigenous leaders who insist on their traditions, ceremon-ies, and values being at the centre of all treaty negotiations and renegotiations.

This land relationship–based treaty heritage offers all of Canadian society a path to renewal: renewing our relations with each other, settler and Indigenous societies, and together, renewing our relations with the earth.

In *Lighting the Eighth Fire*, which she edited and con-tributed to herself, Leanne Betasamosake Simpson, a Michi Saagiig Nishnaabeg scholar, writer, and musician, writes, "In order for the Eighth Fire to be lit, settler society must also choose to change their ways, to decolonize their relationships with the land and Indigenous Nations, and to join with us in building a sustainable future based on mutual recognition, justice and respect."[3]

I'd like to think that one of her children might also be at that council fire, ready to welcome my descendants and per-haps receive any gifts they might have to offer.

Acknowledgments and Important Sources

The journey that became this book took more courage than any of my other books required – emotional, spiritual, and intellectual courage. I drew that courage from others who have shared this journey with me, some of them friends and others mentors, with some of those mentors being books on my shelf and some of the authors of those books in turn becoming friends. I am humbled to have received so much support, and grateful.

Two friends have been beside me all the way. First, Dona Harvey, whose love and steadfast faith in the integrity of my quest kept me going through many dark moments of self-doubt, and who also brought her skills as a retired newspaper editor to offer close readings of every draft. My Ojibwe friend Bev Lubuk has not only been a source of loving support; through her words, her gifts, and her example, she's inspired me to be open to the wisdom of the ancestors, Creator, and Creation. It's partly because of this guidance that I find myself wanting to thank water both for holding me and for teaching me, too: specifically, the waters of Lake Huron and the waters of the Pacific Ocean, beside which I currently live.

I also want to thank the Nishnaabeg of Aazhoodena/Stoney Point who gave me the benefit of the doubt by talking with me in the first place. Four of them opened their homes and their hearts to me as they shared their stories and their knowledge to co-author the book *Our Long Struggle for Home: The Ipperwash Story*: Bonnie Bressette, Carolyn (Cully) George-Mandoka, Marcia Simon, and Kevin Simon. Over nearly five years of relationship and trust building, they have become friends, with one even calling me "treaty sister." They have been my teachers on this journey, and I thank them for all I've learned. There are others who also deserve mention for their willingness to open up to me with warmth, generosity, and stories: Marlin Simon, Gina Johnson, Bernard George, and Janet Cloud. Miigwech to them too.

Two writer friends, Rita Donovan and Sandy Duncan, offered editorial feedback on at least one draft of the memoir each. Other friends with experience in publishing offered valuable insights while also cheering me on: Michelle Benjamin, Sibyl Frei, Louise Rebelle, and Scott McIntyre. A host of other friends, including Jewel Walker, Margo Henniger, Joan Wright, Carol Weaver, Maggie Mooney, and Margaret Singleton, both read the manuscript at various stages and kept me going with meals, chai, hugs, and laughter. And then there's my son, Donald Burton, who has believed in me and been there with love and understanding through all my ups and downs.

On a more professional level, I want to thank Martha Attridge Bufton, Interdisciplinary Studies librarian at Carleton University's MacOdrum Library, who spent many hours on Zoom helping me find sources in my research, plus David Sharp and other Inter-Library Loans staff, who mailed books to me through the pandemic.

Anishnaabe literary agent Stephanie Sinclair was an important source of moral support as she affirmed the legitimacy of my lending my writing skills to the Nishnaabe co-authors of *Our Long Struggle for Home* on the basis of my kinship obligations and ties to them through an 1827 treaty.

And then there are all the fine people at UBC Press with whom I worked; they've been an amazing support team: Melissa Pitt, the publisher, who facilitated important connections, and her assistant Brit Schottelius with her warmth and prompt attention to detail; Darcy Cullen, the rights editor who has been a steadfast source of support through both book projects, including by reaching out to the Nishnaabe co-authors of *Our Long Struggle for Home* to help foster their trust in the publishing process; Ann Macklem, production editor on this memoir, whose intelligence and compassion were palpable across the digital distance of our communication; Merrie-Ellen Wilcox, who edited the manuscript with exquisite sensitivity; Laraine Coates, the head of marketing, who brought such enthusiasm to our Zoom calls planning how to promote the earlier book; Kerry Kilmartin, the publicist who worked tirelessly to create promotional materials and follow up with her many media contacts; and Carmen Tiampo, with whom I worked to solicit pre-publication endorsements of the book. Thank you to you all for turning a lot of work into a source of pleasure, and sometimes fun, that helped sustain me.

SOURCES THAT INSPIRED AND GUIDED ME

Much as I couldn't have written this book without the love and support of friends and mentors, I couldn't have done it without the guidance and support of published works, the authors of which became my mentors.

Some helped drive home for me the price that Indigenous people continue to pay as ordinary Canadians like me allow the status quo to continue. These sources include the reports of the Royal Commission on Aboriginal Peoples (1996), the Ipperwash Inquiry (2007), the Truth and Reconciliation Commission (2015), and the Inquiry into Missing and Murdered Indigenous Women and Girls (2019). There are also numerous books. One that particularly helped to motivate me is Audra Simpson's *Mohawk Interruptus* (Durham, NC: Duke University Press, 2014) as it spelled out the harsh reality that colonial-settler "emplacement" was and still is at the expense of Indigenous displacement and dispossession. Jesse Wente's *Unreconciled* (Toronto: Penguin Random House, 2022) spelled out the ongoing day-to-day-ness of this, especially in the cultural sphere. Thomas King made similar trenchant points in *The Inconvenient Indian* (Toronto: Doubleday Canada, 2012), and his signature wry humour did nothing to weaken his challenge to me: to become an inconvenient settler refusing convenient complicity in the ongoing status quo.

Others challenged me as they showed the hard and often painful work of healing, recovery, and resurgence going on in Indigenous communities across the country. Glen Coulthard's *Red Skin, White Masks* (Minneapolis: University of Minnesota Press, 2014) is a powerful example, documenting the shift in the politics and psychology of "recognition" from a colonial conferred basis to one of mutual respect, as Indigenous peoples get on with their own decolonization and renew their own capacity for self-recognition and self-determination grounded in Indigenous lifeways and worldviews. Much of Leanne Betasamosake Simpson's writing works the same ground, from her lyrical *Dancing on Our Turtle's Back* (Winnipeg: Arbeiter Ring, 2011), the poetic *Islands of Decolonial Love* (Winnipeg: Arbeiter Ring, 2015), and the incisive *As We Have Always Done* (Minneapolis: University of Minnesota Press, 2017), with lines like "land is pedagogy," to her brilliant novel *Noopiming: The Cure for White Ladies* (Toronto: House of Anansi Press, 2020), with its haunting line, "I remember hopeless connection." All of Richard Wagamese's writing has inspired me, too, but his novel *Medicine Walk* (Toronto: Penguin Random House, 2014) moved me particularly as I realized that I was embarking on a healing journey of my own.

Paulette Regan's *Unsettling the Settler Within* (Vancouver: UBC Press, 2020) helped me get on with this as it talked about the necessity of encounter and relationship building for the "transformational learning" that decolonization involves, and tipping me off that this would be a "pedagogy of discomfort," not a walk in the park.

Eva Mackey's *Unsettled Expectations* (Halifax: Fernwood Publishing, 2016) helped me stay the course in showing me how resistance to change lingers even alongside good intentions, but also encouraged me to see that once you welcome that change, the path toward reconciliation starts to open.

Robin DiAngelo's *White Fragility* (Boston: Beacon Press, 2018) helped me recognize the shadow of racism and white privilege as white supremacy reinforcing colonial thinking, and to understand that reparations preparatory to reconciliation require me to "interrupt" and "repair" myself. Dionne Brand's brilliant *Nomenclature: New and Collected Poems* (Toronto: McClelland and Stewart, 2022) offered me a number of word tools to work with and references to people who had informed and inspired her thinking, such as James Baldwin.

Then there were all the sources that encouraged me by showing what was to be gained by learning how to listen, and dismantling the old, colonial ways of thinking that blocked this. Daniel Heath Justice's book, *Why Indigenous Literatures Matter* (Waterloo: Wilfrid Laurier University Press, 2018) showed me that Indigenous stories and storytelling are a medium for learning to become fully human through kinship with all Creation.

James (Sa'ke'j) Youngblood Henderson's gem of an account of how the UN Declaration on the Rights of Indigenous

Peoples came into being, *Indigenous Diplomacy and the Rights of Peoples* (Saskatoon: Purich, 2008), inspired me by showing me what is possible through respectful relating and relationship building. Robin Wall Kimmerer's eloquent essay collection, *Braiding Sweetgrass* (Minneapolis: Milkweed Editions, 2013), helped me build a bridge from my world view to hers and see that becoming "Indigenous to place" was possible for zhaganash (white people) like me by making that choice and committing to the changes that follow.

Abenaki cultural historian Lisa Brooks's *The Common Pot* (Minneapolis: University of Minnesota Press, 2008) took me into the mind space that prevailed in North America at the time of first European contact, the role of kinship in Indigenous treaty-making traditions, and the importance of condolences and reparations in treaty renewal.

Anishnaabe legal scholar John Borrows's work and guidance have been invaluable. His book *Canada's Indigenous Constitution* (Toronto: University of Toronto Press, 2010) taught me not only that treaties are founding constitutional documents of this country but also that the way we constitute ourselves as a society is properly grounded in sacred laws, such as creation stories demonstrating how to live in right relationship with all on this shared land. *Recovering Canada: The Resurgence of Indigenous Law* (Toronto: University of Toronto Press, 2002) challenges settlers like me to learn how to genuinely share this land and reconstitute a shared life on it in a treaty partnership of respectful mutuality. *Law's Indigenous Ethics* (Toronto: University of Toronto Press, 2019) opened my imagination to what this might entail as Borrows flipped the page on still-prevalent colonial perspectives on treaties to reveal the rich Indigenous heritage of treaties originally made with animals, the land, and the Creator. For Borrows, the seven grandmother/grandfather teachings are a metaphor for living earth's interconnectedness with relational empathy.

Not only did I learn from Borrows's writing, but I learned from his example as he started responding to my query emails, and generously put me in touch with colleagues, such as Alan Ojiig Corbiere who, in turn, kindly shared some of what he's learned about the meanings coded into the bead-work of treaty wampum belts. Thank you.

It's hard to know where to stop in listing sources. I want to end by mentioning some other texts that helped me see the challenge and the possibilities in decolonizing, rethinking, and rewriting the larger story of life on this land that colonizers call Canada. Olive Dickason's *Canada's First Nations* (Don Mills: Oxford University Press, 2001) is one of these, and a good place for people to start because it is so inclusive across both space and time. Other, more recent works are more particularly focused but just as helpful for people ready to unlearn the old narrative and make way for the new. One of my favourites is *No Surrender: The Land Remains Indigenous* (Regina: University of Regina Press, 2019) by Sheldon Krasowski; it's an exhaustive correction of the story behind the numbered treaties negotiated in Western Canada. Another is *Our Hearts Are as One Fire* (Vancouver: UBC Press, 2020) by Jerry Fontaine, makwa ogimaa, which re-claims the legacy of three eighteenth- and early-nineteenth-century Anishinaabe leaders to reframe the story of this land around other possibilities. And, on the listening side of this dialogue opening a path toward reconciliation, in *Canada's Odyssey* (Toronto: University of Toronto Press, 2017), historian Peter H. Russell calls for rethinking Canada and its history, as a multinational country.

Last but certainly not least, I want to thank the BC Arts Council for supporting me in my work with a generous writing grant.

Notes

INTRODUCTION

1 Alan Ojiig Corbiere, "'Their Own Forms of which They Take the Most Notice': Diplomatic Metaphors and Symbolism on Wampum Belts," in *Anishinaabewin Niiwin: Four Winds Rising*, ed. Alan Ojiig Corbiere, Mary Ann Naokwegijig Corbiere, Deborah McGregor, and Crystal Migwans (M'Chigeeng, ON: Ojibwe Cultural Foundation, 2014), 62.
2 This is how the Nishnaabe people identify themselves collectively as a nation.
3 In February 1994, the federal government announced plans to shut down the army training program at Ipperwash. There were no cadets or training staff there by 1995.

CHAPTER 1: AT THE FENCE

1 The reserve is traditionally called Stoney Point. But the band council representing the two reserves calls it Stony Point.
2 I later learned, through some archival research, that the man whom the Indian agent had contracted to move houses off Stoney Point had interrupted the work for several months while he did another job, during which time the army camp began operations.

CHAPTER 2: SHOWING UP

1 Paulette Regan, *Unsettling the Settler Within: Indian Residential Schools, Truth Telling, and Reconciliation in Canada* (Vancouver: UBC Press, 2011), 21.
2 Regan, *Unsettling*, 27.

CHAPTER 4: A CHANCE TO REALLY ENGAGE

1 Paulette Regan, *Unsettling the Settler Within: Indian Residential Schools, Truth Telling, and Reconciliation in Canada* (Vancouver: UBC Press, 2011), 196.

CHAPTER 5: WHO DO YOU THINK YOU ARE?

1 The "birth alert" practice was banned in BC in 2019, where it was labelled illegal and unconstitutional. It was banned in Ontario in October 2020.

CHAPTER 6: SHOWING UP AGAIN

1 The term *language nest* is used in many places around the world in relation to Indigenous language recovery efforts. See Lindsay Keegitah Borrows, *Otter's Journey through Indigenous Language and Law* (Vancouver: UBC Press, 2018).

CHAPTER 8: CHALLENGED

1 The forced removal of the Potawatomi is known as the "Trail of Death," not of tears. Graham George, *Aazhoodena: The History of Stoney Point First Nation*, Ipperwash Inquiry, Part II (Aazhoodena and George Family Group, 2006), 11.
2 Patricia and Norman Shawnoo. In sharing this story with Jerry Fontaine for his book about the Three Fires Confederacy, *Our Hearts Are as One Fire* (Vancouver: UBC Press, 2020), they pronounced *Tecumseh* as Tecumtha.
3 The officials drafting the Order in Council for appropriating the Stoney Point Reserve under the authority of the War Measures Act in 1942 inserted a small phrase promising that the land would be returned "when it was no longer needed" by the army.

CHAPTER 9: CHALLENGING MYSELF

1 Thomas King, *The Inconvenient Indian: A Curious Account of Native People in North America* (Toronto: Anchor Canada, 2013), 61.
2 King, *Inconvenient*, 85.
3 *Compact Oxford Dictionary* (Oxford University Press), 415.
4 The term *ethnocentrism* is associated with anthropologist Franz Boas.

CHAPTER 10: CONVERSATIONS DEEPEN

1 Truth and Reconciliation Commission of Canada, *Honouring the Truth, Reconciling for the Future: Summary of the Final Report of the Truth and Reconciliation Commission of Canada* (TRC, 2015), 72, 76.

CHAPTER 11: WITNESSING DENIAL

1 Darlene Johnston, *Connecting People to Place: Great Lakes Aboriginal History in Cultural Context,* research report for Ipperwash Inquiry (2007), 8.
2 Johnston, *Connecting*, 6–7.

CHAPTER 15: LIVING A LAND CLAIM

1 Theresa S. Smith, *The Island of the Anishnaabeg: Thunderers and Water Monsters in the Traditional Ojibwe Life-World* (Lincoln: University of Nebraska Press, 2012).
2 Jerry Fontaine, *Our Hearts Are as One Fire* (Vancouver: UBC Press, 2020), 87.

CHAPTER 16: CONNECTIVE CADENCES

1 I have been inspired to use both genders through the example of Anishnaabe legal scholar John Borrows, who describes the teachings this way in his work.
2 Truth and Reconciliation Commission of Canada, *Honouring the Truth, Reconciling for the Future: Summary of the Final Report of the Truth and Reconciliation Commission of Canada* (TRC, 2015), 93.

3 TRC, *Honouring*, 92.
4 I owe thinking of this simple word here to poet Dionne Brand, understanding poetry's "project to be ... undoing the times we live in. And doing that at the core of where the world gets made and articulated – language." Dionne Brand, *Nomenclature: New and Collected Poems* (Toronto: McClelland and Stewart, 2022), xx.

CHAPTER 17: COLONIALISM ONGOING

1 In 1969, the government of Pierre Elliott Trudeau released a policy paper called a White Paper that "promoted the century-long goal of the Government of Canada of full integration of the First Nations into the dominant society, the end of Indian status, the reserves and the historic Indian treaties." Donald B. Smith, *Seen but Not Seen: Influential Canadians and the First Nations from the 1840s to Today* (Toronto: University of Toronto Press, 2021), xxiii.

CHAPTER 18: PREPARING TO LEAVE

1 Timothy Findley, *The Wars* (Toronto: Clarke, Irwin, 1977), 48.

CHAPTER 19: THE POIGNANT BLESSINGS OF RELATIONSHIP BUILDING

1 This a reference to Nishnaabeg women's fasting rituals which would likely have been frowned upon by Christian churches, especially conservative ones.
2 Marshall McLuhan (with Quentin Fiore), *The Medium Is the Massage: An Inventory of Effects* (New York: Bantam, 1967).

CHAPTER 20: SURRENDERING PROFESSIONALLY

1 Robin DiAngelo, *White Fragility: Why It's So Hard for White People to Talk about Racism* (Boston: Beacon Press, 2018), 145–46. DiAngelo talks about repairing racism, but I found myself making it more personal. Similarly, she uses the concept of "interrupting" a racist discourse, and I have personalized it here.
2 Heather Menzies, "'Structural Racism' vis a vis 'Authorial Voice,'" *Writers' Confidential*, October 1988.

3 David Henry Hwang, *M. Butterfly*, act II, scene 7.

4 Donald B. Smith, *Seen but Not Seen: Influential Canadians and the First Nations from the 1840s to Today* (Toronto: University of Toronto Press, 2021).

5 Lindsay Keegitah Borrows, "Traditional Law Through Indigenous Language Resurgence," webinar, TRC 57 Learning with Syeyutsus speaker series, November 25, 2020, https://trc57speakerseries.ca/speakers/lindsay-keegitah-borrows/.

6 Scholar Eva Mackey writes about the politics of certainty around settler entitlement: "Settled expectations and certainty emerge from having one's ontology of entitlement confirmed through various laws." Eva Mackey, *Unsettled Expectations: Uncertainty, Land and Settler Decolonization* (Halifax: Fernwood Publishing, 2016), 35.

7 George Orwell, "Politics and the English Language," in *Why I Write* (London: Penguin Books, 1984), 118.

CHAPTER 21: HELPING PREPARE A SPIRIT PLATE

1 Joseph W. Graham, *Insatiable Hunger: Colonial Encounters in Context* (Montreal: Black Rose Books, 2021), 245, note 66.

2 Shawn Wilson, *Research Is Ceremony: Indigenous Research Methods* (Halifax: Fernwood Publishing, 2008), 69. Wilson writes: "When ceremonies take place, everyone who is participating needs to be ready to step beyond the everyday and to accept a raised state of consciousness."

3 Maggie Hodgson, Carrier First Nation (and residential school survivor), quoted in Augustine S.J. Park, "Remembering the Children: Decolonizing Community-Based Restorative Justice for Indian Residential Schools," *Contemporary Justice Review* 19, 4 (2016), 439.

4 Warren Cariou, foreword to *Elements of Indigenous Style: A Guide for Writing by and about Indigenous Peoples*, by Gregory Younging (Edmonton, AB: Brush Education, 2018), ix.

5 Cariou, *Elements*, x.

CHAPTER 22: CONTINUING THE JOURNEY

1 Maurice Switzer, "Book Review: *Our Long Struggle for Home: The Ipperwash Story*," *Anishinabek News*, September 6, 2022.

2 Beth Brant, *Writing As Witness: Essay and Talk* (Toronto: Women's Press, 1994), 52.

3 Anishnaabe writer, broadcaster, and arts leader Jesse Wente used this term in the documentary *Reel Injun*, referring to *Atanarjuat: The Fast Runner*, which was filmed entirely in Inuktitut by Inuit filmmaker Zacharias Kunuk and his production company, Isuma Igloolik Productions. Neil Diamond, *Reel Injun* (Montreal: National Film Board, 2010).

4 See, for example, Theresa A. Papp, "A Canadian Study of Coming Full Circle to Traditional Aboriginal Pedagogy: A Pedagogy for the 21st Century," *Diaspora, Indigenous and Minority Education* 14, 1 (2020): 25–42. The article reports on a Saskatchewan case study demonstrating educational success from engaging mainly Aboriginal high school students in holistic, experiential, and relational instruction.

5 One example of this is associated with the Fraser River Discovery Centre in BC. See Marsha Lederman, "How Three Canadian Museums Are Reckoning with Their Past Mishandlings of Indigenous History," *Globe and Mail* (February 5, 2022), https://www.theglobeandmail.com/arts/art-and-architecture/article-how-three-canadian-museums-are-reckoning-with-their-past-mishandlings/.

6 Truth and Reconciliation Commission of Canada, *Honouring the Truth, Reconciling for the Future: Summary of the Final Report of the Truth and Reconciliation Commission of Canada* (TRC, 2015), 18.

7 Alastair McIntosh, *Soil and Soul: People Versus Corporate Power* (London: Aurum Press, 2004), 54.

8 Michael Newton, *Warriors of the Word: The World of Scottish Highlanders* (Edinburgh: Birlinn, 2009), 130.

EPILOGUE: LIGHTING THE EIGHTH FIRE?

1 The idea of recovered languages and customs being the wood for a council fire came from a talk by Haudenosaunee scholar Taiaiake Alfred at a talk he gave on Gabriola Island, BC, on October 5, 2017.

2 Leanne Simpson, ed., in *Lighting the Eighth Fire: The Liberation, Resurgence, and Protection of Indigenous Nations* (Winnipeg, MB: Arbeiter Ring, 2008), 14.

3 Simpson, *Lighting*, 14.

About the Author

HEATHER MENZIES is an award-winning author, activist, and adjunct research professor in the School of Indigenous and Canadian Studies at Carleton University. In 2013, she was appointed to the Order of Canada for her contributions to public discourse. Most recently, she collaborated with the Nishnaabeg at Stoney Point to produce *Our Long Struggle for Home: The Ipperwash Story*. She is also the author of ten books, including *Reclaiming the Commons for the Common Good, No Time: Stress and the Crisis of Modern Life*, and the memoir *Enter Mourning: Death, Dementia and Coming Home*. She has won two book awards and one magazine award, and two of her books appeared on the *Globe and Mail's* top 100 books of the year list. She lives on unceded Snuneymuxw territory in British Columbia.

Printed and bound in Canada by Friesens

Set in Walbaum by Artegraphica Design Co. Ltd.

Copy editor: Merrie-Ellen Wilcox

Proofreader: Sarah Wight

Cover designer: JVDW Designs

Cover images: *(bottom front, and back)* Covenant Chain wampum belt, reproduction by Ken Maracle, Canadian Museum of History, LH2016.48.2, IMG2016-0267-0250